AF522633

CONTESTING FUNDAMENTALISMS

CONTESTING FUNDAMENTALISMS

Edited by
Carol Schick
JoAnn Jaffe
Ailsa M. Watkinson

AAKAR

CONTESTING FUNDAMENTALISMS
Carol Schick, JoAnn Jaffe, Ailsa M. Watkinson (Eds.)

Published in agreement with Fernwood Publishing, Nova Scotia, Canada
for publication and sale only in the Indian Subcontinent
(India, Pakistan, Bangladesh, Nepal, Maldives,
Bhutan & Sri Lanka)

First Published in India, 2006

ISBN 81-87879-67-X (Hb)

Published by
AAKAR BOOKS
28 E Pocket IV, Mayur Vihar Phase I, Delhi-110 091
Phone : 011-2279 5505 Telefax : 011-2279 5641
E-mail : aakarb@del2.vsnl.net.in

Printed at
Mudrak, 30-A, Patparganj, Delhi–110 091

Contents

Acknowledgements

This edited collection has benefited from the contributions of many people. We especially thank the thoughtful help of Naomi Frankel and Lisa Comeau and the administrators of the Transdisciplinary Project Fund at the University of Regina. We commend the copy-editing of Brenda Conroy and the manuscript preparation and typing of Debbie Mathers. Thanks to Larissa Holman for making us look good on the cover and Beverley Rach for the layout. We stand firm in our praise of Wayne Antony for his creativity and patient hand-holding as Fernwood's editor.

JoAnn Jaffe wishes to thank Michael Gertler, Maxim Gertler-Jaffe and Jardena Gertler-Jaffe for their support and indulgence. Ailsa M. Watkinson thanks Allan Wickstrom and their sons, Sheldon, Jeffrey and David. Carol Schick could not do without her Dan.

About the Contributors

Murray Knuttila teaches in the Department of Sociology and Social Studies at the University of Regina, where he is slowly learning that oppressive regimes and the inequalities they generate are harmful to all parties. His books include *That Man Partridge: The Life and Times of E.A. Partridge; Introducing Sociology: A Critical Perspective* (2nd edition): and *State Theories: Classical, Feminist and Global Perspectives* (3rd edition with Wendee Kubik). murray.knutilla@uregina.ca

Joyce Green is Associate Professor of Political Science at the University of Regina and is seconded half-time to the Women's Studies Program for the academic years 2003–05. Her research interests are currently focused on Aboriginal-settler relations and the possibility of decolonization in Canada; and on the theoretical parameters and political significance of Aboriginal feminism. joyce.green@uregina.ca

F. Volker Greifenhagen is Associate Professor of religious Studies at Luther College at the University of Regina. He is author of *Egypt on the Pentateuch's Ideological Map* and various articles on Islam and in biblical subjects. He is especially interested in the dynamics of fundamentalism, sacred texts and religious rhetoric. Franzvolker.greifenhagen@uregina.ca

Jackie Kuikman is Associate Professor and Chair of Religious Studies at the University of Regina. Her interest in Jewish fundamentalism comes from personal and academic studies. Her research interests include Holocaust Studies, Judaism and gender, first century Jewish/Christian relations. Jackie.kuikman@uregina.ca

Verna St. Denis is Associate Professor of Education in the College of Education, University of Saskatchewan. She was born into a Métis road allowance community on the south edge of Prince Albert National Park and is also a member of Beardy's and Okemasis First Nations. She is both a graduate and former faculty of Aboriginal Teacher Education programs in Saskatchewan. She now teaches a required cross-cultural education course to pre-service teacher education students. Her research includes promoting a critical race analysis in Aboriginal education. verna.stdenis @usask.ca

Nayyar Javed is a psychologist in the Saskatoon Adult Community Mental Health Services. She was born and raised in Pakistan. Nayyar was an

Assistant Professor in Peshamar University in Pakistan. Since moving to Canada she has been involved in the feminist movement at local, national and international levels. Nayyar has published several book chapters and articles on women and psychology, the intersection of race, class and gender, and Muslim women. [no e-mail address]

Ailsa M. Watkinson is Associate Professor with the Faculty of Social Work, University of Regina located in the Saskatoon Community Education Centre, St. Andrews's College. Ailsa's research interests centre on human rights issues. In 1999 Ailsa released a book entitled *Education, Student Rights and the Charter*. As well, she has co-edited two books on systemic violence. She has published a number of journal articles that focus on such topics as child sexual abuse, corporal punishment, sexual harassment, employment equity, the Charter as policy advocate, globalization and the administration of equality rights. ailsa.watkinson@uregina.ca; awatkinson@sasktel.net

Carol Schick is Associate Professor at the University of Regina. Her work focuses on anti-oppressive education in teacher preparation programs. Areas of research include critical race theory, whiteness studies and post-structural theories of discourse. Her early experiences in a fundamentalist household help to inform her research and writing on this topic. carol.schick@uregina.ca

Don Mitchell is a community and co-operative developer, writer, researcher, teacher and former Mayor in Moose Jaw, Saskatchewan. He has an M.A. in Political Science from the University of Saskatchewan and has published numerous articles on Canadian food and agriculture. He is the author of *The Politics of Food* (James Lorimer and Company, 1975). He is married to Martha Tracey and co-parent of Dave and Tracey, who are activists in the global community.

JoAnn Jaffe is Associate Professor of Sociology and Social Studies at the University of Regina. She has a Ph.D. in Development Sociology from Cornell University and is an author and co-editor of *Farm Communities at the Crossroads: Challenge and Resistance* (CPRC Press 2003). Reared in the old United States heartland, she has also spent years researching and participating in life in other parts of the world, including Haiti, Israel, Costa Rica, Guatemala, Chile and Grenada. JoAnn became an activist at an early age in the era of civil rights, Vietnam and the women's movement. She remains a true believer in the prospects for liberatory change. JoAnn co-parents Maxim and Jardena with her partner, Michael Gertler, who teaches sociology at the University of Saskatchewan. joann.jaffe@uregina.ca

Chapter One

Considering Fundamentalism

Carol Schick, JoAnn Jaffe, Ailsa M. Watkinson

It is hard to accept the breaking off of a chain of logic that might otherwise be available to discuss the rationality of one position versus another. Suddenly, in the midst of a discussion of competing points, the flow of logic stops. It is as if the other person got off the train, without warning, and got onto another one going in another direction. The discussion comes to a screeching halt because the other side has appealed to a position that can no longer be subjected to common terms of reason. They have made the leap of faith—in some traditions called the "God trick"—to a place impervious to earthly reason. It is a matter of their faith that an unerring principle, a belief system, an ancient text can be called upon unconditionally to support their side. There can be no appeal.

How We Got Started

This collection came together serendipitously shortly after September 11, 2001, when two of us were discussing the rising paranoia that billowed out like toxic dust from the fall of the twin towers. In the aftermath of 9/11 and amid increased sensitivity to U.S. politics, our work as critical thinkers in the academy seemed more intense. We felt the soot and grittiness of the fall settle over us as we tried to define a space from which we could continue to critique hegemonic social practices, of which the complexities of U.S. foreign policy were one example. The debate over what had happened in the U.S. was so polarized that it was hard to say anything without seeming to side with either the destructive acts of terrorism or the hysterical notion of a pristine, victimized United States.

We had each been working independently on the issue of Christian fundamentalism and were alarmed by the influence of fundamentalist thought on public events. In the post-9/11 climate, little if any attention was being paid to the inroads Christian fundamentalism was making in local and international politics. The focus had become riveted on "Islamic fundamentalism" as the only form of extreme religious behaviour. Even though, for instance, Christian fundamentalist, Jerry Falwell had stated publicly that "America got what it deserved" (Saunders 2001: A2)—condemning the fact that gays and lesbians have increasing access to rights, that abortion is a woman's choice and other such "evidence" of the world in decay—the focus barely moved from "Islamic fundamentalism." Our third editor joined us and expanded the discussion to other types of fundamentalism, for example, economic and Jewish.

As a result of our informal discussions in the fall of 2001, we applied for and received funding from a University of Regina initiative, the Transdisciplinary Project, to host a symposium entitled, "The Basics of Fundamentalism." We invited other colleagues to reflect on and write about fundamentalism and the meanings they drew from it in their own areas of expertise. We all wanted to know more about the trains (of thought) going in other directions.

The term "fundamentalism" is most frequently used when referring to systems of religious thought such as are found in types of Christianity, Islam and Judaism. The term, however, is not easy to define, nor is it limited to religious contexts. Fundamentalism can also be used to describe particular types of national pride, cultural exclusion, xenophobia, economic theory and other systems characterized by strongly held beliefs, group formation, boundary development and prescriptive practices. Fundamentalism of all types is increasingly under discussion following recent world events, but some issues remain unexplored. Talk of fundamentalism often lacks precision, leaving unexamined the implications of fundamentalist practices. How can we use the term so that it has analytical meaning and is not just a label used by self-proclaimed non-fundamentalists?

This book has three aims: 1) to explore the meaning of fundamentalism in religious, social, cultural and economic settings; 2) to study concrete examples of fundamentalist practices; and 3) to examine the social and political effects of fundamentalism in Canada and elsewhere. We maintain that fundamentalism is not limited to areas of religious practice but also describes the ideological positions of various social and cultural movements. We invite a multidimensional understanding of who or what may be called fundamentalist and the dilemmas that this naming creates. We also consider the social and cultural effects that fundamentalist thought and practice have for adherents and non-adherents. Whereas some contributors to this volume are concerned with definitions, others examine fundamentalist systems for what they accomplish, deny or permit in a social sense. We are concerned to ensure that we do not label as fundamentalists only those with whom we part company ideologically. Conversely, we consider whether the contributors to this book and the directions they take could be characterized as fundamentalist by those whom the writers are describing. Finally, we contend that the more complete understanding that we are working towards here is a necessary project for contesting the claims of fundamentalism.

Fundamentalist movements profess to be upholding some kind of orthodoxy or right practice and regard themselves as instrumental in preserving the tradition from erosion. Even though they claim to uphold a sacred past, their procedures and institutions are quite new or unprecedented and actually constitute a reinterpretation of the past. Fundamentalist movements tend toward self-separation or exclusivity, as well as prescriptive distinctions that mark adherents from outsiders. Their practices also claim, by tacit or explicit decree, a masculine hegemony, which results in a male-dominated leadership or authority. J.D. Van der Vyver (1996: 1) contends that "these trends, seen in isolation, would not necessarily constitute fundamentalism of any particular kind. It is the combination of all, or most, of those trends that would attract the fundamentalist badge."

Although the fundamentalist label can be applied to many social groups and processes, a reference to religious fundamentalism can provide clues to considering the concept more broadly. For example, the term "Christian fundamentalism" has been used in North America, correctly or not, in reference to the Christian Right, which in popular media is sometimes portrayed as intolerant, extreme and anti-pluralistic (Bolce and DeMajo 1999). Politically, the Christian Right is also associated with the views of the Canadian Alliance in Canada[1] and the Republican Party in the United States. Whether the Christian Right is really fundamentalist is a matter not only of definition but also of perception. These perceptions of fundamentalism operate at a mass level and provide social actors with broad definitions for describing who is siding with whom. Although the term fundamentalist is imprecise and somewhat overworked, it is nevertheless helpful across movements, which although they may have different aims, still "bear a strong family resemblance" (Armstrong 2001b: 17).

The essays in this book investigate the nature of fundamentalism expanded beyond the usual frame of religious experience to include areas such as market economics and hegemonic masculinity. While none of the contributors claims to be an expert on fundamentalism, each is committed to studying a topic that contends with some form of fundamentalist practice. The commonality among us is that we all share an orientation that can be described as feminist, anti-racist and anti-oppressive. In the midst of our various forms of liberatory and/or anti-oppressive activity and scholarship, our work bumps up against some type of fundamentalist thinking. Each area of expertise—economics, gender relations, ethnic studies, Aboriginal politics, nationalism and religious studies—is made clearer, brought into sharper relief or simply shown in a different light by the application of a fundamentalist lens.

Each chapter reflects an aspect of personal experience and involvement, including for some a certain vulnerability, that makes fundamentalism and this treatment of it more than an academic affair. Some experiences come from insider knowledge gained in former times of fundamentalist systems. For other authors, connections with fundamentalist communities, such as family and friends, are still on-going and continue to serve important purposes in their lives. For these authors, there is understandable reluctance to externalize a critique that may be read as a betrayal of their own culture. There may even be negative personal and political repercussions in providing insider criticism of already vulnerable groups.

A similar public/private complexity is described by Linda Kintz (1997), who as a feminist, writes critically of her experiences of living with and researching the lives of conservative, right-wing Christians in the United States. Kintz understands the deep sense of belonging that is experienced by adherents of this religious group; she makes explicit the nature of the public/private appeal of a reactionary spiritual movement even while offering her feminist critique. She closes her book by describing her response to hearing a voice-mail message from an older woman friend, who has invited her to an anti-abortion demonstration. Kintz is torn by the familiarity and the revulsion that she simultaneously feels:

> The mother's voice, at least as this culture teaches it to us, is like the nightingale's song, its promise of fullness symbolically overwhelming me with passion while the mother's actual place—the fact that masculine hatred of her has constructed the edifice of that symbolic power in the first place—leaves me both dizzy with desire for her and devastated by what she represents. (Kintz 1997: 272)

It requires courage and intense honesty to speak critically from an insider position about that to which one is still attached, especially if the attachment is in some oppositional or conflicted way. Externalizing the critique with the level of care found in this volume is evidence that the topics capture us still. The stance of disinterested observer is always an impossibility and nowhere more so than in public and private expression on fundamentalism.

Why is this Investigation Important?

Fundamentalism captures our attention for many reasons. It is perhaps the closed-ness of fundamentalism that one notices first, as it rubs up against an ideological assumption of modernity: that modernity itself is a construct with a low tolerance for intolerance. A lack of critical reflection characterizes fundamentalist beliefs. Ghassan Hage (2001: 30) offers the following, "critical reflexivity is *a priori* negative since it implies that the self [and a particular cause] can be questioned or changed. Fundamentalism is clearly more concerned with the never-changing nature" of its particular expressions—patriarchy, religious orthodoxy, nationalism, ethnicity, market economics. Inevitability, essentialism and fore-ordained status are a few of the cornerstones of a fundamentalist belief system that by definition are not open to debate. Reflection is stifled by convincing insiders that they are imperilled by outsiders who are essentially unlike them. Ironically, the ultimate failure to construct the dangerous "other" is a source of continuing tension both within and without the fundamentalist project, as Carol Schick (chapter 11) explains in her work on public debates over minority rights in schools. She concludes that it is precisely the inability to establish the firm boundaries on which fundamentalist identities and discourses depend that is troubling both for fundamentalists themselves as well as for those outsiders who negotiate the public spaces which fundamentalists claim.

An examination of fundamentalism is important because of the dangerous potential in our society for increasing kinds of violence, of which the invasion of Iraq is a significant example. The prospect of violence has at least two aspects. First, although most fundamentalist groups do not openly espouse violence against their detractors, the stand of religious fundamentalists against justice issues such as homosexuality, birth control and abortion provides licence to the fanatical among their ranks as well as to the irreligious. The repressive aspect of fundamentalism works against marginalized groups and makes them easy targets for the frustration and anger of anyone whose sense of entitlement has not been fulfilled. These acts of violence may seem, at first, to have little to do with fundamentalism, except for the exclusionary talk or the racist, sexist and homophobic examples of "righteous" people. At this time in North America, it is difficult to imagine widespread retrieval of images of Islam without it also releasing prejudice and racism.

Second, religious fundamentalism as representative of an ultra-conservative agenda is worth paying attention to because it is one of the pieces necessary for the development of a fascist state. Although many mainstream conservative Christians wish to be distinguished as separate from the extreme Right, the theological basics are the same: biblical inerrancy and the belief that sooner or later they will be "the saved" (Herman 1997). In Europe prior to World War II, a well organized, extreme right-wing movement was a significant part of the eventual rise of fascism. Religious emphases were merged with nationalism and overt discrimination against minorities—homosexuals, Jews, Gypsies and communists (Swomley 1995: 4). Today, the apocalyptic vision of religious fundamentalists manifests itself in violence against secular society and others identified as enemies, such as is seen in the actions of "Operation Rescue and the lambs of God which engage in terrorist tactics to intimidate women, physicians, and their families; and the Coalition on Revival, which advocates execution of adulterers, homosexuals, and others" (Swomely 1995: 4). The cultivation of violent theologies and a profound sense of disaffection, anger and resentment cannot be safely ignored by any society (Armstrong 2001b). Swomley (1995: 5) concludes: "The purpose of these radical religious demands is not to improve morality or end secularism but to merge the power functions of the state with a particular religious expression and therefore lay the groundwork for a theocracy."

Fundamentalism shares with fascism a nostalgic mythology of an earlier state of purity and glory, an exclusionary exaltation of the authentic people, the idea of the primacy of the homogeneous whole with a concomitant diminution in the importance of individual rights (Griffin 1991), a concern with absolutes. But we should not expect fascism in the 2000s necessarily to look much like fascism in the 1940s. Expectations and sensibilities have changed. History has happened. Communication technologies have opened up new possibilities and new challenges. Nevertheless, in that certain human fragilities and needs remain, there are fresh opportunities for the political demagogue, the charismatic guru, the video game programmer, the military recruiter, the intellectual with little inhibition and much ambition.

It would be a mistake to see Rightist movements conspiratorially, if only because the complexity of fundamentalist activity might be lost in the process. Taking refuge in the binaries of good and bad simplifies what can be learned about the politics of social situations. Studying fundamentalism provides a way of recognizing the use of fixed identities as a causal force ("we cannot be otherwise"). Ruptures and debate involving fundamentalist ideologies reveal the assumptions about society that otherwise remain concealed. Tracing the path of fundamentalist influence illustrates how slippages are suppressed and sameness is prized. It is important not simply to dismiss fundamentalism as an oppositional force when much can be learned by examining the frame of its orthodoxy, to see where debates have got stuck. Apple and Oliver (1998: 92) remind us that by ignoring possible insight about fundamentalist groups, we "ignore the places where decisions could have been made that would not have contributed to the growth of these movements." We ask: What are the ideological boundaries that are unavailable for negotiation? How do systems of authority construct starting points? What are the trains of thought whose tracks never meet?

Causality and the Rise of Fundamentalism

An important consideration is why fundamentalism has, at least in its twentieth-century forms, become an issue. Murray Knuttila, writing on hegemonic masculinity (chapter 7) suggests that fundamentalism is linked to "projects of social reform or political power." Knowing why fundamentalism has come into existence at this time and recognizing who benefits from its ideologies and beliefs are important to understanding what fundamentalism is. Indeed Volker Greifenhagen (chapter 5) writes that fundamentalism is many faceted, and when referring to Islam, fundamentalisms are plural. He therefore calls for the careful and critical application of the label, if it is to retain any descriptive power, especially when applied to Islam. He further differentiates fringe from mainstream Islamic fundamentalisms, although one of the consequences of September

11, 2001, is that the possibility of such a distinction seems to have collapsed.

At a most superficial level, fundamentalism is a label that has served to legitimate prejudice and counter-violence. Put to work, however, fundamentalism is a concept with analytical and explanatory power capable of going beyond stereotypes about religions. As the authors in this volume indicate, the term, although it may be rooted in religious practice and orthodoxy, has a broad application. The fundamentalisms of the affluent and the poor, the American and the Egyptian, the man and the woman, the old and the young, the recent immigrant and the Aboriginal may all be different on the surface and even in some of their deeper manifestations, but it is our argument that they have much in common.

The term fundamentalism derives from the U.S. Protestant evangelical movement that began in the late 1800s (Marsden 1990). Taking its name in 1920 from *The Fundamentals: A Testimony of Truth* (1910–1915), a twelve-volume set of essays that reasserted the five-point fundamental creed[2] of evangelical Christianity in the face of growing liberal theology, the movement took off after World War I. Fundamentalism as a social movement began as a reaction against what was seen as the increasing control of Protestant mainline churches over both government and biblical criticism, as well as against a broad range of liberal/modern social transformations. Successive displacements wrought by the Civil War and post-war Reconstruction, massive non-British immigration, urbanization and World War I were critical in the rise of the fundamentalist movement (Armstrong 2001a). In essence a revitalization movement (Wallace 1956), it sought to restore the "true" religion and to save the United States from becoming Babylon (Marsden 1990). According to George Dollar (1973: XV), "Historic fundamentalism is the literal exposition of all the affirmations and attitudes of the Bible and the militant exposure of all non-Biblical affirmations and attitudes." Militancy is a key term here—fundamentalists saw themselves battling against ethical pluralism and changes to traditional society. Battles were waged for prohibition and blue laws and against the teaching of evolution in the schools (Marsden 1990). The movement sought a return to traditional beliefs, thereby to restore the purity of the nation. While claiming to re-establish the New Jerusalem, however, the fundamentalist movement was actually creating an original translation of the Christian religion based on a mythic and romanticized past (Armstrong 2001a).

Many of the features of fundamentalism can be discerned in this description of its origins. To be satisfied in its right-thinking, a fundamentalist system must claim that its standard of truth is based on objective authority and not subjective interpretations. Whether the belief resides in a sacred text or an infallible economic system, the basic tenets are unavailable for debate. Although inerrancy of scripture is not a characteristic of all religions,[3] the papers in this volume show that the social processes following fundamentalist thinking seem to be more or less replicated in a wide variety of contexts. Fundamentalism is especially strong in times of great social change, particularly in periods of perceived loss for social groups, as in the challenge to hegemonic masculinity through the changing roles of women.

Fundamentalism has important social dimensions and dynamics. In the westernized First World, we have experienced five hundred years of colonialism and nearly two hundred years of industrial capitalism. The last century is marked by accelerated rates of change. Sources of change are multiple and interactive with the shortening of distances through changes in transportation and communications technologies; the heightened contact of cultures and ideas; the growth, centralization and concentration of business and corporations; increased dependence on low wages and urbanization; intermittent war and ongoing conflict; the rise of individualism; new social movements; and the breakdown and reconstitution of community along new (and old) lines being among the most significant causes and effects of transformation.

Didi Herman (1997) describes the ways in which the infusion of a civil rights code moved North American society away from religious roots and toward human rights standards of law. Fundamentalist groups see themselves as victims fighting for survival, saying for example, that gay and lesbian rights constitute an attack on heterosexual culture. Fundamentalism can be seen, in part, as a reactionary movement that aims to regain or restabilize lost power, prerogatives and status. Regardless of the rest of their message, many fundamentalist movements, especially religious groups, are also about returning to the rightful order by putting previously subjugated groups back in their rightful places. This frequently includes (re)gaining societal control over women's sexuality, reproduction and labour. Ailsa M. Watkinson (chapter 10) describes several legal examples in which the teachings and actions of fundamentalist Christians in Canada infringe on the rights of groups protected under the *Canadian Charter of Rights and Freedoms*. The insistence on equality rights for disadvantaged groups represents a move away from the good old days of unquestioned patriarchal authority and compulsory heterosexuality. Not surprisingly, this same move parallels the rise of the Christian Right in the United States.

Fundamentalism and Social Regulation

Fundamentalism may emerge as a movement, but it is also a set of strategies that are about power. The authors in this volume draw attention to the "fundamentalist dividend," defined as the benefits and competitive advantages that may be gained by being part of a fundamentalist group. The fundamentalist methodology involves re-imagining the past and invoking an authentic community with deterministic social characteristics.

In so doing, it produces a paradox—the fundamentalist simultaneously engages in nostalgia for the past while displaying historical amnesia (Jameson 1992) about a system of living that never existed.

The strength of the fundamentalist identity may easily lead to a type of nationalism or contribute to the growth of nationalism where religion and nation coincide, as discussed by JoAnn Jaffe (chapter 8). The fundamentalist project often involves the desire to be both exclusive and universal. For example, the United States acts in an exclusionary fashion when it argues that a preventative war is a morally justifiable act for the United States but not for others with whom it disagrees. At the same time, the U.S. argues that its policies should be universal, that others should hold the same views, especially with respect to political and economic organization. The fundamentalist position claims the social space of true and faithful outsider (although the outsider status may not be desired) and moral guardian of the broader public. This (literally) ambivalent position may be troubling for both fundamentalist insiders and outsiders, as it produces relationships that are at once contradictory and unstable. The efforts that go into regulating conduct and ideologies are a measure of the instability that fundamentalist practices attempt to control.

Given the unstable nature of "true belief," how do fundamentalists guard their own? Karen Armstrong (2001b: 17) says that fundamentalism "begins not as a crusade against outsiders but a hatred of those of the same faith." In spite of the evangelizing imperative of some Christian fundamentalists, there is less of an attempt to regulate the behaviour and habits of those who are outside the range of social persuasion than there is to guard the hearts and minds of committed insiders. Fundamentalist practices glorify the homogeneity of the community as entirely distinct from, at first, co-religionists—such as liberal Christians—and then against outside others and foreigners. This premise accounts for the close scrutiny of the faithful insiders against deviations from or apostasy within their ranks. Purity of belief and behaviour is a mark of the insider and a way of setting the divisions of "with us" versus "against us." The price to be paid for raising questions or stepping outside normative group actions is swift and sure. Terms of persuasion, if not ridicule, are at the ready for disciplining the wayward, as in Kevin Davison's (2000) example of the regulating action that is brought to bear on the less than masculine. Men who fail to uphold hegemonic masculinity are automatically stigmatized as males of lesser status and possibly even as gay. "Hegemonic heterosexual masculinity is enforced through the discrimination of sissies and gay youth" (Kinsman, cited in Davison 2000: 47). Gender-appropriate behaviour is policed by punishing—through physical and emotional abuse that amounts to a kind of social terrorism—that which is deemed inappropriate. Fundamentalist systems require ideological control over their elect insiders and, simultaneously, repudiation of outside others. In fundamentalist

Christianity, the existence of others also represents opportunities for missionary work and prayer. Much depends on this construction of opposites in which the other is desired to the extent that the fundamentalist can be fulfilled through the other's neediness.

Fundamentalism as a social process produces both those who are named and those doing the naming. Indeed, fundamentalism is rarely used as a term of self-identification and is almost always applied by those on the outside who take issue with it. Jackie Kuikman (chapter 4) raises important considerations for use of the term for cases in which the definition of fundamentalism is not fixed or agreed upon and when groups to whom it is applied do not necessarily meet all the criteria all of the time. She calls for a "careful and nuanced" approach when applying the term fundamentalist, not only for accuracy in nomenclature but so as not to obscure important differences between groups who "might seem to resemble one another when the term fundamentalism is applied." Kuikman describes how the term, applied as a condemnation, erases several important distinctions between various Jewish groups, setting them up as easy targets for ongoing anti-Semitism.

A closely articulated and practised ethnicity is often the only response to the denigrating effects of an external power, for example, the colonialism experienced by First Nations people. Joyce Green (chapter 2) describes the powerful Janus face of nationalism that, when fused with fundamentalism, has the potential to conflate communities into singular expressions of ideology. Among First Nations communities, a response to colonizing forces has been the adoption—on the part of some First Nations people—of exclusionary cultural practices adjudicated by insider experts who decide what and who is Aboriginal. What might be cause for positive collective pride is, instead, subject to restricted action to the extent that, in order to be authentic, one must *be* one's culture. In order to belong, one must forgo a critique of this particular form of strict characterization or "any other form of social accounting."

Verna St. Denis (chapter 3) contends that essentialist notions held by and about oppressed people limit the justice claims they can make. She describes the problem of insisting on strict adherence to Aboriginal cultural practices as the overriding keys to Aboriginal identification and "healing." Unwavering faith in cultural revitalization as the means to overcome the effects of colonization operates as a particular form of cultural fundamentalism. Moreover, the emphasis on cultural practices serves to restrict a thorough-going critique of power relations and the consequences of systemic racism and poverty experienced by First Nations people. Most unfortunately, silencing the internal critique of a culturalist ideology perpetuates the on-going unequal distribution of wealth and resources, an outcome that continues to benefit hierarchies operating both within and without the social group. There is a great need for solidarity and little space for self-critique within a group that is already socially disadvantaged. Such cultural fundamentalism has the potential to be doubly restrictive. While the closed system offers safety of association to insiders, it also contributes to the assumption that indigenous people simply *are* their culture, even while it silences internal dissent that cultural practices are not the sum total of their identity.

Nayyar Javed (chapter 6) cautiously negotiates the tenuous ground between liberatory self-naming and traditionalist Islamic practice. Regrettably, stereotyping Islamic peoples and exoticizing Muslim women on the part of the West straitens the women's circumstances rather than offering them any useful solidarity. A common characteristic of fundamentalist groups is the claim that they are under attack from social, religious or political outsiders. It is important to acknowledge that for groups with reduced social and political power as the ones described in chapters by Jackie Kuikman, Joyce A. Green, Verna St. Denis and Nayyar Javed, their ability to claim their rights is a constant struggle. Groups operating through traditional practices, however, need not be fundamentalist or restrictive of human rights as long as dissent does not mean expulsion or coercive conformity. Traditions within a community and a sense of belonging can be reclaimed without reifying the traditions or excluding critical voices.

What is the Appeal of Fundamentalism?

Those who deal in fundamentalisms are often astute in exploiting the insecurities and angst that result from the ongoing revolution in social relations. Fundamentalist patriarchy reassures insecure men of their right to dominate women. A clear sense of entitlement separates the men from the not men, irrespective of whether the patriarchal dividend is forthcoming. Fundamentalist stances provide easy answers to questions of public morality: the response to whether same-sex couples should have the legal right to marry will always be "no." A sense of belonging is offered in exchange for the practice of and belief in prescriptive cultural practices that identify one as secure and at home. There is something very appealing in the promise of an 'authentic' identity and the feeling of belonging that accompanies it. Fundamentalist practitioners offer assuredness, community, acceptance, resolution and a strong set of rules to live by. The fundamentalist dividend may also be manipulative, however, and well able to exploit and cultivate psychological weaknesses and insecurities of all kinds. The promise of fundamentalism is thorough, moving between levels and issues of a most intimate and personal nature, including those having to do with broad historical mega-trends, while offering simplistic answers to complex economic and social relations.

People may be susceptible to the siren song of fundamentalism because they are cast adrift, without compass or anchor, life jacket or life insurance, fearful that the rising tide may lift other boats but not their own—which can only mean their own craft is sinking. Many people spend the bulk of their waking lives in pursuits that carry little intrinsic satisfaction or meaning for them. They are subjected to hierarchies at work and may feel that they have little control over most aspects of their lives. Fundamentalism cuts through the ambivalence, the contradictions and the disturbing unpredictability. It offers instead, stability, a coherent regimen, answers, certainty and support. It frequently comes packaged with some kind of community, one that may offer a new salient identity, resources and psycho-social supports. A person may be out of step, a misfit or an outsider in the wider world but enjoy a sense of belonging within the community of certainty. A community of fundamentalists may demand certain kinds of conformity, but it may also be accepting of other kinds of difference. Fundamentalism holds out a promise of transcendence, peace and security in a world that specializes in upheaval, dissolving all ties, loosening all bonds and rendering contingent all relationships.

Fundamentalism can offer searchers a measure of security in the turbulence of economic and political disorganization and disorder. As the restructuring and cannibalization of economies throw people into higher states of anxiety and self-doubt, they face increasing pressure to take risks and to consume at levels well beyond their means. The stress of coping and striving is high. How attractive it is to learn that there are ready answers, that their predicament is caused by perfidious infidels or other strangers. Fundamentalists learn that in the face of others who lack moral rectitude, they can achieve inner calm and outward confidence by joining with the members of a strong contingent of true believers. In the kind of fundamentalism that borders on fascism, extremist and disaffected people find a common cause in the rhetoric of xenophobia and the certainty of simplistic answers. The "other" is always a necessity for the formation and fervour of fundamentalist dogma. The safety of the fundamentalist is always at risk from toxic ideologies and religious fanaticism of outsiders. As a consequence of continually anticipated, real or imagined harm, the fundamentalist adopts the status of a beleaguered minority, regardless of its social power. Ironically, the doctrine of U.S. exceptionalism carves out a minority position even for a dominant world force such as the United States.

Each of the variations of fundamentalism that we consider has as its centre a critique of the moral decay of society. In each example, a fundamentalist process is designed to safeguard the interests of the harassed; it arises especially at times of ideological uncertainty and retrieves a "historic vision" of the national or cultural self (Melling 1999).

What of the topics of hegemonic masculinity and neo-liberalism? What if critics of these topics are able to point out oppressive characteristics of these systems without recourse to a fundamentalist lens? What can we gain from our approach of examining unconventional areas in this light? It is helpful to see that neo-liberalism and hegemonic masculinity, like religious movements, also offer an ideological determinism much wanted in times of uncertainty. As belief systems, faith in the market or in hegemonic forms of masculinity offer security in the midst of diffusion and loss, even as they confirm adherents in their paranoia. Furthermore, the power relations within these hegemonic systems depend on hierarchies of inequality similar to the way women and minorities are regarded within religious and ethnic forms of fundamentalism. Adherents to fundamentalist systems need not be social minorities in order to feel under attack. In a paradoxical way, they feel beleaguered because they are powerful.

One consistent principle in all fundamentalist orderings is a "radical patriarchalism" (Riesebrodt 1990), which can be described as prescriptive behaviour that favours a masculine authority. The predominance of masculine leadership in areas of public authority is rationalized as if it were naturally occurring rather than operating through a system of unequal access to social and political power. When it is backed by claims of right thinking and the evidence of the status quo, hierarchical ordering is unquestionable. As in religious fundamentalism, a notion of objectivity or right thinking at once admits and defines the faithful. In the Christian example, accepting the circularity of the truth of the Bible because "the Bible tells me so" is a position that can only be arrived at by the proverbial leap of faith—not by logic. A fundamentalist system—whether it is religious, social or economic—depends on unassailable belief in itself regardless of the adjustments the faith has to undergo to keep itself intact. The opening line of Phillip Melling's (1999: ix) *Fundamentalism in America* states: "fundamentalism has been seen as ... the deadly enemy of rational debate and intellectual enquiry." Recognizing the characteristics that neo-liberalism and hegemonic masculinity share with fundamentalist belief systems will explain some of the ways these systems have remained impervious to rational argument even if we cannot always follow where the train of logic stops.

What Does the Process of Fundamentalism Permit?

Some of the writers in this volume speak of fundamentalism as a process, as a set of behaviours, and not only an ideological position. What then is permitted by fundamentalist process? What does it accomplish with its idealized past, inerrant beliefs, fixed boundaries and opposing identifications on both sides of the in/out divide? In spite of the surety of its dogma, fundamentalism is tied to the modernist project of the late nineteenth and twentieth centuries, even as it rejects modernism—or at least the open critique that is said to accompany it. For example, even though religious fundamentalists reject the supremacy of human rights when those rights are at odds with their beliefs, they still appeal to human rights tribunals to uphold exemptions based on freedom of religion. Religious fundamentalists often see themselves as separate from and a corrective to mainstream religious practice. At the same time, they desire to have tremendous influence over public affairs and to see their cause as having central significance. Biblical scholar James Barr (1978: 343) says: "Fundamentalists today are no longer entirely content with their alienation; they are also craving recognition. They want their arguments to be taken notice of; they want their cultural achievements and their scholarship to be recognized." Barr (1978: 343) continues that the religious fundamentalist who is annoyed at being alienated from the academic world of religious scholarship retaliates by "unchurch[ing] those who believed differently and [treating] their theology and their biblical work as if it was an enemy of God." The attention of outsiders is necessary both for the recognition of the fundamentalist cause and for proof that oppositional factions threaten them and their beliefs. A fundamentalist agenda with its promise of reward, if not transcendence, is ostensibly meant for insiders; a main dilemma, however, is that outsiders might take fundamentalists at their word and leave them alone.

Having said that, it would be disingenuous not to acknowledge that outsiders to fundamentalist activities often ignore the violations of human rights that can go on within fundamentalist circles, as Nayyar Javed reminds with respect to the lives of some Muslim women. Further, it is the proselytising activity of certain forms of fundamentalism that renders the movements problematic for outsiders. Indeed, it is the sometimes violent promotion of particular fundamentalist ideologies that brings them to our attention.

Fundamentalism as described here is a phenomenon of true belief and true believers. It can be identified as a process in which a set of binary absolutes are constructed: insiders and outsiders, truth and lies, God and devil. Thus, one can note fundamentalism as a principle in operation in a wide variety of contexts—the true believer may be fundamentalist to the extent of admitting no contradiction. In the area of science, biotechnologists who promote GMO (Genetically Modified Organisms) technology in agriculture, to take an example close to those of us in Saskatchewan, revile their critics and accuse them of being ignorant fear-mongers, anti-progress and anti-poor. Their tactic is to delegitimize detractors and place them outside of the pale of reasonable discourse and decision-making. Similarly, as Don Mitchell explains (chapter 9), belief in economic neo-liberalism has long passed the healthy scepticism that one might expect in relation to scientific theory and has progressed to the status of sacred truth. This dogma of market fundamentalism includes the belief that markets are the best means to allocate resources and rewards; in contrast, the notion of the public or common good is regarded as heretical. In circular fashion, social problems that result from market fundamentalism are cited as proof that there is still too much public control over the markets. Like other fundamentalisms, its imagined utopian past is being used to control the present.

The Left is not immune to fundamentalist impulses either. Marx's idea that the working class would make society into a place where together everyone could reach their full potential led quickly to accusations of false consciousness when the workers did not behave correctly in the interest of all the people. Lenin's prescription was vanguardism, rule by a group of intellectuals and bureaucrats who would determine and then lead the people to understand their own interests. Stalin's fundamentalist/totalitarian answer, like Pol Pot's in Cambodia, was to purge the wrong-thinking worker.

Are We Fundamentalists in Doing this Work?

Throughout this project of defining and examining the social phenomena of fundamentalisms, we ask how we are produced through this naming. Is our work, which we identify as feminist, anti-racist and anti-oppressive—that we intend as liberatory—ultimately fundamentalist? Are we anxious to find distinctions that will not include us, or to locate others as more extreme, so that our own positions are reasonable in comparison? We think these are important questions because we recognize some qualities shared with fundamentalist thinkers such as the passionate holding of a sustained, systematic set of beliefs. Like fundamentalists, we are convinced that what we have learned—in our case, about social justice—is worth working toward and teaching others about. We have concluded, however, that if anyone who is passionate about something can be labelled a fundamentalist, then the word means nothing.

We differ significantly from fundamentalists in that we do not pine for a reconstructed pristine past but instead look toward increased transparency of and political accountability in power relations. The doctrine of fundamentalism is prescriptive and must be enforced, and, by definition, is not open to interpretation or critique. After all, in the case of religious fundamentalism, the authority is prophetic, leaving followers with the duty to remain faithful. While we admit that our projects of social and political change are also enmeshed in ideology, we claim that attention to openness and justice can help us to avoid the pitfalls of fundamentalist practice.

How do we engage differences, tolerate them and avoid sliding into relativism while maintaining our own convictions? How do we decide between competing claims when there is no objective notion of truth that stands outside and from which we take unerring direction? A good counter is to return to the question of whose interests are being served by each particular set of ideas and practices. Who benefits by the social ordering that accompanies each set of fundamentalist principles—what is the fundamentalist dividend? We know that our work is guided by an emancipatory project and that we are taking a stand for social justice issues. We are not consumed by the relativism that "anything goes." Indeed, we believe that some ideas are more powerful than others—and that what we choose does make a difference.

At the same time, we want to be aware that the term fundamentalist can be used simply to obfuscate difference or to refuse the possibility that we are the other of whom we speak. We want to avoid using the term simplistically to demonize others who are dialectically opposed to our work for a variety of reasons. Rather than painting fundamentalist ideologies with broad strokes as if all instances were homogeneous, it is important to see the careful negotiations of people living in tension within and on the edges of fundamentalist communities, like some of the writers in this volume. One's location also matters in how criticism can be heard. "Insider" criticism may hold the highest value; the work of critical insiders also involves the greatest risk, and, most likely, the greatest subtleties.

We return to Linda Kintz (1997) and her reaction to the intimately familiar message on her voice-mail that delivers its hate-filled invitation in all sincerity and righteousness.

> If those of us who want to understand contemporary conservatism could only decipher what we hear in this voice, we might also momentarily come much closer to understanding the passions of reactionary politics. And if there are conservatives who are appalled at being symbolically associated with these absolutist conservatives perhaps they too need to understand a bit better the dangers of resonance.... For in contemporary America, where passion and media blur all boundaries, responsibility has far less to do with intentions than it does with the recognition of the dangers of those sympathetic vibrations. (Kintz 1997: 272)

Ruptures in the social fabric, such as 9/11, allow examination of practices such as fundamentalism that otherwise might be taken for granted. Such opportunities for deconstruction are most useful if we also examine our own understandings for intransigence and tendency towards closed thought. Here is where we hope to part company: We take fundamentalist frames to be systems of thought and action that, by definition, remain closed to critical scrutiny. The effects of a particular system will vary, but the closed system itself has every potential to contribute to oppressive acts and prescriptive behaviour. Extreme versions of fundamentalism result in zealotry and fanaticism. A fundamentalist system is an effect of power relations that are bounded by an internal logic that is beyond examination. What remains the same is a fundamentalist notion of a pure past and a pure identity; what changes are the local and historical explanations for why purity cannot be achieved at this particular moment, such as the persistence of evil-doers or feminists or the moral decay of society. In this volume, it is the closed systems of thought, the resistance to scrutiny and the unassailable logic that captures our attention to and interest in fundamentalism.

Notes

1. In late 2003, the Canadian Alliance of Canada merged with the Progressive Conservative Party of Canada to become the new Conservative Party of Canada.
2. The five-point creed is: the inerrancy of scriptures, the deity of Christ, his virgin birth, the substitutionary atonement of Christ, and his physical resurrection and coming bodily return to earth (Cole 1931: 34).
3. For example, in Judaism, all readings of holy texts are considered to be interpretations, and a large part of Orthodox Jewish religious practice is engaging in different levels of interpretation (Kuikman, this volume). As regards Islam, the Qur'an is considered inerrant and read literally as God's word by the vast majority of Muslims. People who are typically regarded as Muslim fundamentalists are interested in the political extension of Islam and focus on the establishment of an Islamic government (Greifenhagen, this volume).

References

Apple, M., and Oliver, A. 1998. "Becoming Right: Education and the Formation of Conservative Movements." In C.A. Torres and T.R. Mitchell (eds.), *Sociology of Education: Emerging Perspectives*. New York: SUNY Press.

Armstrong, Karen. 2001a. *The Battle for God*. New York: Ballantine Books.

_____. 2001b. "Cries of Rage and Frustration. *New Statesman (1996)*, 130(4556).

Barr, James. 1978. *Fundamentalism*. Philadelphia: Westminster Press.

Bolce, L., and DeMajo, G. 1999. "The Anti-Christian Fundamentalist Factor in Contemporary Politics." *Public Opinion Quarterly 63(4)*: 508.

Cole, Stewart Grant. 1931. *The History of Fundamentalism*. New York: R.R. Smith.

Davison, Kevin. 2000. "Masculinities, Sexualities and the Student Body: 'Sorting' Gender Identities in School." In Carl E. James (ed.), *Experiencing Difference*. Halifax: Fernwood.

Dollar, George. 1973. *A History of Fundamentalism in America*. Greenville, SC: Bob Jones University Press.

Griffin, Roger. 1991. *The Nature of Fascism*. New York: St. Martin's Press.

Hage, Ghassan. 2001. "The politics of Australian fundamentalism: Reflections on the rule of Ayatollah Johnny." *Arena Magazine* 51.

Herman, Didi. 1997. "'Then I Saw a New Heaven and a New Earth': Thoughts on the Christian Right and the Problem of 'Backlash.'" In Leslie G. Roman and Linda Eyre (eds.), *Dangerous Territories: Struggles for Difference and Equality in Education*. New York: Routledge.

Jameson, Frederic. 1992. *Postmodernism, Or, the Cultural Logic of Late Capitalism*. Durham, NC: Duke University Press.

Kintz, Linda. 1997. *Between Jesus and the Market: The Emotions that Matter in Right-Wing America*. Durham, NC: Duke University Press.

Laqueur, Walter. 1996. *Fascism: Past, Present, Future*. New York, Oxford: Oxford

University Press.
Marsden, George. 1990. "Defining American Fundamentalism." In Norman J. Cohen, (ed.), *The Fundamentalist Phenomenon: A View From Within, A Response From Without*. Grand Rapids, MI: Wm. B. Erdmans Publishing.
Melling, Philip. 1999. *Fundamentalism in America: Millennialism, Identity and Militant Religion*. Edinburgh: Edinburgh University Press.
Riesebrodt, Martin. 1990. *Pious Passion: The Emergence of Modern Fundamentalism in the United States and Iran*. Translated by Don Reneau. Berkeley: University of California Press.
Saunders, Doug. 2001. "U.S. got what it deserved, Falwell says." *Globe and Mail* September 15, A2.
Swomley, J.M. 1995. Neo-Fascism and the Religious Right. *The Humanist* 55(1).
van der Vyver, J.D. 1996. "Religious Fundamentalism and Human Rights." *Journal of International Affairs* 50(1).
Wallace, Anthony F.C.1956. "Revitalization Movements." *American Anthropologist* 8(2).

Chapter Two

Cultural and Ethnic Fundamentalism

Identity, Liberation and Oppression[1]

Joyce A. Green

Fundamentalism is characterized by nostalgia for a mythical time of goodness in an earlier order, which can be reacquired by adhering to fundamentalists' representation of the code of that tradition. Tradition becomes the social prescription for national or cultural rejuvenation and its practice reinforces boundaries and behaviour. Many Aboriginal activists and intellectuals have claimed that cultural traditions provide the formula for healthy indigenous communities today. For some, these arguments have included racialized notions of how "the people," or the relevant community, will be determined. These are not uncontested questions. Necessarily, the political questions of who decides, who is authoritative, how the truths are maintained and how deviance is disciplined emerge from these kinds of claims.

My intention is not to dismiss the inestimable value of cultural practices but to problematize political arguments that invoke tradition as absolute authority for fundamentalist formulations of cultural practices, community and politics. I use the work of Emma LaRocque and Taiaiake (Gerald) Alfred to explore these themes. It is my contention that fundamentalism leads to rigid, exclusionary political processes that are likely to violate human rights and that it should therefore be eschewed by Aboriginal liberationists as well as by post-colonial vanguards. Ultimately, fundamentalist conceptions of liberation are oppressive and potentially place governments outside of the community of nations that subscribe to the collective discipline of human rights and international law.

"Fundamentalism," according to the *Oxford Canadian Dictionary*, is a "(1) strict maintenance of traditional Protestant beliefs ... (2) strict maintenance of ancient or fundamental doctrines of any religion, esp. Islam" (2001: 565). The notion is drawn from theological positions in which doctrinaire prescriptive approaches establish a correct practice, in contrast with incorrect or apostate or unholy practices. Fundamentalism is also typically thought of as "militant" and "reactionary." Anson Shupe and Jeffrey Hadden define fundamentalism as "a proclamation of re-claimed authority over a sacred tradition which is to be reinstated as an antidote for a society that has strayed from its cultural moorings" (1989: 110–11). They suggest that the sociopolitical template of fundamentalism is global, consisting of "a pattern of many contemporary sociopolitical movements that share certain characteristics in their responses to a common *globalization process,* [which instigates a search] for ultimate meaning, values, and *resacralization* of social institutions" in the search for meaningful community identity (116, emphasis in the original).

This globalization process is a contemporary phenomenon and part of what makes fundamentalism itself thoroughly modern. Fundamentalism is reactive against the rapid transformation of societies, cultures, economies and politics. Globalization is an ever-more rapid set of transformations associated with technologies, especially communication technologies. It is also characterized by the evolving practices of global capitalism, including the emergence of regulatory mechanisms that are above national jurisdictions, such as the World Trade Organization and other trade agreements. Globalization is associated with the permeability of all cultures to the dominant consumer and cultural ethos embedded in mass entertainment media, especially that exported from the U.S.

The themes of culture, tradition and identity also emerge in indigenous contestation of colonialism. It is in the search for authentic socio-political practices for anti-colonial praxis and theoretically informed political action that fundamentalism takes on a less theological but more cultural and political character. Yet the process of fundamentalism remains consistent: prophetic identification of sets of practices that invoke authenticity, against the violations of culture committed by colonial powers and inherent in their assimilative strategy.

This chapter aims to explore the process that is characteristic of fundamentalism, as well as its political purchase. The objective is not to invoke barriers to liberation but to trace the potential for non-oppressive politics of liberation. In so doing, I take up what I see as essentialist and fundamentalist impulses in arguments invoking tradition uncritically as a formula for contemporary social, political and, less often, economic organization. This formula has the potential for foreclosing liberation and for legitimating human-rights violations in the service of cultural redemption. Truly liberatory programs will have to create carefully the path between the imperatives and values of threatened traditions and the social and political limitations that traditional frameworks place on contemporary peoples. Liberatory programs must be mindful of the oppression inherent in any sociopolitical framework when that framework is constructed as incontestable.

Between Fundamentalism and Fundamentals

Religious fundamentalism strictly encodes tradition, which is treated by its adherents as inviolate. The *process* of fundamentalism is dualism: binary categories of right and wrong, good and evil, are established by elites who presume to know the content of the categories and who judge and prescribe sanctions for those who deviate from the correct formulations.

In the language of politics, the closest approximation to fundamentalism is totalitarianism, characterized by ideological control. Contrast the nature of fundamentalism with the definition of "fundamental": "of affecting, or serving as a base or foundation, essential, primary, original" *(Oxford Canadian Dictionary* 2001: 564). The tension between the two, then, revolves around the distinction between that which is essential and original, and a coercive approach towards enforcing behaviours in respect of that fundamental essence.

It is the authoritarian sociopolitical prescription, not the specifically religious content, that is characteristic of fundamentalism. This is a question of who knows, and how, and what kinds of coercive authority the knowers may invoke to compel conformity to their program. Fundamentalism is about process, not about issues, and it is the process that shares attributes across different kinds of fundamentalism that deal variously with ideology, religion, politics, economics, social mores and gender relations. Fundamentalism relies for its authority on fundamentals, but whose? And that authority is represented as unassailable, beyond debate. The fundamentalism formula consists of a (self-selected) prophet's call for "the people" to return to a lost tradition, the repository of social and theological rightness. Posed as an alternative to evil (identified by the prophet), the return is to an Edenic state of being to which there are clear cultural and faith ties, and of which the prophetic class are guardians (Shupe and Hadden 1989: 112).

E.J. Hobsbawm writes: "The 'fundamentals' that fundamentalism stresses always come from some earlier, presumably primal and pure ... stage in one's own sacred history. They are used for setting boundaries, for attracting one's kind and alienating other kinds, for demarcating" (1990: 167). The code of an earlier tradition, described by fundamentalists through myth and nostalgia, becomes the social prescription for national rejuvenation, and its practice reinforces boundaries and behaviour. The narratives of fundamentalism are particularistic and prescriptive, as are national narratives. Each represents a selective history, and a selective theology, to explain and glorify the past and to chart the future through practices in the present. Fundamentalism is antithetical to plurality, to tolerance, to differences.

Fundamentals simply exist as argumentative tools on which subsequent claims are based: "Our traditions served us well in the past and ensured the reproduction of healthy communities. Therefore, the values carried in those traditions ought to be resurrected in the interests of contemporary healthy communities." On the other hand, when the argument is transformed to one proposing: "Our traditions are these specific practices, done in these ways, by these people; therefore, these practices must be replicated precisely in order to achieve culturally authentic and healthy communities," fundamentalism rears its head. The proposition implicitly frames the speaker as the knower, able to discern infallibly, against whose knowledge others will be measured.

Fundamentalism cannot withstand intellectual contestation; it relies on its invocation of fundamentals in terms defined by its authorities. In this respect, fundamentalism leads to insularity and to exclusion of those who are not acceptable (or who do not accept), based on the assessment of the knowers. In such a climate, human rights cannot thrive, for they are always conditional on their fit with the sociopolitical frame determined by the fundamentalists. Democracy cannot thrive, for no oppositional propositions can be presented for serious consideration. Self-determination cannot thrive, for the community of interest must not be able to make a critical determination based on information and alternatives, and it must also not subject itself to the human-rights regime sustained (however imperfectly) by international law.[2]

The Politics of Fundamentalism

These habits of fundamentalism are political. Religion may have the highest profile, but the social-regulation aspects of fundamentalism also permeate areas that are only incidentally religious or are non-religious. The absolutist thinking and the resistance to critique and to critical thinking are characteristics of all fundamentalisms and, most perniciously, of politicized fundamentalism.

Politicized fundamentalism has become the scourge of our times, generating the terrorist reactions against hegemony and also the hegemonic imperial responses to terrorism. The reactive politics range from rejection of imperialism and colonialism, to rejection of Western political culture and social forms, to outrage about the radical material and political inequities inherent in the global economic order, which is in turn associated with the (Christian) West. The kinds of fundamentalism that are implicit in the Al Qu'eda program of terrorist violence against the American hegemony, for example, cannot be captured by the limited analysis of fundamentalism as a purely socio-religious position. It embodies a socio-religious preference and certainly has all of the totalitarian characteristics named above, but it emerges as a political response to a political condition, one in which the global political economy, with its concomitant cultural imperialism, is writ large. And this is the lesson to be learned: fundamentalism is reactive and can only be understood in its politico-historical context. Comprehension, not condemnation, is the first step in dealing with fundamentalism and also with terrorism.

Fundamentalism as Nationalism

How does fundamentalism, the ultimate essentialism, shape ideology, identity and nationalism? The political use of essentialism has produced a formula I call ethnic or cultural fundamentalism, which constructs historically and nationally located identity as legitimate only when a precise set of cultural, ideological and, most worryingly, genetic markers or "blood quantum" are met. This form of fundamentalist rhetoric has emerged in some claims to self-determination. Nationalist fundamentalism is the oppositional and reactive construction of "nation" in relation to the existing social formation, as identifiable by known and essential practices and beliefs, which both identify in/outsiders and perpetuate the nation. These essential characteristics become idealized, policed and enforced, in defence of the politics and social purity of the nation. The nation is conceptualized as anti-modernist relative to the multi-national state.

The desire to belong is a common human need, and nationalism and related forms of collective identity formation and celebration are expressions of that need. The search for belonging plagues those whose socio-political context is bereft of meaningful community. Belonging seems to be most meaningful when it affirms one's origins, identity, values and relationships. This is precisely why Marx's call for workers of the world to unite has had little mobilizing effect, for "workers of the world" is too large and diffuse a category to be emotionally resonant for most of us. We seem to need community that not only affirms us in our contexts but that also has boundaries. The community that is not bounded is emotionally irrelevant. Boundaries return us to the *problematique* of schemas determining who is in, who is out and who decides. For states, this is called citizenship, a relationship between individuals and the political power embodied in the institutions of political power. When ethno-nationalists claim state-like powers to determine membership, or citizenship, they are drawing boundaries around a "*relational* concept" (Thomas 2001) in order to determine who is in. When the criteria for who is in revolve around notions of ethnic purity or cultural purity, the filter becomes very fine and very problematic. For where will disputes be heard, and how can those who have been defined as "not community" challenge the filters of the community?

There is little likelihood of eliminating nationalism. Any viable human community will, over a relatively short time, see itself through political and historical accounts that are nationalist.[3] And nationalism frequently takes as its reference point a mythical past, lost to the contemporary community. That mythical past is sometimes invoked as the standard for the community, known to a few and imposed on the many in the name of cultural or national regeneration. Still, without the power inherent in the "nation" concept, communities will be hard pressed to act autonomously within the multi-national state. And without exclusivity of membership, definition becomes problematic. In sum, nationalism is a fraught concept and set of political assumptions; yet it is also imbued with much of the political muscle necessary to achieve a measure of the self-determination that is itself a human right. The challenge is to find the path to self-determination across terrain littered with conceptual material antithetical to human rights.

The interpretation of the past (or historically resonant tradition) in a contemporary program is not a neutral exercise. Selected experts decide, and to the extent that the experts are sustained by political power, others must acquiesce. Therefore, the power relations within communities set the stage for the political programs that inevitably are encoded within nationalist narratives. "Imagined history" (and all history emerges from selective memory and imagination) must also be understood as a political and prescriptive narrative, the details of which suggest a political agenda (Levinger and Lytle 2001). The invocation of essential values is both a call to re-inscribe culturally relevant meaning on social life and a rejection of critique by any other form of social accounting.

"Chameleon-like, nationalism takes its colour from its context," writes Anthony Smith (1991: 79). Fundamentalism is sometimes fused with nationalism in ways that conflate the community with ideology and culture, and sometimes with ethnicity. Nationalism shares some characteristics with fundamentalism. Committed to the nation, a necessarily exclusive community, nationalism becomes problematic for the multi-nation state. Nationalism can create a positive sense of identity and common cause. When it is a valorization of some and an erasure of others; when its fictive and mythical elements resonate for some and alienate others, it is at best irrelevant; at worst, it dramatizes oppressive and offensive strands within the political culture. Such a culture, according to Monserrat Guibernau, is precisely what nation-states try to create.[4]

Nationalism "as a political principle holds that the nation and the state should be congruent" (Guibernau 1996: 62). Typically, nationalism is understood by academics to refer to a sense of allegiance on the part of a self-conscious community to a territorially bounded, politically constructed entity known as the state—or to the idea of creating such an entity. Nationalism is about collective aspirations and boundary maintenance in achieving them. The nation is an "imagined community," in Benedict Anderson's phrase (1983, cited in Hobsbawm 1990: 46), or a "narration" in Edward Said's (1994: xiii). In Hobsbawm's view, it can meet the "emotional void" that exists because of a lack of real human communities. Nationalism depends on an authoritative conception of the nation, which typically includes language and ethnicity.[5] Yet, especially in colonized societies, language is often either a political imposition or a form of political resistance; and ethnicity may only impute a cultural affiliation (sometimes erroneously) as culture is a social phenomenon, not a biological or genetic one. But ethnicity can, according to Hobsbawm, contribute to the conceptualization of what he calls a "proto-nation," because it functions to bind populations that are physically dispersed and that lack a common polity (Hobsbawm 1990). The markers of ethnicity have been used with racist intent, so that "visible differences ... have too often been used to mark or reinforce [class] distinctions between 'us' and 'them'" (Hobsbawm 1990: 65–66). Rather than being primarily about nationality, ethnic and cultural differences are not politicized unless repressed or associated with the exploitative power relations of class, colonialism and imperialism.

National identity is composed of the characteristics of historical territory, common myths and history, common culture, shared legal rights and duties and a common economy with territorial mobility for members (Smith 1991). The signal attributes of ethnic communities (or *ethnie*) include collective consciousness manifested in a name, a myth of common ancestry, shared historical memories, differentiating elements of common culture, a "homeland" and a widely shared sense of internal solidarity (Smith 1991). Ethno-nationalism fuses the two into a political program for the *ethnie*, generally in opposition to an existing, sometimes colonial, authority.

Ethno-nationalism consists of a political national discourse and program for the culturally bounded, if not always geographically or politically bounded, community. Walker Conner (1994) suggests that ethno-nationalism (which seems to be identical to what Hobsbawm calls "proto-nationalism") has been inadequately studied in part because of the vague terms used for the phenomenon and because of the reluctance of scholars to use the term "nationalism" in relation to ethno-nationalism.

Nationalism has been defined as "a strategic program or agenda whereby a given nation or nationality seeks to promote its autonomy, freedom, cultural priorities, prosperity, and (sometimes) sheer power" (Dallmayr and Rosales 2001: xvi). Matthew Levinger and Paula Lytle identify three elements of nationalist rhetoric that are remarkably similar to the attributes of fundamentalism: "the glorious past," "the degraded present," and "the utopian future" associated with national resurgence (2001: 178). Nationalism wears the Janus face of positive collective pride in common identification and the dangers of xenophobia and the legitimation of intolerance. Expressed as a declaration of primacy against all others, these kinds of collective identity are reactive, insular and ethically suspect. Nor do they offer a political program for change. E.J. Hobsbawm declares, "the call of ethnicity or language provides no guidance to the future at all. It is merely a protest against the status quo or, more precisely, against 'the others' who threaten the ethnically defined group" (1990: 168). Yet nationalism has also been a liberatory declaration against the imposition of external power, especially colonial power. Colonialism, in its typical processes of denigration of indigenous political and cultural forms and imposition of colonial ones, constructs the colonized as subordinate and deficient, save for the ameliorating effects of colonial influences. National and cultural resistance, therefore, are a reclaiming of authenticity, of dignity and of an anti-colonial frame for political and cultural reference. "To identify with the nation is to identify with more than a cause of a collectivity. It is to be offered personal renewal and dignity in and through national regeneration" (Smith 1991: 161).

Contemporary existence provides a set of challenges to traditional forms of social, political and economic life in the context of Aboriginal peoples in Canada. In response, some activists and theorists have recommended traditional formulae for politics, family, culture and so on, collapsing what David Lynes calls "the complicated relation between the commitment to cultural verity on the one hand and the appropriate means of defending this from the continued influence of colonialism on the other" (2002: 1044). This has been interpreted by some as nationalism, for the most part as ethno-nationalism, but occasionally as a claim to sovereignty equivalent to that of the colonial state. This linkage between culture, colonial occupation, resistance and nationalism is one of political possibility for both liberatory and oppressive consequences.

Ethno-nationalism draws communities of interest together under the umbrella of shared culture, history and language, to be a shield against the dominating and fragmenting colonial culture. It provides a collective frame for identity, based on essential elements of "continuity over time and differentiation from others" (Guibernau 1996: 72–73). This shared sense of community is a powerful human need, made more acute in the face of racist oppression such as that to which Aboriginal peoples are routinely subjected. Yet ethno-nationalism (like generic nationalism) is also problematic, for it sharpens the focus on cleavages between communities and against an "enemy-image" (Wilson 2001: 376). It has fundamentalist characteristics. It does not tolerate dissent within, but requires acceptance of an elite-determined "group voice" (Nira Yuval-Davis, cited in Wilson 2001: 376). It thrives on oppositional differences rather than on affirmative political agendas. It draws on "elements of racist and fascist discourses" (Guibernau 1996: 85). In Robin Wilson's view, ethno-nationalism escalates conflict (2001). Infamously, ethno-nationalism has a racist potential, constructing the "we" community as fundamentally racially pure and distinct from others, who are political competitors. At its worst, this has resulted in fascism, ethnic "cleansing," mass atrocities and genocide.

Whatever the superficial differences in appearances, it is the human species that is the "race"; different communities are not in fact fundamentally, biologically different. (Relatedly, scientists have recently proposed including chimpanzees in the genus *homo*, as chimps and *homo sapiens* share 99.4 percent of their genes. Not only are humans not fundamentally different from each other, but we're barely distinct from chimpanzees.) Yet, as Conner reminds us, "it is not *what is*, but *what people believe is* that has behavioural consequences" (1994: 75).

Canada has developed a set of practices to facilitate some ethno-national accommodation within the practices of federalism and within the text of the Constitution (Asch 1984). Until 1982 this accommodation was limited to the province of Quebec, implicitly understood to be the geographical heartland of the Quebecois, conceptualized as *pur laine* descendants of French colonists. In the wake of the 1982 constitutional recognition of "aboriginal and treaty rights" and of Indians, Inuit and Métis as the peoples referred to, a body of jurisprudence and of scholarship is emerging that links, approvingly, (ethno)-nationalism to decolonization, within the boundaries of the Canadian state and with the support of the Canadian polity. This nationalism is never called such, but it may be time to start calling it a duck if it walks like a duck; "self-government" demands look more like nationalism than like requests for administration of colonial programs and policies. These claims are made on behalf of nations, against what Guibernau might classify as an "illegitimate" state.[6]

Culture and Identity

Culture remains an essential context for individual and collective identity and is politically resonant in virtually all societies (Smith 1995). Culture is the context in which our individuality is made meaningful. Where culture has been suppressed, as in colonial relationships, recovery of culture and strategies for resurrecting political power flowing from culture are parts of a decolonization narrative. Indigenous nations around the world have formulated a nationalism that claims difference from the colonial states as a justification for self-determination (Macklem 2001). At the same time, cultures that have been subordinated undergo a variety of transformations that radically change them, even as they can become ossified in memory and practice at the time of subordination. Applying Frantz Fanon's analysis, Lynes writes, "an indigenous culture under a colonial regime lives continually under the strain of knowing that its very existence is at risk. Faced with the perpetual need to resist this threat, very old traditions are forced into service playing new roles in defence of the culture which gives rise to the tradition in the first instance" (2002: 1056). In other words, the political project of cultural recovery is limited to what resources are available, be they imperfect, disputable or historically located at some distant time. Yet it is that culture which bears with it the claim for political liberation in the form of self-determination, as well as the potential for meaningful human community for those who are in the circle.

These twin impulses—change precipitated by external forces and contemporary reification of a particular previous cultural frame—vex those who would resurrect cultural practices, both for authentic identity and for political resistance. As Lynes argues,

> The problem is that what will count as an adequate defence of traditional culture is itself subject to the inevitable influence of the

> many forms this defence has assumed in the persons of innumerable, *legitimate* Indigenous and non-Indigenous advocates of Aboriginal culture. The defence itself, in other words, will not always be merely or exclusively conservative in its orientations or its aims. As new ways of formulating the defence are developed and expressed, the very nature of what is being defended inevitably evolves as well. (2002: 1046, emphasis in original)

To the extent that political power within the decolonizing nations is derived from cultural invocation, culture becomes a site of political struggle, and the authorities determining what and who is valid become political elites. Culture can be associated with the nation or state in xenophobic ways. It becomes a source of identity, sometimes characterized as "a return" to culture and tradition, that asserts codes of intellectual and moral behaviour (Said 1994). And, like fundamentalism, culture is also contemporary, shaped by the forces of "globalization" and communication technologies, and a powerful source of identity, as well as a connection to an apparently more authentic past (Bhabha 1994).

From Scepticism to Enthusiasm: LaRocque and Alfred

Several indigenous scholars have commented on the virtues and limitations of tradition in the context of decolonization and the recovery of indigenous power and authenticity. Apropos of this discussion of fundamentalism, identity and decolonization, it is useful to examine their premises and prescriptions against the characteristics of fundamentalism. Scholarship demonstrates the breadth of opinion and analysis and the contestations within indigenous communities over theory, analysis and praxis. Moreover, because liberatory projects can also fall prey to the oppressions they contest, a valid (equitable, sustainable, non-oppressive, authentic) decolonization process must take care that its intellectuals and, therefore, its programs and projects, are not damaged by logic and claims that would so taint them.

Here, I briefly take up the work of two powerful and very different voices. Emma LaRocque, Ph.D., is a Métis professor of Native Studies at the University of Manitoba. She has contributed to historiography, literary criticism and a gendered and feminist analysis of culture discourse for many years.[7] She is also theoretically and in her praxis a feminist. Taiaiake (Gerald) Alfred, Ph.D., is a Mohawk political scientist who heads the Indigenous Governance Program at the University of Victoria. His two books argue that indigenous liberation is found in the practice of cultural traditions and in the maintenance of Canada–indigenous relations via formal mechanisms such as treaty relationships (1995; 1999). He also takes a more polemical and prescriptive approach in his popular writing in indigenous presses, where he lays out a program for action based on cultural authenticity, boundary maintenance and rejection of compromises (such as policy like British Columbia's treaty commission) with the colonial state (2000 a and b). His work seems implicitly anti-feminist in its insistence on an uncritical reification of tradition, which of course has always been a site of contestation for feminists.

LaRocque argues:

> Aboriginal peoples are, *ipso facto*, dynamic peoples, whose cultures were seriously disturbed but not entirely erased by colonization processes. In part, the task is to know (or try to) the places (where) we have been imposed upon, and the places of our resistances, which has led to some significant maintenance of crucial cultural spaces. In other words, how do we read our many changes: where have we changed due to colonial force(s), or due to "natural" change as ordinary human beings who respond to our environments? In any case, I do believe in the value of Aboriginal peoples, cultures, nations' right to their distinctive identities. For example, I value my Métis landbased and linguistically Cree-rooted cultural background, along with a particular worldview that this embeds us/me with. However, I have never viewed or experienced my distinctiveness (intellectually and/or spiritually) as static, or as Hiawathian. Nor do I believe that oppression makes us morally superior or extra sensitive. (LaRocque, personal communication 2003)

LaRocque warns of the dangers of politicized tradition and essentialism when she expresses concern with the potential for human rights abuses through the imposition of traditions "created from the context of colonization" (1997: 76). "Terms such as 'traditional' or 'culturally appropriate' appear as a matter of course in discussions on Aboriginal governance.... The result has been a growing complex of reinvented 'traditions' which have become extremely popular even while lacking historical or anthropological contextualization. This is particularly true with respect to notions of justice and the role of women in Aboriginal societies, past and present" (1997: 76). For LaRocque, culture is always contestable, and she is especially interested to see how culturalist politics play in the lives of the marginal, especially marginal women. In her view, Aboriginal women find their interests subsumed in male-dominated institutions within Aboriginal communities—and in the external colonial society. Culture, supported by male colonial politicians and claimed for its political force by Aboriginal male politicians, can become a weapon to maintain women's subordination. LaRocque's is a minority view, but a cogent and substantive one.

Contrast LaRocque's view with the more prescriptive nationalist program of Taiaiake (Gerald) Alfred. Alfred argues that dominant western theories of nationalism are blind to the power relations in colonial states and are indifferent to the proposition that indigenous societies' resistance takes on characteristics of nationalism, articulated within the historic conditions of colonialism. "If we are to become strong nations again, we must move far beyond the politics of pity and begin to take action to free ourselves from the colonizer's cage" (2000b). Alfred considers that indigenous resistance to colonialism ultimately takes on a nationalist character, which is itself grounded on authentic traditional cultural and institutional bases (1995; 2000b) and corresponds most closely to the nationalism that western scholars call "ethnic" (1995). Ethno-nationalism "seeks to achieve self-determination not through the creation of a new state, but through the achievement of a cultural sovereignty and a political relationship based on group autonomy reflected in formal self-government arrangements in co-operation with existing state institutions" (1995: 14). This nationalism is directed not at construction of a separate state but at autonomy and a formal political relationship with the colonial entity.

Alfred's conceptualization of institutions and communities requires a very precise definition of who is who, and how we know. Alfred's model is silent on these issues as well as on the difficulties posed by hybridity. It does not address the problems that LaRocque raises of the syncretic nature of cultures (which makes absolute characteristics problematic) and of the many contingent choices individuals make in their cultural selections. Rather, for Alfred, the native cultural *corpus* is essentially fixed and not transient, in contrast with the fluidity (and hence the less politically significant) ethnic identities in the settler population. It is in these details that potential for oppressive fundamentalist formulations arises. "In Native societies, the various cultural, spiritual and political affiliations which comprise ethnicity are at root primordial and fixed, whereas in the general population there is a transience of ethnic identity" (1995: 11). Yet he also conceptualizes traditionalism as a self-conscious political strategy, a tool in the struggle for indigenous authenticity in the context of colonial occupation and hegemony. Tradition involves "changing attitudes, not looks or lifestyles" (1999: 134).

Identity formation is an important component of Alfred's conception of indigenous nationalism. Indeed, but for the distinctness of identity, native nationalism would lose its purchase in the popular indigenous imagination. Therefore, the cultivation of a distinct indigenous identity is both a strategy for, as well as a condition for, liberation. He notes approvingly that his Mohawk community has "enacted a membership law with strict provisions against marriage to non-Indians and membership criteria based on lineage." This is important lest "down the road we will be overwhelmed by people who have some Indian blood but no knowledge of the culture, no desire to participate in the community and no stake in the future of our nations" (2000a). It is in defining the community of identity that politics again manifest themselves, along with the potential for essentialism and fundamentalism. Like nationalism, then, identity formation and identity politics offer both community coherence and radical exclusion. "The various permutations of the collective identity are understood as forms of nationalism because they maintain traditional cultural boundaries and create group self-identification as a political community distinct from the state, and consistently committed to the right of self-determination (1995: 182). Identity is fused with a political project, and made dependent on it. Yet Alfred is not unaware of the problems associated with boundary maintenance: he suggests communities should be self-determining and that membership will involve "blood and belonging" determined *via* particular processes (1999).

Towards a Non-Oppressive Politics of Liberation

I have argued that fundamentalism is about process, not about content. I have shown how culture and nationalism, not only religion, can be fundamentalist. I have suggested that while indigenous liberatory struggles are necessarily located in history and culture, they, like all political movements, can become fundamentalist in ways that are unhelpful to the liberatory project and can constitute violations of fundamental human rights, if they are framed in dualistic and totalizing terms. The challenge, then, is to retain the political space for resistance to colonialism latent in cultural authenticity, while avoiding imposing social roles or racist and sexist boundaries for the community. Necessarily, this strategy must avoid conflating cultural authenticity with genetic purity in ways that are racist and that deny the existence of hybridity. The challenge extends to keeping culture vital and relevant, while recognizing that all cultures are syncretic and evolving. In relation to decolonization of Canada, LaRocque and Alfred have differing degrees of faith in the power of culture as a liberatory formula. LaRocque warns of the oppressive potential when culture and belonging are deployed politically to the disadvantage and disenfranchisement of marginal members of communities of resistance. Alfred is more sanguine about the ability of indigenous communities to negotiate the definition and maintenance of boundaries of belonging. Yet feminist theory and analysis would indicate that LaRocque's concerns must be attended to, as it is precisely in tradition that women and marginalized others have identified the most deeply held beliefs that sustain oppressive practices. While all tradition is not pernicious, neither is it all innocent of relations of dominance and subordination, nor of exclusion, and liberatory theories will have to attend to concerns of oppression within.

Culture is the repository of much collective wisdom; it provides meaning and context for human existence, but it is not infallible and it is not universal. This suggests that both critique and boundaries should be maintained. Nationalist and culturalist agendas serve both "in constructing identity and in mobilising popular support" and so must be considered in light of their strategic power (Levinger and Lytle 2001: 177). Nationalism, especially ethno-nationalism, relies on particularity for its force—boundaries matter, and they are often demarcated by shared culture. This, according to Andrew Robinson, limits cultural dynamism and the subjects of and parameters for contestability (personal communication 2003). However, liberation agendas should rely on claims of liberation from oppression rather than on cultural redemption, for in the latter way lies the potential for much anguish and oppression. Fundamentalism is never emancipatory. Finally, cultural redemption itself can still be a collective project of decolonizing societies, most safely when it is not tied too closely to political power, and when it is a dynamic, contestable process involving even those who dissent.

Notes

1. A version of this chapter appeared as "Cultural and Ethnic Fundamentalism: The Mixed Potential for Identity, Liberation and Oppression" in The Scholar Series, Saskatchewan Institute of Public Policy, University of Regina. Thanks to Andrew Robinson, Assistant Professor, Political Science and Contemporary Studies, Wilfred Laurier University, Brantford Campus, for his helpful comments on this chapter. I acknowledge the excellent assistance of Courtney England, MA student, University of Regina; and of Kathy McNutt, PhD student, Simon Fraser University. I also gratefully acknowledge the support of the Saskatchewan Institute of Public Policy, where I was Senior Fellow for the academic year 2002–03.
2. For a discussion of the wisdom of subjecting indigenous governments to the international human rights regime, see Joyce Green (forthcoming).
3. Dallmayr and Rosales note that "the most decisive criterion of proto-nationalism [is] the consciousness of belonging or having belonged to a lasting political entity" (2001: 73).
4. "While the national has a common culture, values and symbols, the nation-state has as an objective the creation of a common culture, symbols and values. The members of a nation can look back to their common past; if the members of a nation-state do likewise, they may be confronted with a blank picture—because the nation-state simply did not exist in the past—or with a fragmented and diversified one, because they previously belonged to different ethno-nations" (1996: 47–48; see also 62–64).
5. Hobsbawm also considers national languages to be politically motivated constructs imposed over a variety of languages or dialects (1990: 51).
6. Guibernau classifies states as illegitimate when there is inclusion of different nations or parts of nations under the predominance of one nation. While all citizens are treated equally, "there exists some kind of discrimination that derives from the fact that the state tries ... to instil a common culture, a set of symbols and values and pursues a programme of homogenization among its citizens" (1996: 60).
7. LaRocque's work includes (but is not limited to) "Teaching Native Literatures:

Margins and Mainstreams," *Reading Aboriginal Literatures: Epistemological, Pedagogical and Cononical Concerns* (R. Eigenbrod and J. Thom, eds.), Bearpaw Publishing (at press); "From the Land to the Classroom: Broadening Aboriginal Epistemology," *Pushing the Margins* (J. Oakes et al., eds.), Winnipeg: Native Studies Press, 2000; "Tides, Towns and Trains," *Reinventing the Enemy's Language: Contemporary Native Women's Writings of North America* (Joy Harjo and Gloria Bird, eds.), New York: W.W. Norton & Co., 1997; and "The Colonization of a Native Woman Scholar," *Women of the First Nations* (P. Chuchryk and C. Miller, eds.), 1996.

References

Alfred, Taiaiake. 2000a. "Manifesto for a New Century. *Windspeaker* 18(9) January.

_____. 2000b. "Solving the Indian Problem." *Windspeaker* 17(10) February.

_____. 1999. *Peace, Power, Righteousness: An Indigenous Manifesto.* Toronto: Oxford Press.

Alfred, Gerald R. (Taiaiake). 1995. *Heeding the Voices of our Ancestors: Kahnawake Mohawk Politics and the Rise of Native Nationalism.* Toronto: Oxford University Press.

Asch, Michael. 1984. *Home and Native Land: Aboriginal Rights and the Canadian Constitution.* Toronto: Methuen.

Bhabha, Homi. 1994. *The Location of Culture.* London: Routledge.

Conner, Walker. 1994. *Ethnonationalism: The Quest for Understanding.* Princeton: Princeton University Press.

Dallmayr, Fred R., and Jose M. Rosales, eds. 2001. *Beyond Nationalism? Sovereignty and Citizenship.* Lanham, MD: Lexington Books.

Green, Joyce. (Forthcoming). "Towards Conceptual Precision: Citizenship and Rights Talk for Aboriginal Canadians." In Gerald Kernerman and Philip Resnick, (eds.), *Insiders and Outsiders: Alan Cairns and the Reshaping of Canadian Citizenship* (provisional title). Vancouver: UBC Press, anticipated 2004; also forthcoming in Darlene Juschka and Leona Anderson (eds.),*The Great Escape: Scaling the Walls of Ideology.* Vancouver: UBC Press, anticipated 2004.

Guibernau, Montserrat. 1996. *Nationalism: The Nation-State and Nationalism in the Twentieth Century.* Cambridge: Polity Press.

Hobsbawm, E.J. 1990. *Nations and Nationalism Since 1780: Programme, Myth, Reality.* Cambridge: Cambridge University Press.

LaRocque, Emma. 1997. "Re-examining Culturally Appropriate Models in Criminal Justice Applications." In M. Asch (ed.), *Aboriginal and Treaty Rights in Canada.* Vancouver: University of British Columbia Press.

Levinger, Matthew, and Paula Franklin Lytle. 2001. "Myth and Mobilisation: The Triadic Structure of Nationalist Rhetoric." *Nations and Nationalism* 7 (2).

Lynes, David A. 2002. "Cultural Pain vs. Political Gain: Aboriginal Sovereignty in the Context of Decolonization." *Ethnic and Racial Studies* 25 (6).

Macklem, Patrick. 2001. *Indigenous Difference and the Constitution of Canada.* Toronto: University of Toronto Press.

McCarthy Brown, Karen. 1994. "Fundamentalism and the Control of Women." In J. Stratton Hawley(ed.), *Fundamentalism and Gender.* New York: Oxford University Press.

Said, Edward. 1994. *Culture and Imperialism*. New York: Vintage Books, Random House.

Shupe, Anson, and Jeffrey K. Hadden. 1989. "Is There Such a Thing as Global Fundamentalism?" In J.K. Hadden and A.S. Shupe (eds.), *Secularization and Fundamentalism Reconsidered*. New York: Paragon House.

Smith, Anthony D. 1995. *Nations and Nationalism in a Global Era*. Cambridge: Polity Press.

———. 1991. *National Identity*. Reno: University of Nevada Press.

Thomas, Paul. 2001. "Modalities of Consent, Compliance, and Non-Compliance." In Dallmayr and Rosales.

Wilson, Robin. 2001. "The Politics of Contemporary Ethno-nationalist Conflicts." *Nations and Nationalism* 7 (3).

Chapter Three

Real Indians

Cultural Revitalization and Fundamentalism in Aboriginal Education

Verna St. Denis

A relatively new Red Power consciousness, which contributed to a climate of hope and optimism, was evident when I entered the Indian Teacher Education Program in 1978. I am one of many beneficiaries of the National Indian Brotherhood (1972) policy—*Indian Control of Indian Education*—that called for the establishment of such programs. This was my first experience with an education equity program and the first time I would be in a learning environment supportive of the educational concerns of and responsive to the humanity of Aboriginal people.

Having survived and graduated from grade twelve in spite of the neglect and lack of interest on the part of my public school teachers, I thought I would burst from pride at being a student in the Indian Teacher Education Program. For the first time I felt pride in my identification as a Cree and Métis woman. My Cree, Mitcif, French and English speaking father was both delighted and bewildered with his daughter's enthusiastic interest in his history. I asked my devout Christian mother not to speak in English to me any more, and I became even more ambivalent about her devotion to Christianity. I wanted her to teach me about Cree cultural traditions and practices, to learn how to bead and to pick herbs and medicines. I wanted to wear as much Indian jewellery as possible. I wanted to learn about and participate in traditional spiritual practices. These moments of having one's life and cultural heritage acknowledged and legitimated are profoundly moving and powerful at the same time as they are disconcerting. It is the disconcerting effects that I struggle to understand.

Whereas previous Indian education policy and practice had actually facilitated the dehumanization of Aboriginal people, these new directives called for the celebration, affirmation and revitalization of Indian cultures and peoples. *Indian Control of Indian Education* (National Indian Brotherhood 1972) called for radical change by proposing that Indian education be culturally relevant to the philosophy and needs of Indian people. A culturally relevant education would recognize "Indian culture, values, customs, languages and the Indian contribution to Canadian development. Courses in Indian history and culture should promote pride in the Indian child, and respect in the non-Indian student" (National Indian Brotherhood 1972: 9). Although it is important to provide a historical account of how this shift in educational policy and practice came about, the focus of this analysis will be on some of the contradictory and paradoxical effects a program of cultural revitalization has in Aboriginal education. One way in which to highlight the contradictions of cultural revitalization is through the concept and practices of fundamentalism.

What About Fundamentalism?

Fundamentalism is most often associated with religious beliefs and practices and is sometimes intertwined with nationalism. Falkenberg (2002) suggests that fundamentalism, particularly Christian fundamentalism, is committed to simplistic interpretations of the faith, to simplistic notions of morality and right and wrong. Fundamentalism encourages dedication to cultural homogeneity and fixed behaviour patterns, to unchanging traditions and conventions for governing social interactions (Falkenberg 2002). In some of these characteristics, fundamentalism parallels the goals and strategies of cultural revitalization in Aboriginal communities, especially in the expectation of homogeneity, cultural preservation, unchanging traditions and historically anchored cultural values and conventions for governing social interactions.

The discussions of fundamentalism in the chapters by Joyce Green and Carol Schick (both in this volume) overlap in the critique of fundamentalism. For example, Schick is interested in the way fundamentalism is intent on preserving traditions, partly through a glorification of the past in a spirit of "repristination" that hopes to restore the "good old days" and a practice by which outsiders and insiders can be determined and maintained as separate. Green is interested in how fundamentalism seeks to establish doctrinaire prescriptive approaches that produce a kind of essentialist nationalism. The practices of traditional culture come to stand in for racial identification to the effect that one simply *is* one's culture.

I argue that the assumption that cultural revitalization and restoration are the primary goal of those involved in promoting Aboriginal education can also be described as having achieved fundamentalist status. Cultural analyses have assumed a level of sacredness and/or orthodoxy in Aboriginal education such that other analyses of the on-going marginalization, exclusion and oppression of Aboriginal people are not adequately explored. As a form of fundamentalism, cultural restoration and revitalization encourages Aboriginal people to assert their authenticity and to accept cultural nationalism and cultural pride as solutions to systemic inequality; ironically, this helps to keep racial domination intact.

Cultural Authenticity and Cultural Revitalization

I have not arrived easily at a place from which to critique cultural revitalization in Aboriginal education. Cultural revitalization has long been the focus of our educational interventions in the education of Aboriginal students. For example, a recent review of policy on Aboriginal education states that between 1967 and 1982 Aboriginal education was increasingly regarded as a "means for the revitalization of Indian cultures and economies" (Abele, Dittburner and Graham 2000: 8).

Interestingly, in 1967, the Hawthorne Report recommended cultural revitalization, ironically suggesting back then that Indian people must reclaim and develop a positive cultural identity. The report states: "the Indian must be brought to greater awareness of what he [sic] once was, of what he is and above all, what he can become if he is given the necessary means to develop" (Hawthorne 1967: 170). Further, the Hawthorne report suggests that by "freeing himself [sic] from the shackles of poverty and cultural exclusion, the Indian will retrieve his pride and dignity which are qualities essential to his development and progress" (166). In this Canadian government analysis, the development of pride and dignity among Indian people is touted as the solution to systemic problems resulting from the colonialism and racism it had perpetrated against Aboriginal people. Increasingly, reclaiming and developing a positive cultural identity would become mainstream thinking as the solution to educational inequality.

Adherence to cultural revitalization encourages the valorization of cultural authenticity and cultural purity among Aboriginal people and has helped to produce the notion and the structure of a cultural hierarchy. "Authentic" cultural Aboriginal identity has become high currency. Some of the markers of cultural authenticity include speaking one's Aboriginal language, having knowledge of and participating in a myriad of spiritual practices, and having knowledge of traditional stories and other practices of the past. Quetone, an American Indian elder, explains:

> There is a sudden awareness of being Indian, and everybody is going back, or at least making a grand search for some identity and some tie-in with traditionalism. The college kids are grasping for some tie-in through their Indian Studies programs. On the reservations, the kids are now trying to find more authentic information, more of their own traditions, and I think it must be very difficult, with so few elders who can give this kind of information. (quoted in Morey and Gilliam 1974: 156)

The problem of finding elders knowledgeable of cultural traditions and practices became increasingly paramount in the 1970s. One could already detect the development of a socio-cultural hierarchy among practitioners and those regarded as repositories of traditional knowledge. Whereas in an earlier period, those Indian people able to exhibit signs of "cultural assimilation" received some rewards, such as support to pursue religious studies, the table had now turned and those who exhibited signs of "cultural and linguistic retention" were now regarded with esteem.

This interest in revitalizing culture and language encouraged the production of categories of Indians: real, traditional and assimilated. For example, realizing that "traditionals" were increasingly in demand, Henry Old Coyote, a Crow Indian from Montana, explains:

> Now we have Indian experts popping up all over the country. Everybody's trying to tell us that this is the correct way, the authentic way of presenting our customs and beliefs. But the real traditional Indian is staying in the background, trying to see what goes on. I consider myself a traditional Indian.... And according to the advice I've been getting, I keep my ears open and my mouth shut. (quoted in Morey and Gilliam 1974: 4)

In an example closer to home, Sarah Whitecalf discusses the relationship between the Cree language and identity and the merits of speaking English. She explains:

> It is indeed very valuable for you, you put English to very good use in your work; of course it is not good if a person cannot speak English—such as I myself, for instance, look, I am an old woman, I am approaching seventy, I never went to school, I never set foot in a school, and *because of that I am truly a Cree, I am truly a Cree woman*. (1993: 27–28, emphasis added)

Language as an important sign of one's cultural authenticity continues to pose a challenge for many Aboriginal people. Although there have been many calls for Aboriginal language maintenance and reclamation, Aboriginal languages are continually eroding. Aboriginal teachers charged with the responsibility of supporting the development of a positive and strong cultural identity in their Aboriginal students must struggle with their own challenges of reclamation and revitalization. In the end, Aboriginal teachers must defend the actions of their parents and grandparents, who also struggled to make good decisions for their children, only to be told that they now had to try to reverse language and cultural loss.

Our Parents and Grandparents Have Not Forsaken Us

Aboriginal parents often remark on the shifting language demands that are made of them. These shifts are daunting for many Aboriginal parents.

> A Yup'ik instructor at the local community college noted, "Back when parents were told to speak only English to their kids, they did that but had very limited vocabulary in English. With limited vocabulary, children aren't going to learn that much." Now, however, parents are hearing that they should speak Yup'ik to their children. This change has caused some parents to mistrust the advice of educators. A Yup'ik parent voiced this mistrust at a school board meeting: "first I was told one thing, then another. If the advice changes every five or ten years, why should I listen?" (Henze and Vanette 1993: 128)

In some respects, a project of cultural revitalization and cultural affirmation places Aboriginal parents and grandparents in a similar dilemma. A strategy of cultural revitalization can have the effect of blaming our Aboriginal ancestors as having made the wrong decisions, holding them accountable for cultural and social change they did not singularly or always determine.

Aboriginal teachers also struggle to come to terms with the contradictory notions of cultural authenticity. One Aboriginal teacher explains that when he was about sixteen years old, he asked his parents why he and his siblings were never taught to speak Cree (St. Denis 2002). He explains that his grandfather had requested his parents not teach them Cree but have them learn English instead because it was going to be more profitable. Learning English would enable his grandchildren to move out of the reserve.

> I asked my mom, "Why is it that we didn't get to learn the Cree language? Why didn't you speak to us when we were kids, and teach us how to speak Cree?" And she told me that my mushum said "don't teach your kids Cree. I want your children to learn English," and the reason why is because, in his day, to learn the English language was going to be more profitable for you in the long run than it would be to learn Cree and I only analyzed it later on and realized that the reason why he wants me to learn English instead of Cree is because to be stuck on the Reserve and not have the skills that are necessary to move out of the Reserve would be detrimental to anyone. Then you would have to stay on the Reserve. He kind of looked at it as being, education was the key to success, and you had to learn the White man ways to be able to profit. (quoted in St. Denis 2002: 116)

This same teacher suggests that he should not be penalized for not speaking his language, as it was "not what I was taught":

> My reserve uses the provincial curriculum and I just kind of feel it's hypocritical to say that you have to have a Cree language to be able to teach, because that is not what I was taught. It seems to be a disadvantage for those who don't speak their own language. (quoted in St. Denis 2002: 117)

An Aboriginal educator, who is also regarded as an elder, explains her history:

> I think that the basis of survival is knowing your language, whatever it is, and for myself I never taught my kids because I had to relearn my own, relearn my own language, and once I grew up and got married I never lived in Saskatchewan, so there was nobody there to guide me or nobody there to talk and to speak Cree… even my dad never wanted us to learn our language, to relearn our language. He used to say, "I don't want any Indian spoken in this house." (quoted in St. Denis 2002: 117)

Another Aboriginal teacher shares with me the ways in which her father resisted the negative and stigmatized identification associated with being Indian. She explains that "he had his hair cut short" and denied that he spoke any First Nation language, even though she would later realize that not only could he speak Saulteaux, but he was also familiar with Cree and Sioux, so that "he lied to us about not knowing his language":

> I think part of his whole identity as being Indian was shaped during the residential school. He had his hair cut short. He didn't speak English until he was twelve when he went to school. He spoke Saulteaux before that and now the story is that he doesn't speak or understand it any more, but when I see him with his friends, he not only can understand what they say in Saulteaux, he knows Cree and Sioux as well … a few words of Sioux, and Dakota from the fellows he chums around with, so, he lied to us about not knowing his language, but he didn't see ... any value in it and he only used it when he was with his friends who spoke it. (quoted in St. Denis 2002: 118)

Here we have Aboriginal teachers and educators commenting on decisions their parents and grandparents made in attempts to participate in the promise of assimilation, namely, that once their children had learned English they would be able to avoid oppression and racism and be accepted into the dominant white society. Aboriginal parents and grandparents, in trying to protect their children from white supremacy, attempted to pass for white and actively denied their Aboriginal identity.

In a strategy of cultural revitalization, these efforts to resist racial exclusion would come back to haunt Aboriginal people who had lost their languages and were no longer familiar with their historical cultural practices and customs. In these respects, a strategy of cultural revitalization holds Aboriginal parents and grandparents accountable for colonization and responsible for their own downfall as a people.

Koyukuk Alaskan elder, Madeline Solomon, explains:

> We were told not to talk in Indian to our kids so we start talking in English to them. Then as they were growing up they don't know how to talk in Indian. Now they change their minds and start this Bilingual, but it's pretty hard to teach these kids. They just don't believe in learning the language again. (quoted in Madison and Yarber 1981: back cover)

Rethinking Cultural Revitalization, Authenticity and Inequality

As a cure for systemic social inequality, I argue that cultural revitalization is problematic. Education that promotes cultural revitalization as a primary solution to the educational inequality and marginalization of Aboriginal people has contradictory and paradoxical effects for Aboriginal people. First of all, in placing the burden of change on Aboriginal peoples, it ignores those larger issues of racism and economic imperialism that are not of our own making. Cultural revitalization as a strategy to counter inequality actually encourages the minimizing of historical and contemporary effects of racial inequality in Canada. In some respects, a strategy of cultural revitalization encourages the denial of history and socio-cultural change.

But cultural revitalization also shares several characteristics with fundamentalist orthodoxies that ultimately limit rather than liberate its adherents. Cultural revitalization, acting as a system of true beliefs, depends on a construction of Aboriginality as a timeless, unchanging essence. It operates with a fixed notion of culture and a social stratification that regulates degrees of authenticity. Cultural revitalization supports the development of national and cultural fundamentalism, especially by encouraging a hierarchy of Indianness, partly through the valorization of authenticity and pristine traditions. This solution of cultural revitalization operates in a fundamentalist fashion that is closed to a critique about its effectiveness as a liberatory strategy.

This analysis is not altogether original, as over three decades ago, the well known Lakota scholar, Vine Deloria (1969), was already reflecting critically on the belief that claims to cultural authenticity will alleviate problems in Indian education. In response to proposals that suggested the Oglala Sioux languished because they mourned the passing of their warrior practices, Deloria asked questions that are still relevant today:

> how ... can the Oglala Sioux make any headway in education when their lack of education is ascribed to a desire to go to war? Would not perhaps an incredibly low per capita income, virtually non-existent housing, extremely inadequate roads, and domination by white farmers and ranchers make some difference?... Real problems and real people become invisible before the great romantic notion that the Sioux yearn for the days of Crazy Horse and Red Cloud and will do nothing until those days return....The conclusion has been reached—Indians must be redefined in terms that white men will accept, even if that means re-Indianizing them according to a white man's idea of what they were like in the past and should logically become in the future. (Deloria 1969/1988: 91–92)

Cultural revitalization has problematic implications because of a kind of cultural absolutism it imposes on the native Other. In particular, it encourages incompatibility with socio-cultural change as the native must remain Other, distinctly different and identifiable.

N. Thomas, who analyzes the uses of authentic Aboriginal identity in Australia and New Zealand, comments on how the celebration of authentic Aboriginal identity demands a certain kind of native. He argues that the celebration of authenticity

> fixes the proper identity of those peoples in their preservation and display of a folkloric and primitivized culture and denigrates and marginalizes urbanized or apparently acculturated members of these populations who speak English, lack ethnic dress, do not obviously conduct ceremonies and do not count as real natives to the same extent as those who continue to live in the bush and practice something closer to traditional subsistence. Compared with, and at times comparing themselves with, the "real Aborigines," Aboriginal people are caught between attributions of unchanging essences (with the implications of an inability to change) and the reproach of inauthenticity. (Thomas 1994: 30)

Vine Deloria noted that Indian people "begin to feel that they are merely shadows of a mythical super-Indian. Many anthros spare no expense to reinforce this sense of inadequacy in order to further support their influence over Indian people" (Deloria 1969: 82). In response to anthropologists' queries of why Indians no longer danced, Deloria explains:

> the people did Indian dances. BUT THEY DIDN'T DO THEM ALL THE TIME. Suddenly the Sioux were presented with an authority

> figure who bemoaned the fact that whenever he visited the reservations the Sioux were not out dancing in the manner of their ancestors. In a real sense, they were not real. (Deloria 1969: 87, emphasis in the original)

Cultural revitalization, in its fundamentalist form, harkens back to a pristine past that is uncritically regarded as good. Moreover, regaining that lost culture, in its more or less unchanged form, is offered as the way of salvation. In the process, culture itself has become objectified through the practice of referring to one's culture as existing outside of self, family and community. In other words, culture as a "thing" existing outside oneself is something one can lose or regain. Culture, in the fundamentalist sense, has become something one can choose to engage with or not.

It is difficult to question the benefits of instilling cultural nationalism and cultural pride in people who have experienced colonization. The uncritical acceptance of these claims is evident in the contradictions that cultural revitalization, as a decolonizing strategy, manifests in the area of Aboriginal education. This is particularly so when Aboriginal people and especially teachers are held accountable for failing to exhibit the characteristics of traditional cultural identity. In these ways, cultural revitalization 'blames the victim' of colonization, in part, by denying history and social change.

U.S. Indian elders gathered in the late 1960s to discuss among themselves "The modern Indian's dilemma" (Morey and Gilliam 1974: 147), which included the challenges to revitalizing and reclaiming cultural traditions and practices. Henry Old Coyote explains, "We have teenagers today who have *lost* their identity as Indians but want to regain it" (quoted in Morey and Gilliam 1974: 158, emphasis added). Yet he lamented that these young people go around "indiscriminately" taking up traditions and customs of various tribes, and cultures, such as hairstyles and distinguishing ornaments, which are not appropriate to them (quoted in Morey and Gilliam 1974: 158). How does the cultural change brought about as a result of colonial domination get rephrased as something Indian teenagers have merely "lost"?

The popular notion that one has lost one's culture, as opposed to having one's culture stolen, places the responsibility for making appropriate cultural adjustments on those who for so long were the target of systemic and individual cultural change. In a project of cultural revitalization, Indian people are unwittingly held responsible for the problem of losing culture; they are produced as reckless caretakers of their culture. Describing Aboriginal youth as lost is a benign way to describe the effects of the discrimination, exclusion and sustained violence and aggression they face on a daily basis.

Cultural revitalization also suggests that Aboriginal youth merge the two worlds of Aboriginal and dominant white society. The expectation that Aboriginal youth will become bicultural/bilingual people "ignores the reality that the world of the Anglos is only marginally available to them as a choice because of poverty, racism, discrimination, and lowered teacher expectations, regardless of their potential for success" (Deyhle 1998: 5). The focus on cultural revitalization helps to distract and minimize the effects of racialization and racial discrimination in Aboriginal education (St. Denis 2002). In fact, "there is little research on the role racial prejudice plays as a barrier in the Indian educational experience. Quite often, the racial prejudice encountered by Indian students is simply included under the rather generic label of 'cultural conflict'" (Huffman 1991: 1; see also St. Denis and Hampton 2002).

Foley (1996) and Ledlow (1992) challenge the assumption that culture is the cause of failure in the education of Aboriginal and Indian students (Foley 1996; Ledlow 1992). Ledlow (1992:29) suggests that pointing to cultural factors as a cause of school dropout precludes "overwhelming evidence that economic and social issues which are not culturally specific to being Indian (although they may be specific to being a minority) are very significant in causing students to drop out of school." Brady (1996) also argues that Aboriginal student drop out must be understood in the context of socio-economic status, which also shapes and limits the quality of education of low-income adolescents. Quite simply, Aboriginal culture "cannot be accepted as the only explanation for their lack of success" (Wilson 1991: 368).

Perhaps the Royal Commission on Aboriginal Peoples (RCAP) also helps us to recognize these structural constraints, as they reported that many problems in education remain despite many positive changes and program initiatives. Aboriginal people expressed "the same concerns that Aboriginal people have been bringing forward since the first studies were done" (RCAP 1996, Vol. 3: 440). For example, there continue to be "too many youth who do not complete high school, they do not have skills for employment, they do not have the language and cultural knowledge of their people" (RCAP 1996, Vol. 3: 434). Perhaps it is time to re-examine both the causes of inequality and the strategies we embarked on over three decades ago and become more critical of our approaches.

> We need to scrutinize and understand the limits of cultural-difference approaches, which may inadvertently further stereotype peoples, and recognize that such an approach might lead to a superficial reading of difference, making power relations invisible and keeping dominant cultural norms in place. (St. Denis, Bouvier and Battiste 1998: 76)

The irony of cultural revitalization in Aboriginal education is that it has facilitated the holding of Aboriginal teachers responsible for the effects of colonization. Perhaps it is time to redefine the problems that contribute to the educational failure of Aboriginal students. In addition to reporting that Aboriginal youth still face the same problems since the first studies were done, the Royal Commission also states, "Many Aboriginal community members and education leaders have expressed frustrations that Aboriginal teachers are not fully grounded in the teaching traditions of their nations" (RCAP 1996, Vol. 3: 492). In some respects, these charges against Aboriginal teachers are similar to what has occurred among the Maori of New Zealand, where "Maori are no longer seen as deficient in relation to Pakehas [white New Zealanders], they are seen as deficient as Maoris" (Wetherell and Potter 1992: 131).

Conclusions, Consequences and Contradictions

Cultural revitalization for Aboriginal peoples is a double-edged sword. On one hand it is liberating because it challenges the goals of colonization that eradicate the cultural practices and identities of Aboriginal peoples. But on the other hand, it proposes new and difficult, and perhaps misplaced, emphasis on finding and restoring our cultural traditions and practices. Cultural revitalization can also have the effect of encouraging cultural authenticity and cultural purity in a fundamentalist manner. Through encouraging Aboriginal peoples to seek out and perform authenticity as compensation for our exploitation and oppression, cultural revitalization becomes oppressive itself; in fact, it becomes a form of "blaming the victim."

In this chapter, I have suggested that the strategy of cultural revitalization through Aboriginal education has assumed a form of fundamentalism. It is fundamentalist in the sense that a cultural discourse reigns supreme in explanations of both educational failure and success of Aboriginal students. A cultural discourse has assumed a level of sacredness and/or orthodoxy for explaining the social and educational conditions of Aboriginal people in Canada, so much so that other explanations for the on-going marginalization, exclusion, and oppression of Aboriginal people are denied and minimized. It is possible that seeing a strategy of cultural revitalization as a form of fundamentalism can help to dislodge the supremacy of such discourses in explaining both the conditions and solutions for the inequality that marks so many Aboriginal communities. Perhaps cultural revitalization misdiagnoses the problem and places far too much responsibility on the marginalized and oppressed to change yet again, and once again, lets those in positions of dominance off the hook.

References

Abele, F., C. Dittburner, and K.A. Graham. 2000. "Towards a Shared Understanding in the Policy Discussion about Aboriginal Education." In M.B. Castellano, L. Davis and L. Lahache (eds.), *Aboriginal Education: Fulfilling the Promise*. Vancouver: University of British Columbia Press.

Brady, P. 1996. "Native Dropouts and Non-Native Dropouts in Canada: Two Solitudes or a Solitude Shared?" *Journal of American Indian Education* 35(2).

Deloria, Vine Jr. 1969/1988. *Custer Died for Your Sins: An Indian Manifesto*. Norman: University of Oklahoma Press (originally published in 1969/New York: Macmillan).

Deyhle, D. 1998. "From Break Dancing to Heavy Metal: Navajo Youth, Resistance, and Identity." *Youth and Society* 30(1).

Falkenberg, S. 2002. *What is Fundamentalism and Why is It So Dangerous?* Available at www.newreformation.org/fundamentalism.htm [Accessed Oct. 27/03].

Foley, D. 1996. "The Silent Indian as a Cultural Production." In A. Levinson, D. Foley and D. Holland (eds.), *The Cultural Production of the Educated Person*. New York: State University of New York Press.

Hawthorne, H.B. (ed.). 1967. *A Survey of the Contemporary Indians of Canada: Economic, Political, Educational Needs and Policies*. Volume II. Ottawa: Indian Affairs Branch.

Henze, R., and L. Vanett. 1993. "To Walk in Two Worlds—Or More? Challenging a Common Metaphor of Native Education." *Anthropology and Education Quarterly*, 24.

Huffman, T.E. 1991. "The Experiences, Perceptions, and Consequences of Campus Racism among Northern Plains Indians." *Journal of American Indian Education*, 30(2).

Ledlow, S. 1992. "Is Cultural Discontinuity an Adequate Explanation for Dropping Out?" *Journal of American Indian Education* 31.

Madison, C., and Y. Yarber. 1981. *Madeline Solomon: Koyukuk*. Blaine, WA: Hancock House.

Morey, S.M., and Gilliam, O. (eds.). 1974. *Respect for Life: The Traditional Upbringing of American Indian Children*. New York: Myrin Institute Books. Report on a conference at Harper's Ferry, West Virginia.

National Indian Brotherhood. 1972. *Indian Control of Indian Education*. Ottawa: National Indian Brotherhood.

Royal Commission on Aboriginal Peoples. 1996. *Report on the Royal Commission on Aboriginal Peoples*. Vols. 1–5. Ottawa: Canada Communications Group.

St. Denis, V. 2002. *An Exploration of the Socio-cultural Production of Aboriginal Identities: Implications for Education*. Unpublished doctoral dissertation. Stanford, CA: Stanford University.

St. Denis, V., R. Bouvier, and M. Battiste. 1998. *Okiskinahamakewak—Aboriginal Teachers in Saskatchewan's Publicly Funded Schools: Responding to the Flux* (Final Report—October 31). Regina: Saskatchewan Education Research Networking Project.

St. Denis, V., and E. Hampton. 2002. *Racism and Its Effects on Aboriginal Education: A Review of Literature*. Prepared for the Minister's National Working Group on Education. Indian and Northern Affairs Canada. Ottawa, Ontario.

Thomas, N. 1994. *Colonialism's Culture: Anthropology, Travel and Government.* Cambridge, UK: Polity Press.

Wetherell, M., and J. Potter. 1992. *Mapping the Language of Racism: Discourse and the Legitimation of Exploitation.* New York: Columbia University Press.

Whitecalf, S. 1993. "Lecture 1." In Wolhart and Ahenakew.

Wilson, P. 1991. "Trauma of Sioux Indian High School Students." *Anthropology and Education Quarterly* 22.

Wolhart, H.C., and F. Ahenakew. 1993. *kinehiyawininaw nehiyawewin The Cree Language is Our Identity: The La Ronge Lectures of Sarah Whitecalf.* Winnipeg: The University of Manitoba Press.

Chapter Four

Jewish Fundamentalisms and a Critical Politics of Identity

The Makings of a Post-Zionist Discourse

Jackie Kuikman

From the place where we are right
flowers will never grow
in the Spring.

The place where we are right
is hard and trampled
like a yard.

But doubts and loves
dig up the world
like a mole, a plough.
And a whisper will be heard in the place
where the ruined
house once stood. (Amichai 2001)

Muslim fundamentalism has received wide media attention in the West, especially since September 11, 2001. Jewish fundamentalism, concentrated mainly within the state of Israel, the West Bank and the Gaza Strip, has received less coverage, even though it is closely linked to concerns in the Middle East. Examples of efforts of this fundamentalism include the Palestinian refugees who fled Israeli territories after the inception of the state in 1948, Israel's victory in the War of Independence against its Arab neighbours and the Dome of the Rock—one of Islam's holiest shrines and the place where the Jewish temple in Jerusalem once stood. The city of Jerusalem itself is disputed territory, claimed by both Israelis and Palestinians as their capital. Whether the current (October 2003) United States-sponsored peace plan—the "road map" to peace in the Middle East—and future peace talks succeed depends, on the Israeli side, to a large degree on the responses of the various Jewish religious groups and coalitions that are considered fundamentalists. Many of these groups believe, for example, that the West Bank of the Jordan River and the Gaza Strip, territories gained by the Israelis during the 1967 war, were given to them by God and that the Palestinians have no claim to them. Some groups believe that the temple destroyed in 70 CE should be rebuilt on the site of the Dome of the Rock.

In this chapter, I analyze and critique various Jewish fundamentalisms particularly within the state of Israel today. I begin with a brief history of the ideology of Zionism from its inception as a political enterprise at the turn of the twentieth century in Europe to what it is today, a predominantly religious Zionism combined with a political system infiltrated by Jewish orthodoxy. What follows is a consideration of the characteristics often ascribed to religious fundamentalist groups, including the use of vicious, dehumanizing rhetoric, and an examination of how these characteristics are linked to violence in various expressions of Jewish fundamentalism, especially in Israel. Finally, I examine recent attempts to construct an alternative Jewish discourse, termed post-Zionism, and an alternative politics of identity.

Zionism is the national movement for the return of the Jewish people to Zion, or Jerusalem, and their homeland in Palestine. The term has roots in the eighteenth-century European intellectual movement known as the Enlightenment, which granted Jews equal rights as citizens in Gentile society. Mainstream society feared their successes and rapid assimilation, however, especially as Jews became more difficult to identify. Religious anti-Judaism was replaced with anti-Semitism, the belief that Jews, as Semites, constituted an inferior race. In France, anti-Semitism reached a nadir with the Dreyfus trial in 1894. Alfred Dreyfus, a Jewish army captain, was indicted for allegedly selling military secrets to Germany. Theodor Herzl (1860–1904), a Jewish journalist from Vienna, was sent to Paris to cover the trial. Convinced that anti-Semitism could only be solved with the creation of a Jewish state, he devoted the rest of his life to this cause. He is considered the father of Zionism and thus is the primary founder of the state of Israel.

Before the actual creation of the state in 1948, many European Jews who felt themselves persecuted moved to Palestine, bought Palestinian land and built collective farms (the *kibbutz).* They transformed Hebrew, the dead language of Jewish religion, into a vital modern language. Many orthodox religious Jews, however, protested that the Jewish return to the "promised land" could occur only with the appearance of the promised Messiah. Those Jews who adhered to Zionism were never united, and a multiplicity of Zionisms emerged. The labour Zionism of the early collective farmers has largely disappeared. Today, religious and biblical Zionism, melded with a right-wing government dominates Israel. This situation is complicated by the growing support of Israel as a state by right-wing Christian Zionists, who regard the modern-day restoration of the state as a herald of the imminent return of Jesus as Messiah.

Characteristics of Fundamentalism

Recent years have seen a proliferation of analyses of religious fundamentalism (see, for example, the five-volume *Fundamentalism Project*, 1991–1995, edited by Martin E. Marty and R. Scott Appleby). Some of this material is marked by a lack of clear consensus about what constitutes fundamentalism, what its distinctive features are and which groups might be described as such. Another difficulty is that labelling some groups as fundamentalist has become a strategy for silencing, used to dismiss or marginalize. Jay Harris notes that a fundamentalist is regarded as one who has a view of the world that is considered by the name-caller to be anti-intellectual, bigoted and intolerant (Harris 1994). What and who one determines to be fundamentalist depends on one's social and ideological location—it is the different other who is "fundamentalist." The anti-Zionist Naturei Karta (Aramaic for "guardians of the city"), for example, are often referred to as fundamentalists by those who are Zionist. Those who regard the biblical text as metaphor or simply as literature frequently label Jews and Christians who believe that the Bible is the literal, revealed word of God as fundamentalist. In some ways, then, as Harris (1994) points out, fundamentalism is the "demonized creation of the modernist." It has become a term that obfuscates and erases important distinctions among groups. The unique historical context of a fundamentalist group is ignored in the political interest of marginalizing or delegitimating those we seek to silence. But analysis and comparisons are impossible without taking into account specific contexts, particularly in Israel today.

While keeping these caveats in mind, it is useful to examine some of the characteristics that have become associated with fundamentalism. A book on gender and fundamentalism includes the following characteristics as comprising a series of "family resemblances" that make comparison of religious groups possible: opposition to modernity, a literal or inerrant approach to sacred texts, an ideology of patriarchy and a perception of being beset (Hawley and Proudfoot 1994). Jay Harris in the same volume argues, however, that these four characteristics are not applicable to Judaism (see below). Recently familiar to us is the descent of political debate into name-calling. Examples include reference to the United States by certain predominantly Muslim states as the "Great Satan" and the counter-vilifying of these Muslim states as the "Axis of Evil." This kind of rhetoric is addressed in the context of the discussion on the "fundamentalist ideologies of gender" by Hawley and Proudfoot (1994: 32) and is termed "religious machismo."

Less well known is the virulent rhetoric within Israel/Palestine itself, but it is the most overtly visible characteristic of fundamentalism there. The rhetoric, with its primary purpose to dehumanize the other, is vicious and potentially deadly. Palestinians lash out against Israeli Jews with names such as "Nazi" and "bloodsucker." The latter epithet hearkens back to the medieval myth that Jews captured Christian children in order to use their blood as an ingredient in unleavened bread for Passover. Conservative Jews denounce secular Jews as "apostates," those who have abandoned their faith. Some Jewish groups in Palestine/Israel refer to Palestinians and other Arabs as "dogs,"[1] considered in the Jewish religious tradition as unclean animals with no reason to exist.

One does not have to look hard to find other characteristics of fundamentalism. Related to textual literalism is the adherence to absolute-truth claims. Enslavement to particular ideas or teachings can take a religion on a path to violence. "Blind obedience" to a charismatic leader (Kimball 2002) was evident in the case of Osama bin Laden. The use of coercive force (Lincoln 1989) is ubiquitous in Israeli dealings with Palestinians. However, groups do not and need not share all of these characteristics to be considered fundamentalist.

Harris (1994) is an articulate voice for those disputing the fundamentalist label. Applying various fundamentalist characteristics to Judaism, he argues that groups in Israel generally considered fundamentalist, such as the Gush Emmunim, do not exhibit features described as fundamentalist. For example, Harris explores the issue of the Gush's supposed opposition to modernity. For him, this is an example of the "politics of nomenclature," using language in a way that normalizes a western way of life. As such, modernity is a construct. The right-wing Zionist Gush Emmunim is not opposed to modernity, Harris argues; it is opposed to democracy and pluralism. "The goal of greater Israel transcends the claims of the democratic process and outweighs—perhaps negates—any claims Arabs[2] might make to the possession and exercise of certain civil and human rights" (Harris 1994: 155). In the case of the Gush Emmunim, Harris is correct, but that does not exclude the Gush from being considered fundamentalist on other grounds.

Harris also maintains that Jewish religious tradition, at least ideally, does not take a literal approach to biblical texts, because three distinct claims must apply. First, if God is the author of scripture, then the text can be considered without error, or inerrant. Second, the receiving and interpreting community must be able to comprehend the meaning of the text inerrantly. And third, inerrancy implies a text that has only one meaning. The first claim is affirmed by orthodox Jews (and presumably by fundamentalist Christians). The second claim may apply to certain Christian and Jewish groups who insist they have the authoritative interpretation of a text. As for the third claim, Jewish tradition has always affirmed that the literal meaning of a text does not exhaust scripture. Different contexts bring forth new interpretations and different layers of meaning. Moreover, there have always been disputes among exegetes, such as the medieval biblical interpreter Rashi, and resolution depends on the majority opinion. The majority may rule but that does not mean they have the correct interpretation.

A Talmudic story illustrates this God-given creative interpretative ability. A group of sages meet to read and interpret a text over which they all disagree. One of them appeals to God to support his interpretation, whereupon God's voice is heard: "Eleazar is right." But the other rabbis ruled God out of order on the grounds that the majority opinion rules. God's reaction was to laugh and say, "My children have defeated me."

Harris's points are well taken as part of the history of Jewish interpretation of texts. But it is evident that certain Jewish religious groups in Israel today have simply decided to remain at the first step; they insist they have a clear interpretation from God.

The ideology of patriarchal control over women as a characteristic of fundamentalism also depends on perspective. Harris argues that women who accept the presuppositions of the *halachic,* or Jewish religious law, (which excludes women from the study of Torah and relegates them to the private sphere of the home as wife and mother) regard themselves "as living within a world defined by God's will, not by a male power structure." These women do not as a rule see themselves as powerless and miserable. Their lives are the "continuity of traditional gender patterns" (Harris 1994: 164). To say this isn't fundamentalist masks the ways women are still covertly subjugated in modern societies. And Harris does not address the harmful, iron grip on laws concerning marriage and divorce by the Jewish orthodoxy, especially in Israel.[3] Further, Jewish women who move into the public realm, such as those who pray with a Torah scroll at the Western Wall (the last remains of the Second Temple and Judaism's holiest religious site), risk verbal and physical abuse by religious men praying on the other side of the *mechitzah* (barrier segregating men from women).

Finally, to speak of the perception of being beset implies that those who feel beset are more or less irrational or paranoid, Harris argues. If this is a characteristic of fundamentalism, then centuries of hostility against Jews and Judaism have made all Jews fundamentalists (Harris 1994).

Harris's objections are well taken. But because he is so defensive, he does not properly analyze the oppressive, hegemonic policies and Zionist discourses in Israeli politics today. Harris's work is, however, a reminder that a careful and nuanced approach is required towards groups that seem to resemble one another from a fundamentalist perspective.

Jewish Fundamentalism in Israel

It is astounding that such a small country as Israel can harbour so many varieties of Jewish fundamentalism. Because Israeli politics and religion are so profoundly intertwined, however, it is not surprising to find also a multiplicity of political parties, each influenced by religious fundamentalist groups. In order to make sense of the complexity of Israeli society and its many internal divisions, it is helpful to note that Israeli Jews comprise largely two political categories: the Left, represented mostly by the Labour Party—the oldest and largest leftist party—and the Right, all the other parties who are right-wing and religious and many of whom are fundamentalists. The largest Israeli right-wing and territorial expansionist party is Likud, or Consolidation, a coalition of various right-wing parties. Both the left-wing and right-wing groups adhere to some form of Zionist ideology, the Left for secular and political reasons and the Right for religious reasons. The exceptions on the Right are religious Jews who descended from the Lithuanian and German opponents to the dominant chasidic traditions of eighteenth and nineteenth-century Europe, or mitnagdim. Today they comprise various small fundamentalist movements, such as the Naturei Karta, who believe that religious scholars, not soldiers, are the true guardians of the city (Jerusalem), and the Satmar Chasidim. Both groups oppose Zionism on the biblical grounds that redemption, or return to the holy land, depends on the coming of the Messiah.

Fundamentalist Zionist Israeli Jews fall into one of two groups: the Haredim, or Fearing, in the biblical sense of God-fearing, and the more religiously moderate settler movement known as the Gush Emmunim, or Block of the Faithful. The Haredim are further divided into the Ashkenazi Haredim, or Lubavitcher Chasidim, who are Jews of eastern European descent, and the Sephardi Haredim, Jews of middle eastern descent. The latter certainly have reason to feel beset as they are often treated as second-class citizens by other Israeli religious Jews.

Of all these groups, two represent best the complexities of Jewish and Israeli fundamentalism: the Gush Emmunim and the Lubavitcher Chasidim. Both are politically active in Israel and promote Jewish settlement of the West Bank and Gaza. Both groups are growing rapidly and have spawned violence in support of their expansionist agendas.

The Gush Emmunim is the organizational core of the fundamentalist movement—an umbrella organization of approximately twenty thousand Israeli Jews, many of whom enjoy dual citizenship in the United States and Israel. It is an ultra-nationalist and religious movement influenced by their guru, Rabbi Isaac HaCohen Kook (1865–1935, commonly known as Rav Kook), an early religious Zionist who became the first Chief Rabbi of twentieth-century Palestine. The Gush saw the 1967 victory of the Six Days War[4] and occupation of the West Bank as a miracle of God. With its Manichean approach to the world—good versus evil, Jew versus Arab—the Gush regards the land as divinely ordained for the Jews and polluted by the Arabs. Since 1967, more than 150 settlements have been established in areas the Gush refers to as Judea, Samaria and the Gaza District. Settlement projects are justified through a selective reading of biblical texts, typical of fundamentalism, such as Genesis 23, which outlines

Abraham's purchase of the cave of Makhpelah. Hence the deep conviction that not only did God give the land to Jews, but Abraham paid for it.

The Gush Emmunim's practical political goal of incorporating the occupied territories into the state of Israel is related to the long awaited process of redemption. The Gush's religious rhetoric underpins this goal. Its slogan is: "The Land of Israel for the People of Israel, according to the Torah of Israel." Eventually, all Jews will return to the land, *halachah* (Jewish religious law) will be enforced, the temple will be rebuilt in Jerusalem and the Messiah will appear (Lustick 1988). Although officially non-partisan, the Gush's messianic ideas are represented in the Israeli parliament by the ultra-right National Religious Party, which represents those Jews who are not Haredim, Likud or various other right-wing parties (Lustick 1993). The Gush recruits new members from the religious youth movement, Benei Akiva (a network of paramilitary seminaries), the religious education system and new immigrants. Its organizational system is comprised of an association of local councils known as Yesha (salvation) (Lustick 1993). Thus, the Gush is deeply integrated into Israeli society, drawing from various religious and social elements of Israel's culture. Followers of the Gush can be distinguished from other religious Israeli Jews by their distinctive knitted skullcaps and army clothing, such as commando boots. They have contributed deeply to the image and reality of Israel as a military culture. While they are as opposed to secular Israeli lifestyles as the Haredim, they believe that all Jewish people, both secular and religious, have a role in the process of redemption of the land.

Since 1980, various plots have been uncovered to blow up the el-Aksa mosque, Islam's third holiest site (after those in Mecca and Medina), and the Dome of the Rock by underground Gush activists (Lustick 1988). The magnificent Dome of the Rock, referred to by Muslims as Haram el Sharif (noble sanctuary), stands on the location where Mohammad ascended to heaven as well as where Herod's Temple once stood; it is therefore sacred to both Muslims and Jews. For virtually all fundamentalist Jews (and fundamentalist Christians), this is the site for the third and future temple. These organized attempts to destroy the Temple Mount, nothing short of terrorism, were undertaken by Gush activists, settlers on the West Bank and respected members of the Gush movement. In some cases these activists had strong ties to the Gush leadership (Lustick 1988: 69). Between 1978 and 1982 a major effort to destroy the el-Aksa mosque and the Dome of the Rock was aborted when leading Gush rabbis failed to approve the plot. Many of the Gush activists engaged in this conspiracy were arrested and convicted and several served prison sentences (Lustick 1988: 69–70).

On November 4, 1995, Yigal Amir, a religious, messianic Jew with ties to the Gush Emmunim murdered Yitzchak Rabin, Prime Minister of Israel, as he left a peace rally. The attack was an attempt to halt the implementation of the Oslo Accords[5] and the Israeli withdrawal from large Palestinian cities in the West Bank.

The Lubavitcher Chasidim, also known as Chabad, an acronym of the Kabbalistic terms for wisdom, knowledge and understanding—attributes of God—is perhaps the fastest growing Jewish religious group (Bob Dylan is a supporter). There are currently more than seventeen hundred Chabad centres around the world. They are best known for their *mitzvah* mobiles, vans that drive major city streets in search of Jews, with the purpose of bringing them home to the true Judaism (i.e., Chabad). The movement is responsible for erecting huge Chanukah menorahs in public spaces, such as city halls, during the Christmas season. The majority of these Chasidim affirms that the late Lubavitcher Rebbe, Menachem Mendel Schneerson (who died in 1994), initiated the messianic era and will return soon to complete the redemption of the world in his role as Messiah.[6] In 1996, the standard messianist slogan "may our master, teacher and the King Messiah live forever" was modified to state "may our master, teacher and Creator, the King Messiah, live forever." The Rebbe is seen as "divinity in physical garb" (Berger 2001: 79).

Today Chabad constitutes one of the most extreme groups of religious settlers on the West Bank (Shahak and Mezvinsky 1999). Baruch Goldstein, a physician and West Bank settler from Brooklyn, New York, murdered Muslim worshippers in a mosque in Hebron on February 25, 1994. He was a follower of the Lubavitcher Rebbe and of Kahane of the Jewish Defence League. This horrific incident may be linked to Chabad's dehumanizing religious rhetoric concerning the essential difference of the Jewish soul from that of a non-Jew. This official Lubavitch belief is based on teachings of the Lurianic Kabbalah,[7] which emphasize that salvation is only for Jews. Israel Shahak and Norton Mezvinsky (1999) allege that translators of these mystical texts from Hebrew into English, such as Gershom Scholem, deliberately omitted these ideas from the texts.[8] Readers of Hebrew, however, such as members of the Lubavitcher Chasidim, have access to the kabbalistic notion of the radical inferiority of the non-Jewish soul.

Shahak, endorsed by Edward Said (1997), has been accused of hanging out dirty Jewish laundry in public and has been dismissed as a self-hating Jew. One website notes that material similar to that in Shahak and Mezvinsky's 1999 book is found on neo-Nazi and Holocaust denial websites and that Shahak is inciting hatred of Jews (Bialoguski 2001). However, Friedland and Hecht's (1996) account of an interview with a Chabad woman in Jerusalem concerning the superiority of the Jewish soul supports Shahak's allegations.

Critique of Chabad has been more or less limited, unfortunately, to its messianic and christianizing tendencies. The actual and potential violence within the movement has not received as much attention as that of the Gush Emmunim. Critics such as Berger and Lockshin regard the veneration of the late Rebbe Schneerson as *avodah zarah* (literally "foreign worship" or idolatry), a Christianization of Judaism or a cult[9] (Berger 2001).

The only difference now between Judaism and Christianity is "a matter of mistaken identity" (Berger 2001: 130). Lockshin writes that it is inevitable that Jews for Jesus (a highly organized group of Jews who believe in Jesus as the Messiah) will take their place alongside other Jewish denominations, in which case the definition of Jewishness will devolve into a "state of anarchy" (Berger 2001: 131). The Chabad revile their critics as pigs, snakes and asses. A source of political critique is Rabbi Eliezer Shach, an influential Lithuanian *mitnagid* and a dove, who disliked the Chasidim but positively hated Chabad for its support of the Ashkenazi Haredim party, which had allied itself with Likud. He calls the Chabad Rebbe "insane, an infidel and a false Messiah" whose followers are "eaters of treyf"[10] (Friedland and Hecht 1996: 88).

Critiques from the Left

Edward Said (1997)—from a position on the Left and as an outsider, i.e., a non-Jew—critiques Israel's policies of building Israeli settlements in the Palestinian territories of the West Bank and Gaza Strip as "colonialism." His critical analysis deconstructs the rhetorical discourse of the kind one finds among the Chabad and the Gush Emmunim that "proves" Jews own the land. Because he is an outsider, he is either not heard or dismissed as an anti-Semite. However, Noam Chomsky, a Jew, who uses an analysis similar to Said's in his critiques of Israeli treatment of Palestinians, is a prime example of how Jewish identity is contested inside and outside of Israel. Chomsky's criticisms have taken him outside the pale of Jewish boundaries. Considered the quintessential self-hating Jew, no better than the average anti-Semite, the Jewish community in both Israel and the United States has ostracized him. Neither the *New York Times* nor the *Washington Post* publishes his writing. As a Jew, Chomsky is in a political and theoretical bind. He is what Shanaz Khan (2002) has termed, in another context, a "native informant." Although his critique may serve to fuel anti-Semitism, he is compelled to speak out for justice. Chomsky reflects what Joan Scott sees as the "dangers," the "benefits" and the ambiguity of a "fluctuating identity" or "multiple identifications" (Scott 1995: 11). To label Chomsky an anti-Semite weakens the term. It is a way of dismissing and silencing his kind of critique and obstructs analysis of what has in Israel become an extremely complex and volatile environment.

There is, however, a virulent strain of anti-Semitism among many Muslims in general and Palestinians in particular that blurs all distinctions among Jews. It appropriates symbols and motifs from classic European anti-Jewish bigotry and from Nazi propaganda. In literature of Arab states and in the occupied territories one sees images of Jews with hook noses or as devil figures, Israelis with swastikas or as drinkers of the blood of

Palestinian children. The notorious nineteenth-century forgery, *The Protocols of the Elders of Zion*, which outlines the alleged Jewish takeover of the world, has been resurrected and published in Arabic throughout the Arab world. Holocaust denial is popular in Arab media. Israelis are caricatured as the new Nazi plague breeding in Israel. Hitler's *Mein Kampf* has been translated and circulated. Given the hateful nature of this anti-Semitic rhetoric, the suicide bombings and other forms of terrorism come as little surprise. One example of the violence occurred on March 27, 2002: 29 people were murdered and 140 injured when a Palestinian detonated an explosive device in the Park Hotel in Netanya, where 250 guests were gathered for a Passover Seder meal. Hamas[11] claimed responsibility.

Employment of anti-Semitism drawn from medieval Christianity and the Nazi period requires serious analysis. The experience of the Palestinians, dispossessed and humiliated, partially explains their use of anti-Semitic rhetoric already available, perhaps their only recourse to being silenced. The 1967 victory and occupation of the West Bank may have fuelled the notion of a Jewish plot to control the world. But should justice and human rights prevail for the Palestinians, one would hope that some of the deadly rhetoric will subside. It is important to remember that there are groups in Israel that agitate for peace and justice. Women in Black, for example, is a network of women committed to justice for oppressed peoples throughout the world. Group members dress in black and demonstrate in non-violent vigils wherever a certain context of injustice demands opposition. The movement began in Israel in 1988 with Israeli and Palestinian women and their supporters protesting the Israeli occupation of the West Bank and Gaza Strip. Another such group is Bat Shalom, a feminist organization of Israeli women working together with Palestinian women's groups towards peaceful co-operation between Israelis and Palestinians.

Noam Chomsky, Edward Said and Israelis such as Israel Shahak perform the important task of exposing events in Israel/Palestine that are often omitted or glossed over in conventional Zionist discourse and Israeli politics. They also deconstruct the myths of Zionism, naming Israeli occupation for what it is, colonialism. However, their deconstructive enterprise and Palestinian violence leave little or nothing in place from which to build a future for Israeli identity and existence. Furthermore, they fuel anti-Semitism both within and outside of Israel. Yet Zionism warrants serious critique for the way it has legitimated Israeli possession and exercise of power in the course of historical events such as the continuing occupation of the conquered territories and the Israeli invasion of Lebanon in 1982.

Post-Zionism

Uri Ram, a sociologist from Ben Gurion University, has coined the term "post-Zionist" as an alternative to the dominant Zionist discourse that legitimates current power relations (Silberstein 1996). So-called post-Zionists take certain theoretical tools from the other "posts"—post-modernism, post-structuralism and post-colonialism—and from feminist studies. Although post-Zionism in some ways calls Zionism into question, it should not be equated with anti-Semitism. Anti-Zionism, on the other hand, is not far from anti-Semitism when problems in other middle eastern countries such as Iraq are connected with Israel and Zionism.[12]

Most Jewish scholars take an essentialist view of both Jewish identity and Zionism—that is, underlying the perceived multiplicity of Jewish expressions is a core, an authentic Jewish self with attitudes and traits that are "constitutive or essential to Jewish identity" (Silberstein 2000: 1–2). This so-called pure Jewish identity is in reality Ashkenazi identity and excludes others within the Jewish community, Sephardi Jews, women and non- or anti-Zionist Jews. Post-Zionism challenges the ideas of a single, pure Jewish identity and constructs one that more realistically acknowledges multiple and competing identities. In this context, identity is not fixed but always changing; essentialist notions of identity have given way to multiple shifting identities, constructed through the discourses of gender, religion, sexual orientation, race and so forth (see, for example, Butler 1990 on gender identities).

Zionism has had an enormous impact on how Jewish identity is constructed, either positively if one perceives oneself as a Zionist or negatively if one defines one's Jewishness over or against Zionism. In either case, Zionism is a process; it is fluid and has several variations. Ideological discourses such as the Zionism embraced by the Gush Emmunim and Chabad legitimate their exercise of power over the Palestinians, or generally over the other, by "universalizing, and naturalizing historically contingent social arrangements and hierarchies of power" (Silberstein 1996: 330–31). Deconstruction of Zionist discourse allows one to understand that Zionism is temporal; it does and will change over time. It enables one to see how hegemonic Zionist discourse has relied heavily on the notion that essential to Jewish identity is the role of perpetual victim. Conventional Zionist discourse has represented Israeli Jews as heirs to Holocaust victims, who sought refuge in their homeland only to become victims of Arab violence (Ophir 2000). The official Israeli line is that Israel is an "innocent victim of gratuitous, anti-Semitic Islamic terror" (Said 1997: 78).

Adi Ophir (2000), an Israeli, analyzes the way the Holocaust is remembered and used in Israel to position Israeli Jews as victims. The loss of the temple and a renewed fear of loss of the land, coupled with the loss of the six-million Jews in the Holocaust, constructs an identity that justifies colonization and victimization of the other.[13] In both cases the losses are irrecoverable and absolute. The nature of the mythic messianic redemption of the land is its perpetual incompleteness or irrevocability. The loss of the six million is also "incarnated," or represented as irrecoverable (Ophir 2000).

Therapy may help an individual Jew discover what is to be gained through clinging to the victim position. The therapy required for a whole culture that positions itself as victim is cultural and social criticism. Critical analysis of the dominant Zionist narrative of the Gush, for example, as well as the notion of the Jew as perpetual victim, will force Israeli Jews to face the fact that Zionism has created its own victims: Palestinians and, ironically, Israeli Jews themselves. Such criticism problematizes identity and "exposes the ideological work through which the victim position is constructed and maintained" (Ophir 2000: 181–83). Deconstruction of victim rhetoric reveals it to be an exploitative tool in Israel's power relations with Palestinians and others. It reveals Palestinians, among others, to be the silenced, voiceless other over and against which Zionism and the victim identity so crucial to it defines itself (Silberstein 1996).

Post-Zionists are breaking down hegemonic Zionist rhetoric and creating new non-Zionist political and civic discourses rooted in the current realities of the Israeli state. They say "to immigrate" to Israel rather than "to make *Alijah*."[14] They speak of occupation or colonization rather than "redemption of the land" or "liberation" (Ophir 2000) or even "making the desert bloom," the quest of the early labour Zionists. A reconstruction of Zionist rhetoric does not abrogate one's responsibility to ensure the survival of Jews and one's culture, however. Rather it may be seen as "clearing the space necessary for new and more adequate formulations of Jewish identity and culture" (Silberstein 1996: 348). A commitment to the construction of new and stronger Jewish identities is where the post-Zionist enterprise differs from the work of scholars such as Shahak and Chomsky, who seem to lack such commitment.

Still, the path to peace is not easy. Post-Zionists are labelled as "mean, heartless, cynical and full of self-hatred," because they challenge the dominant myth of Zionist discourse, the Israeli Jew as victim. Post-Zionists are considered by hegemonic Zionists to have been "corrupted" by post-modernist ideas. Therefore, post-Zionism is a "deviation," whose arguments need not be taken seriously. In this way, the label "post-Zionist" functions as a mechanism of silencing that obstructs critique and dialogue: "in other words, it encloses Zionist ideology in a dogmatic position" (Ophir 2000: 189).

Conclusion

The term "fundamentalism" is a slippery one, and as Harris illustrates, it must be used with care. It can be misused to silence, dismiss or marginalize. However, Harris seems to advocate too narrow a definition of fundamentalism, a definition that, in the end, does little to analyze groups such as the Lubavitch Chasidim or the Gush Emmunim. The terms anti-Semite or "self-hating Jew" also function to silence or dismiss Jewish scholars who attempt to analyze and critique dominant narratives. Anti-Semitic rhetoric can serve to justify and fuel violence against Jews, while religious rhetoric similarly is useful in Israel today among those with right-wing ideologies.

Post-modern theories are useful in criticizing dominant discourses such as the Zionism of the Gush and the Chabad. Post-Zionism represents an opportunity for Israeli Jews to accept others as victims and understand the ways in which Israelis oppress others. At the same time, post-Zionism neither trivializes the historical Jewish experience nor dismisses all Jewish claims to a homeland. Even though post-Zionists, as both Jewish insiders and critical outsiders, have been rhetorically marginalized by Israeli Jews, post-Zionism moves Israeli Jews away from Jewish fundamentalism. Such a move is one of our best hopes for a true roadmap to peace in the Middle East.

Notes

1. The late Rabbi Meir Kahane, founder of the Brooklyn-based Jewish Defence League in the 1980s, addressed Palestinians as dogs. His *Kach* party in Israel openly favours annexation of the occupied territories and complete expulsion of Arabs, the only party in Israel to do so.
2. Israeli and Zionist discourse tends to speak of the Palestinian population of Israel using the generic concept "Arab," with the overall effect of effacing the Palestinian reality (Silberstein 2000).
3. Only a man can initiate divorce. If he refuses to give a divorce, the female partner cannot rebuild her life with another man. If she does, she is considered a whore and her children bastards. Her husband can have relations with as many women as he wants, as long as they are not married.
4. In 1967 Egypt and its Arab allies threatened a war that would mark the end of the State of Israel. They were able to obtain the withdrawal of United Nations border guards. In a pre-emptive attack, Israel destroyed the Egyptian air force while it was still on the ground. They occupied much of the Sinai peninsula and the West Bank of the Jordan River, and they captured the Golan Heights—a hill overlooking the entire northern area of Israel, the site from which Syria had repeatedly shelled Jewish settlements below. They united east and west Jerusalem, allowing Jews access to the sacred western wall of the second temple.
5. The Declaration of Principles (Oslo Accords) on Interim Self-Government Arrangements was the agreement signed between Israel and the Palestinian Liberation Organization in 1993. Many of the declaration's provisions, such as the handover of some land to Palestinian control and the formation of the Palestinian security forces, were implemented. But Palestinian and Israeli negotiations flagged in terms of agreement on issues involving Jerusalem,

borders and refugees.

6. We have here the notion of a resurrected Messiah whose redemptive mission was interrupted by an untimely death (Berger 2001).
7. Rabbi Isaac Luria founded the latest school of *Kabbalah* (literally, "tradition") in the late sixteenth century CE. According to Shahak and Mezvinsky (1999), his ideas had an impact on the theology of Rav Kook and underpin the ideologies of Chabad as well as those of the Gush Emmunim.
8. A similar strategy to avoid embarrassment in the Lutheran Protestant tradition was to leave Martin Luther's hateful and scatological diatribes against Jews in the original German, that is, not to translate them.
9. "Cult," the media buzzword for new religious movements, of course carries negative connotations. One thinks of killer cults and mind control. The kind of person who joins a cult is commonly thought of as brainwashed and somehow defective. In reality, all mainstream religions have started out as new religious movements, as cults.
10. *Treyf* is a derogatory Yiddish word for non-kosher food.
11. The movement of Islamic Resistance, the principal Islamist organization in the West Bank and Gaza Strip, a branch of the larger Muslim Brotherhood Movement.
12. Recently at a peace rally in Regina, Saskatchewan, the problems in Iraq were combined with a blanket condemnation of Zionism. This is highly problematic when the connection is questionable and incites hatred for Jews rather than right-wing capitalists, for example.
13. Israel's Independence Day culminates observance of Holocaust Memorial Day and Memorial Day for Israel's Fallen Soldiers.
14. Jews who immigrate to Israel speak of themselves as "making *Alijah*," that is, "going up [to Zion]," a biblical image.

References

Amichai, Yehuda. 2001. "From the Place Where We are Right." Epigraph in Richard Holloway, *Doubts and Loves: What is Left of Christianity*. Edinburgh, Canongate.

Berger, David. 2001. *The Rebbe, the Messiah and Scandal of Orthodox Indifference*. Oxford and Portland, Oregon: The Littman Library of Jewish Civilization.

Bialoguski, Stefan. 2001. "The Challenge." Available at www.cactus48.com/jewishlaw.html [accessed February 19, 2003].

Butler, Judith. 1990. *Gender Trouble: Feminism and the Subversion of Identity*. New York and London: Routledge.

Friedland, Roger, and Richard Hecht. 1996. *To Rule Jerusalem*. New York: Cambridge University Press.

Harris, Jay M. 1994. "Fundamentalism: Objections from a Modern Jewish Historian." In Hawley.

Hawley, John Stratton (ed.). 1994. *Fundamentalism and Gender*. New York and London: Oxford University Press.

Hawley, John S., and Wayne Proudfoot. 1994. "Introduction." In Hawley.

Khan, Shanaz. 2002. "Performing the Native Informant: Doing Ethnography from the Margins." *Canadian Journal of Women and the Law* 13 (2).

Kimball, Charles. 2002. *When Religion Becomes Evil*. New York: HarperSanFrancisco.

Lincoln, Bruce. 1989. *Discourse and the Construction of Society: Comparative Studies of Myth, Ritual, and Classification*. New York and Oxford: Oxford University Press.

Lustick, Ian S. 1993. "Jewish Fundamentalism and the Israeli-Palestinian Impasse." In Laurence J. Silberstein (ed.), *Jewish Fundamentalism in Comparative Perspective: Religion, Ideology, and the Crisis of Modernity*. New York and London: New York University Press.

_____. 1988. *For the Land and the Lord: Jewish Fundamentalism in Israel*. New York: Council on Foreign Relations.

Marty, Martin E., and R. Scott Appleby, (eds.). 1991–1995. *The Fundamentalism Project*. 5 volumes. Chicago: University of Chicago Press.

Ophir, Adi. 2000 "The Identity of the Victims and the Victims of Identity: A Critique of Zionist Ideology for a Post-Zionist Age." In Laurence J. Silberstein (ed.), *Mapping Jewish Identities*. New York and London: New York University Press.

Said, Edward. 1997. *Covering Islam: How the Media and the Experts Determine How We See the Rest of the World*. New York: Vintage Books, Random House.

Scott, Joan W. 1995. "Multiculturalism and the Politics of Identity." In John Rajchman (ed.), *The Identity in Question*. New York and London: Routledge.

Shahak, Israel, and Norton Mezvinsky. 1999. *Jewish Fundamentalism in Israel*. London and Sterling, Virginia: Pluto Press.

Silberstein, Laurence J. 2000. "Mapping, Not Tracing: Opening Reflection." In Laurence J. Silberstein (ed.), *Mapping Jewish Identities*. New York and London: New York University Press.

_____. 1996. "Cultural Criticism, Ideology, and the Interpretation of Zionism: Toward a Post-Zionist Discourse." In Steven Kepnes (ed.), *Interpreting Judaism in a Postmodern Age*. New York and London: New York University Press.

Chapter Five

Islamic Fundamentalism(s)

More Than a Pejorative Epithet?[1]

F. Volker Greifenhagen

Islamic fundamentalism emerged into worldwide prominence in the late twentieth century and seemed to set the stage for the twenty-first century with the terrorist attacks of September 11, 2001. The perpetrators and supporters of these attacks, and of other similar attacks in various parts of the world (for example, Indonesia, Afghanistan, Iraq, Palestine and Israel), legitimated their actions with reference to the religion of Islam. Predictably, these events supported an already established Western perception of Islam as an atavistic religion that promotes violence and of all Muslims as fanatical extremists. The result is that the term "Islamic fundamentalism" functions in common western discourse largely as a pejorative epithet or label, obscuring the realities it is supposed to describe under a blanket of fear and revulsion. It further functions to homogenize Islam in the western imagination and cast suspicion on all Muslims as potential threats. Against this emotionally laden background, it is necessary to bring some clarity to the notion of Islamic fundamentalism, so that it may it may serve a descriptive and explanatory purpose.

The following description and analysis of Islamic fundamentalism are not comprehensive or definitive but rather suggestive, providing points of departure for comparisons with fundamentalisms in other traditions. Furthermore, an understanding of Islamic fundamentalism will contribute to considerations of how religiously motivated and/or legitimated violence in various world religions might be better understood and ameliorated. Recognizing that fundamentalism is not a uniquely Muslim phenomenon (see the comparative analyses of, for example, Antoun 2001, Lawrence 1995 and Marty and Appleby 1991–1995) is an obvious but necessary first step towards rescuing the term from the domain of purely anti-Muslim sentiment.

Terminology

The term "fundamentalism," is commonly used as a negative label when it comes to Islam, serving to legitimate prejudice and counter-violence, and many scholars question whether the term can help us understand anything beyond the stereotypes (for example, see Sidahmed and Ehteshami 1996, to whom I am particularly indebted for the following analysis). That it cannot, they argue, is because of the origins and history of the term "fundamentalism" in Christianity.

In the early 1900s, fundamentalists were Protestant Christians who saw themselves set apart as true believers from all other Christians by two practices: 1) a literalist reading of the Bible, viewed as an inerrant document; and 2) an adherence to a core of fundamental doctrines, such as the virgin birth of Jesus. The problem in applying this description to Muslim fundamentalists is likewise twofold:

1. Muslims traditionally regard their scripture, the Qur'an, as inerrant and read it literally as God's word. Yet those who are described as Muslim fundamentalists are typically not concerned with defending the inerrancy of the Qur'an but rather with quoting it to support their political activism. Thus, it is their particular political activism, not their literal reading of the Qur'an, which sets them apart from other Muslims.
2. Muslims in general share a core of common religious practices—the five pillars of Islam (witness to the faith, daily prayer, fasting during the month of Ramadan, almsgiving, and pilgrimage to Mecca)—and common beliefs (in God, God's angels, God's messengers, God's books, judgment, the hereafter, and the divine decree). Those regarded as Muslim fundamentalists typically do not stress these core practices and beliefs but instead focus on the establishment of an Islamic government.

Thus, the term "fundamentalism," as it was originally used of a certain Christian movement, does not seem to fit the phenomenon in Islam. An analogous confusion exists in the case of the Arabic term for fundamentalism, *usūlīya*, because it is based on the root *usūl* (meaning "roots, principles, fundamentals"), traditionally referring to the roots or foundational principles of Islamic jurisprudence (Sidahmed and Ehteshami 1996: 4).

However, fundamentalism in the Christian world has changed and developed since its beginnings and has taken on characteristics of political activism. It is the combination of religious literalism and political activism that seems to make fundamentalism a category that can now be analytically applied to religious traditions other than Christianity, such as Islam. And so one now finds trans-religious definitions of fundamentalism such as the following: "new religiopolitical movements that pose themselves, in one way or another, as a political as well as ideological and sociocultural alternative to secular modern states and discourses" (Tohidi and Bayes 2001: 37).

Some scholars, uncomfortable with the use of "fundamentalism" in reference to Islam, avoid confusion with Christian prototypes by the use of such terms as "Islamism," "radical Islamism," "revivalist Islam," "Islamic resurgence" and "Islamic rigorism." However, as the term has become deeply entrenched in both popular and academic western discourse to describe a trans-religious phenomenon that also appears among Muslims, it seems more useful not to reject it but to transform it from a pejorative label into a concept with descriptive and explanatory power. In the case of Islamic fundamentalism, this task requires an examination of the history of the emergence of this phenomenon.

Historical Context

Fundamentalism (in all religions) is commonly associated with the attempt to revive archaic modes of conduct and belief from the past. At the same time, fundamentalism is a uniquely modern phenomenon. In order to sort out this confusion in the case of Islamic fundamentalism, it is useful to make a distinction between it as an ideology and as a style of action. As an ideology, Islamic fundamentalism is uniquely modern; as a style of action, it has its roots in pre-modern revivalist movements.

In Islamic history, one can broadly discern three main styles of action. The first, adaptationist, involves change and evolution in order to meet new circumstances. It is a style of action evident, for example, during the early years of Muslim history, from the origins of Islam in Arabia in the seventh century CE, to the expansion of Islam into a worldwide empire in the eighth century, to the establishment of Islamic social institutions and intellectual traditions in the ninth and tenth centuries CE. As the Muslim polity expanded, its various components changed and evolved in response to varying circumstances and cultural contexts.

The second style of action can be termed conservative or traditionalist. Once the new Islamic synthesis was established as orthodox—approximately in 1000 CE—it became entrenched and in need of defence against new forces for change. In subsequent centuries, this process was repeated each time a new synthesis emerged.

The third style of action, revivalist, rejects recent adaptations as too compromising and seeks to return to a more "authentic way that is imagined to have existed in some past golden age—usually identified as the period during which Mohammad and his first four successors, the "rightly-guided" caliphs, lived. (This conceptualization of the Muslim golden age is particular to Sunni Islam. Shi'ite Muslims have a somewhat different interpretation of Islamic history). This style of action is evoked most often as a response to a particular crisis.

In the seventh century, during the crisis of leadership of the Muslim community precipitated by the death of Mohammad in 634, the Kharijites emerged as a revivalist movement that sought to reinstate what was imagined as the pristine state of affairs at the origins of Islam. Other revivalist movements or dynamics included various Shi'ite revolts, the formulation of Islamic law or Shari'a under the Abbasids and various mystical or Sufi movements. The eighteenth century witnessed a proliferation of Muslim revivalist movements responding to various financial, demographic and agricultural crises (see Esposito 1998 for further details on the dynamics described in the following). Some of these were internal, but they were complicated by European intrusions into local markets and the diversion of commodity trade to Atlantic Ocean routes following the "discovery" of the New World. Eventually, the outcome was European colonization or control of most of the world's Muslim societies. Islamic revival movements during this period were very much a reaction to and protest against these losses. Best known of these pre-modern revivalist movements is the Wahhabi, founded by Mohammad ibn Abd al-Wahhab (1703–1792) and based on the writings of the strict Hanbali jurist Ibn Taymiyya (d. 1328). The Wahhabi movement allied itself to the ibn Saud family, and its vision of the golden age of Mohammad and the early Muslim community became the basis of the modern Saudi Arabian polity.

This period of reaction to internal disintegration and the external challenges of European colonialism and imperialism was followed in the first half of the twentieth century by a period of secular nationalism. This was a period of adaptation. Muslim societies sought a place in the emerging modern world by adapting to western concepts (often forced upon them), such as that of the independent nation state, western-style education and western political structures. In other words, the Muslim world became subject not only to the process of modernity but also to the influence of the ideology of modernism.

Bruce Lawrence (1995: 27) distinguishes between modernity and modernism as follows:

> Modernity is the emergence of a new index of human life shaped, above all, by increasing bureaucratization and rationalization as well as technical capacities and global exchange unthinkable in the premodern era. Modernism is the search for individual autonomy, driven by a set of socially encoded values emphasizing change over continuity; quantity over quality; efficient production, power and profit over sympathy for traditional values or vocations, in both the public and private spheres. At its utopian extreme, it enthrones one economic strategy, consumer-oriented capitalism, as the surest means to technological progress that will also eliminate social unrest and physical discomfort. (Lawrence 1989: 27)

Many of the elements of modernism with which Muslim societies had to contend were legacies of the previous period of colonization, but they were now being promulgated by indigenous ruling elites. Muslim societies attempted to integrate modern western models in order to reap the economic and political benefits enjoyed by the western developed nations. The traditional or conservative elements of society resisted these changes, especially insofar as they entailed the introduction of the non-traditional ideas of modernism.

This secular nationalist phase was severely undermined in the 1960s by a cumulative sense of failure and loss of esteem, precipitating a massive crisis in many parts of the Muslim world. The paradigmatic event was the Six Days War in 1967 between Israel and a coalition of Arab armies from Egypt, Jordan and Syria. This coalition was led by the immensely popular and charismatic Gamal 'Abd al-Nasser of Egypt, a figure who epitomized and personified the promise of secular nationalism in the Muslim world. The Arab forces were decisively routed and suffered a humiliating loss of territory, most significantly East Jerusalem, which subsequently became Israel's capital.

This war, commonly referred to as The Disaster among Arabs, was widely considered to be symptomatic of an overarching crisis in modern Muslim societies. First, Muslim societies seemed to be experiencing a crisis of identity, unable to find a valued and independent place in the modern world. The model of the secular nation state was not working: Muslim societies continued to suffer corruption and misrule despite independence. The reason for this decline, from a religious perspective, was either that Islam had failed Muslims because it is an outmoded religion, or that Muslims had failed Islam, being seduced away from it by the empty promises of modernism. It is the second explanation that was increasingly embraced. The cry was raised that Islam—not nationalism or some other ideology or concept imported from the West—was the solution to the problems of the modern Muslim world.

Second, The Disaster was symptomatic of an overwhelming disillusionment with the West and an acute sense of betrayal. In general, the promises of western allies and mentors that secular modernization would work were seen as empty or, worse, as subterfuges for continued western control of Muslim societies. More specifically, western duplicity was revealed by what was perceived as the West's continued unfair support for Israel, a country that was widely regarded as a western colony established in Muslim territory and thus a continuation of the West's legacy of imperialism and colonialism. Western double standards were seen to be at work in, for example, the United States's differential treatment of, and intervention in, the affairs of other countries, on the one hand, and its espousal of democratic values on the other. Modernization and development raised expectations in the Muslim world but seemed only to materially benefit a small, urban upper-class elite, while at the same time disrupting the stable certainties of traditional village life.

The West was considered a source of Muslim decline and the problems associated with it. Therefore, the West should be rejected, and authentically Islamic solutions were to be generated from within, without outside help. Islam was believed to be self-sufficient and able to address on its own any modern problems. This belief lies behind the turn from secular nationalism to Islamic revival or resurgence, a turn marked internally by a call for a return to the Shari'a, God's law, and externally by a call to struggle against the West, which was said to be involved in a conspiracy to destroy Muslim societies.

The 1970s seemed to vindicate or support this turn to Islamic revivalism or fundamentalism. For instance, in the October War of 1973 with Israel, Egypt performed significantly better than in previous wars. More importantly, the leader of Egypt, Anwar Sadat, used overt Islamic symbols and terminology in prosecuting this war (in contrast to Nasser's secular nationalistic approach). Also in 1973, the organization of largely Muslim oil producing countries (OPEC) cut back production of crude oil to such an extent that the West seemed to be dependent on the Muslim world for the first time in modern history. The wealth and power of the Muslim oil states were seen as a sign of God's blessing; petro-dollars were used to foster Islamic revival by financing mosques, hospitals, schools, publications and revivalist organizations worldwide. And finally, the Iranian revolution of 1978–79, which toppled the Iranian monarchy and instituted a republican form of government, was the only successful revolt against a western-supported regime in the Muslim world, and it was openly based on an ideology of Islamic revival. The success of the Iranian revolution seemed to vindicate both the turn to Islam and an anti-western stance. The failure of other Muslim countries that tried to modernize according to western expectations but failed stood out in stark contrast.

The initial surge of enthusiasm for a revivalist return to Islamic roots and rejection of the West was tempered by the sobering realities of the 1980s, which brought Muslim-versus-Muslim warfare between Iran and Iraq, the Gulf War of 1991, and state suppression of Islamic revivalism in Muslim countries such as Egypt, Iraq and Syria. Nonetheless, as a style of action, revivalism had gripped the imagination of many Muslims worldwide. However, while this style of action is firmly rooted in the past, the ideological content of these movements is decidedly modern.

Characteristics of Modern Islamic Revivalism

The ideologies of modern Islamic revivalism, or Islamic fundamentalism, have been described by a variety of experts, who have each generated their own list of characteristics (see, for example, Lawrence 1995, Esposito 1998, Armstrong 2000 and Halliday 2002). I suggest that there are five ideological assertions most characteristic of the worldview of Islamic fundamentalism.

1. Islam is seen as a total, comprehensive way of life, sufficient in and of itself to provide adequate—even superior—values and

strategies for living in the modern world. This emphasis on the centrality of religion is deliberately in marked contrast to western secularism.

2. The cause for the perceived contemporary failure of Muslim societies is identified as a turning away from Islam and a turning towards the West and its values and strategies. Therefore, the solution is to reverse this trend. Emblematic of this turn is the call to replace imported western law codes with traditional Islamic religious law, or Shari'a. The Islam to which people are to (re)turn is an idealized version, imagined as having existed in the golden age of the rightly guided caliphs, and based on a selective and ahistorical reading of sources such as the scripture or Qur'an, the *ḥadīth* and *sīra* literature on the life and words of Mohammad and his companions, and works of jurisprudence.
3. The rejection of the West is ideological in that the tenets of modernism (e.g., secularism, pluralism and individualism) are rejected. The fruits of modernity, however, are embraced. Western science and technology, and even to some extent western political and economic strategies, are eagerly accepted and used, as long as their use is governed by Islamic values. As well, sometimes it is argued that these western products and strategies actually originated in Islam or that they have Islamic equivalents. For example, Muslim Spain is seen as having provided the catalyst for the European Renaissance, which in turn provided the impetus for the later developments in science and technology of western societies. Similarly, the western idea of democracy is seen as a mere version of the original Islamic idea of *shūrā* or consultation between the rulers and the ruled.
4. Islamic renewal requires the dedication, training and struggle of ordinary Muslims, not just the class of religious specialists or scholars (the *'ulamā'*). In fact, more often than not, the traditional authority of the *'ulamā'* is rejected, viewed as hopelessly mired in obscure traditionalism or as having been co-opted by the elites intent on staying in power. An emphasis is placed on the notion of *jihad*, erroneously understood by many outside observers as "holy war." While the concept of *jihad* can encompass notions of armed struggle, Islamic jurists over the centuries have formulated strict guidelines for the declaration and prosecution of such an armed struggle, guidelines that have not been satisfied by extremist Muslims, who legitimate their terrorism with reference to jihad. The word itself basically denotes "strenuous exertion" and is much more

widely used today to call Muslims to take an activist stand in rejecting western values and reinstating Islamic values and institutions. (See Noorani 2002, who argues that the most relevant notion of *jihad* for Muslims today is the struggle for social justice).

5. Finally, concepts of the "proper place of women" are prominent in the call for a renewed Islamic society. It has been noted that "almost all fundamentalisms have conservative and retrogressive gender ideologies" (Tohidi and Bayes 2001: 39). So also Muslim fundamentalists, while rejecting premodern institutions such as slavery and feudalism, are intent on reinvigorating patriarchal family codes of the past, focusing on the control and segregation of women. The prominence of this ideological characteristic has led at least one scholar to see fundamentalism largely as a "patriarchal protest movement" (Riesebrodt 1993). Ironically, in mobilizing women to support their political activism (characteristic number four above), Islamic fundamentalist movements actually undermine their program of patriarchal control by creating areas of acceptable political and public agency for women. This accounts in part for the appeal of fundamentalist movements to women (Bauer 1997), an appeal that constitutes part of the fundamentalist "dividend" discussed below.

These are the general characteristics of modern Islamic revivalism, widely articulated, if not necessarily accepted, in many Muslim communities today. But are all Muslims who adhere to these ideological concepts fundamentalists? The problem of the pejorative nature of the fundamentalism label again appears. A further distinction must be made between these broad ideological characteristics—indicative of what I shall call mainstream (i.e., moderate and activist) Islamic fundamentalism—and a much more radicalized version of them, shared by a tiny group of Muslims, and which might be more accurately called fringe (i.e., extreme and militant) Islamic fundamentalism. Fringe Islamic fundamentalist groups add three more elements to the fundamentalist ideological worldview:

1. A stark line is drawn between true believers and infidels. The discourse of these groups contains a sharp dichotomy between us and them, based on an underlying binary of God versus Satan. Usually only members of the group itself and those who sympathize with it are seen as true believers; all others, whether non-Muslim or Muslim, are defined as infidels. Thus, not only the West but even other members of Muslim societies must be opposed and rejected. Struggle against even the traditional

Muslim authorities is legitimized. The Egyptian, Sayyid Qutb, in many ways the intellectual father[2] of modern Islamic fundamentalism redefined rejection of *jāhilīya* (ignorance) to refer not just to the rejection of pre-Islamic Arabian idolatry (the traditional referent for this term) but also to the rejection of contemporary Muslim societies who do not follow a rigorous revivalist style of action and ideology.

2. *Jihad*, or struggle against western influence and models and geared towards the establishment of an overtly Islamic government, is seen as a divine imperative. Thus, it is not a choice that Muslims can make but a command that all "true" Muslims will obey. Those who resist this imperative are, by definition, unbelievers. Furthermore, jihad can, and often must, include violent action in order to be effective. An infamous example of this ideological precept in action is the assassination of President Anwar Sadat of Egypt by an extremist fundamentalist group in 1981 (Lawrence 1995: 213; Esposito 1998: 172–73).
3. Christians and Jews are redefined: rather than being regarded, as in traditional Islamic theology, as "people of the book"—that is, co-religionists or allies of a sort—they are now seen as infidels because they are believed to be part of a western conspiracy against Islam and thus are to be opposed.

Mainstream and Fringe Fundamentalisms

The two lists of ideological characteristics above suggest that one cannot speak of a monolithic modern Islamic fundamentalism, but must rather make distinctions between various Islamic fundamentalisms.[3] These fundamentalisms portray a spectrum of ideological characteristics ranging from moderate to extreme; furthermore, while generally revivalist in their style of action, they exhibit a spectrum of behaviour, ranging from a mainstream activist style to a fringe militant style (see Esposito 1998, especially chapter 5, for further details).

The mainstream style seeks to make society more Islamic by generally non-violent means such as education, social justice initiatives, preaching, publications, running in elections where allowed, moral advocacy and political agitation. Examples include the activities of the Muslim Brotherhood in Egypt, the Jamaat-i-Islami party in Pakistan and the Refah party in Turkey. This strategy can be termed "Islamization from below"—a gradual evolution spearheaded by grassroots efforts and campaigns. In contrast, the fringe militant style seeks to make society more Islamic by toppling the government by whatever means possible and replacing it with a more authentic Islamic governing polity. The coercive power of the state can then be used to impose a particular version of "orthodox" Islamic belief and behaviour. This strategy can be termed "Islamization from above."

At first glance, it seems that the Iranian revolution of 1978–79 is a good example of "Islamization from above." However, the toppling of the western-supported monarchy in Iran was the result of a sustained grassroots movement that grew into a populist revolt. Only when Ayatollah Khomeini consolidated his political power and imposed clerical rule did the Iranian revolution start to lose its populist character. Better examples of "Islamization from above" are found in the small militant groups that deal in assassinations, suicide bombings and murder of western tourists and journalists.

Who, typically, are such militants? It must be noted that they are a relatively small segment of the Muslim population, and their influence—or at least their visibility—is quite out of proportion to their actual numbers. Mainstream Muslim activists are far more numerous. The research of Saad Edden Ibrahim (1980) with some thirty-four Egyptian Muslim militants imprisoned in the 1980s identified the following common characteristics:

- They tend to be urban, with a rural or small-town background, and therefore have been subject to the dislocations involved in the global phenomenon of migration to urban centres.
- They are relatively young.
- They tend to be employed in, or at least trained for, modern clerical and professional jobs rather than in more traditional crafts and trades; i.e., they tend to be teachers, lawyers, engineers, civil servants, doctors or military officers.
- They usually have a higher status job or position than their parents.
- They tend to have a higher education, often a university degree.
- They do not come from what might conventionally be labelled broken homes or troubled childhoods; rather they are the products of a so-called normal upbringing.

These findings indicate that Muslim fundamentalism of the extreme or militant variety does not mainly appeal to the marginalized and dispossessed in Muslim societies. Rather, it draws on the most promising young people, who have experienced educational success and initial upward social mobility, but whose high qualifications and aspirations do not meet with the economic and political opportunities they expect. If these persons are suffering deprivation, it is only of a relative sort. (Ibrahim's research in Egypt has been corroborated by studies of militants in Iran and Turkey; see Van Bruinessen 1995: 165).

It can be further asked why these individuals turn to religious militancy rather than to left-wing secular militancy. The answers lie with circumstances and context: the religious climate of the family of origin, access to certain fundamentalist literature, contacts with recruiters for religious militant groups, the motivating examples of the Iranian revolution and of the religious resistance to the Soviet occupation of Afghanistan, and the fact that political repression in Muslim societies is more successful against left-wing militants than it is against religious militants, all contribute to the higher appeal of religious rather than secular extremism.

Thus, a certain relatively small, disaffected element of the Muslim world population is recruited into violently militant forms of Islamic fundamentalism. This type of extreme fundamentalism is properly the target of various efforts at containment, while at the same time, attention needs to be given to its underlying causes in the upheavals and broken promises of modernity and globalization. However, just as important is that various aspects of activist or revivalist Islam have influenced a much broader sweep of the Muslim population. In many ways the style and ideology of Islamic fundamentalisms of the less extreme sort have become part of the mainstream of many Muslim societies. As already mentioned, the sobering realities following the relative euphoria of the revivalist upsurge of the 1970s led to a certain tempering of fundamentalist rhetoric and action. Oil prices dropped and with them the power of petro-dollars to finance revivalism and militancy. The Muslim-versus-Muslim war between Iran and Iraq shattered the euphoria generated by the Iranian revolution. The militant actions of the radical minority overshadowed the more moderate actions of the majority. Also, fundamentalist movements evolved from being sect-like to being more institutionalized. R. Hrair Dekmejian's (1985) analysis of some 175 Islamist groups revealed that the older, more established ones tended to be less radical, more politically quietist and have a more bureaucratic organization. In contrast, more recently founded movements tended to be more militant and exhibit more charismatic leadership.

Some Islamic fundamentalist ideas and behaviours have become mainstream (Van Bruinessen 1995). For example, the idea of interest-free Islamic investment banks, derived from attempts to literally apply the Shari'a, has been adopted and experimented with in many parts of the Muslim world. Most visible is a conspicuous increase in public religiosity in the Muslim world: greater attendance at mosques for prayer, increasing use of the veil by women in public, avoidance of alcohol and an aversion to western indulgences such as night clubs and movies with violent or sexual content (Dekmejian 1995: 50–54). While these changes are not necessarily directly attributable to the influence of Islamic fundamentalisms, they indicate that various behaviours and beliefs associated with fundamentalism, such as literal adherence to scriptural mandates and rejection of western liberalisms, have caught on widely in the Muslim world. For many Western analysts, this movement of various Islamic fundamentalist ideas and behaviours into the Muslim mainstream is a frightening prospect. It strengthens the negative stereotype of the violent, fanatic Muslim and encourages a hard-line condemnation of, and pre-emptive strikes against, Muslims and their worldview, culture and associations.

Yet one might ask why Islamic fundamentalisms (or any other kind of religious fundamentalisms) are attractive to people in the first place. Is it merely the case that those attracted to fundamentalism have been deceived or coerced in some fashion? Western liberals must here beware of letting their often visceral revulsion against fundamentalism cloud their analysis of this human phenomenon. Fundamentalisms, to borrow an economic analogy, offer a dividend of sorts that appeals to human longings for security and well-being. Embedded in Islamic fundamentalisms, as in all fundamentalisms, are utopic impulses that resonate with universal values, despite blatantly exclusive ideologies, and engender strong bonds of human solidarity. Dialogue and engagement, not blind confrontation, with Islamic fundamentalisms, particularly of the mainstream type, are thus called for since fundamentalisms offer sites of resistance to, and critiques of, the limitations of modernity and globalization (Huff 2000).

Before September 11, 2001, it might have been supposed that mainstream Islamic fundamentalisms would slowly take their place in a world that necessarily works according to the politics of the possible. And perhaps it is precisely because this seemed to be the case that the perpetrators of the attacks made their plans. It can be argued that the events of that day were meant, not so much to strike a blow at the United States, but rather to revive an Islamic fundamentalism and activism that was seen to be flagging, becoming too moderate and mainstream. In any case, one of the consequences of September 11, 2001, is that the possibility of a distinction between mainstream and fringe Islamic fundamentalisms seems largely to have collapsed. And yet, if the world is not to descend into an absolutely destructive "clash of barbarisms" (Achcar 2002), such a distinction must be made operative again.

Notes

1. This chapter had its genesis in a presentation on Islamic fundamentalism(s) to a sociology of religion class. It was further discussed and refined in a faculty colloquy on fundamentalism convened at the University of Regina. The usual diacritical marks have been omitted for Arabic terms such as jihad, Shari'a and Qur'an that have entered into English discourse, but are retained for other Arabic terms.
2. His book *Ma'ālim fī al-Ṭarīq*, translated into English as *Milestones*, first published in 1964, continues to appear in numerous editions throughout the Muslim world.
3. It should further be mentioned that the Islamic fundamentalisms examined in this paper are largely those that are identifiably from the majority Sunni

form of Islam. Shi'ite Islam adds its own particular nuances, requiring a separate analysis.

References

Achcar, Gilbert. 2002. *The Clash of Barbarisms: September 11 and the Making of the New World Disorder*. New York: Monthly Review Press.

Antoun, Richard T. 2001. *Understanding Fundamentalism: Christian, Islamic, and Jewish Movements*. Walnut Creek, CA: Altamira Press.

Armstrong, Karen. 2000. *The Battle for God*. New York: Alfred A. Knopf.

Bauer, Janet. 1997. "Conclusion: The Mixed Blessings of Women's Fundamentalism: Democratic Impulses in a Patriarchal World." In Judy Brink and Joan Mencher (eds.), *Mixed Blessings: Gender and Religious Fundamentalism Cross-Culturally*, New York: Routledge.

Dekmejian, R. Hrair. 1995. *Islam in Revolution: Fundamentalism in the Arab World*. (2nd ed.) Syracuse: Syracuse University Press.

Esposito, John L. 1998. *Islam: The Straight Path*. (3rd ed.) New York: Oxford University Press.

Halliday, Fred. 2002. *Two Hours That Shook the World: September 11, 2001: Causes and Consequences*. London: Saqi Books.

Huff, Peter A. 2000. "The Challenge of Fundamentalism for Interreligious Dialogue." *Cross Currents* 50,1–2. Available at www.crosscurrents.org/Huff.htm (accessed Sept. 15, 2003).

Ibrahim, Saad Edden. 1980. "Anatomy of Egypt's Militant Islamic Groups: Methodological Note and Preliminary Findings." *International Journal of Middle Eastern Studies* 12,4.

Lawrence, Bruce B. 1995. *Defenders of God: The Fundamentalist Revolt against the Modern Age*. (2nd ed.) Columbia: South Carolina University Press.

Marty, Martin E., and R. Scott Appleby, (eds.). 1991–1995. *The Fundamentalism Project*. Five volumes. Chicago: University of Chicago Press.

Noorani, A.G. 2002. *Islam & Jihad: Prejudice versus Reality*. New York: Zed Books.

Riesebrodt, Martin. 1993. *Pious Passion: The Emergence of Modern Fundamentalism in the United States and Iran*, trans. Don Renau. Berkeley: University of California Press.

Sidahmed, Abdel Salam, and Anoushiravan Ehteshami. 1996. "Introduction." In A.S. Sidahmed and A. Ehteshami (eds.), *Islamic Fundamentalism*. Boulder: Westview Press.

Tohidi, Nayereh and Jane H. Bayes. 2001. "Women Redefining Modernity and Religion in the Globalized Context." In Jane H. Bayes and Nayereh Tohidi (eds.), *Globalization, Gender, and Religion: The Politics of Women's Rights in Catholic and Muslim Contexts*. New York: Palgrave.

Van Bruinessen, Martin. 1995. "Muslim Fundamentalism: Something to be understood or to be explained away?" *Islam and Christian-Muslim Relations* 6,2.

Chapter Six

Sifting Islam from Fundamentalism

Muslim Feminists Struggle

Nayyar S. Javed

Writing this chapter has not been easy for me. It has forced me to reflect on my personal struggle, growing up as a Muslim woman in a remote village in the northwest province of Pakistan. I am now a middle-class, older woman, who works as a psychologist. I have been living in Canada since I arrived with my husband in 1969. My gender training was a mixture of orthodox Islam and my father's liberal interpretations of the religion.

During the earlier years of my youth, I found myself being pulled and pushed by the tensions between orthodoxy and liberalism. This struggle helped me to become critical of the contradictions between the claims made by orthodoxy and the real lives of Muslim women. We are told that Islam is exceptionally generous to women as it gives us so many rights, but our experiences contradict this claim. I struggled to find out the truth, and what I discovered did not match with what I was told. "Did my faith lie to me?" was a question that dominated my struggle. I was afraid to openly ask this question.

Some of my fears have continued and intensified even though I have been in Canada for more than thirty years. Others have dissipated. I am no longer afraid of betraying my family, culture and faith. I am now more willing to share my truth. However, I am also aware that what I say may be used against the very women whose lives are already made unsafe by patriarchal assumptions about women in Muslim as well as western countries.

In writing this chapter, I emphasize that many Muslim women live in contradictory spaces, in which their allegiance to their faith and culture is subject to exploitation by insiders as well as outsiders. These contradictory spaces are created by the polarization between their faith and the peculiarities of their respective cultures. The popular assumption about the existence of an Islamic culture put forward by Islamists allows very little room for cultural diversity. Interestingly, there is no historical evidence for the existence of a homogeneous Islamic culture, and no one can deny the presence of cultural diversity within the *umma* (the worldwide community of Muslims), since Muslims live in many different parts of the world.

Attachment to imaginary Islamic culture has far-reaching implications for women. Many indigenous cultures throughout the world have existed since long before the advent of Islam. Even though many are patriarchal, they allow room for self-expression and participation in the public domain. The pressures of faith to repress cultural identity and allegiance to culture itself—for the purpose of strengthening religious identity—can mean giving up this freedom, however restricted it may be. This tension between religious versus cultural allegiance exists everywhere but gains an enormous salience in the lives of millions of Muslim women who have immigrated to the West, including Canada. It is a tension that sets them apart, not only from the mainstream, but also from other radicalized women. Consequently, they experience race, gender and class oppression in isolation. Muslim women have become targets of racism since the collapse of the World Trade Center in the United States. Their struggle to cope with racism is made more painful and their isolation exacerbated in the post-September 11 context. In this chapter I describe the conflicting nature of Muslim women's lives within religious and ideological orthodoxy of the East and the West.

In the contemporary world, little distinction is made between Islam and fundamentalism in both Islamic and North Islamic discourses. Islamists portray Islam as a homogeneous body of knowledge and legal system, and Muslims as a unified *umma*. Both these representations are misleading and both contribute to silencing dissent. Islam is not monolithic but rather includes many schools of thought. Each may claim a monopoly on the truth. However, while the orthodox Muslims, e.g., the Wahabis, allow little freedom for dissent, Islamic mysticism, most popularly known as Sufism, promotes diversity of thoughts, rejects hierarchies and espouses egalitarian ethics. Sufism is built upon the principle of fundamental equality for all human beings and therefore assumes the inherent value of each individual. Such supremacy of individual autonomy is the opposite of what fundamentalism espouses. Not surprisingly, Islamists ignore Sufism and other more liberal versions of Islam. Ironically, this ignoring of liberal versions to some extent privileges U.S. domination.

Islamists espouse a form of Islam that disempowers women and disadvantaged classes in Islamic countries. The escalation of women's oppression in many Islamic countries, such as Iran, Pakistan and Afghanistan, is an outcome of the rise of fundamentalism during the last twenty-five years (Shaheed 1995). Liberal Muslims, including some Muslim feminists, attribute this upsurge of fundamentalism to the problematic interpretations of the religious text and misleading accounts of the sayings and lifestyle of the prophet of Islam—Mohammad (Peace be upon Him).[1] Fundamentalists have focused on literal meanings of the text, highlighting the rituals and repression that promote intolerance. In doing so, the "egalitarian ethic" of Islam, pointed out by scholars like Ahmed (1992), has been obscured. This ethic is the fundamental aspect of the social justice the prophet promoted in his sayings and lifestyle. It is an ethic based on a human-rights approach and offers concrete strategies for equity in wealth distribution and respect for human dignity. This ethic acknowledges an innate potential of all human beings for attaining high levels of spiritual growth by engaging in *taqiva,* or transcendence from material needs. No gender distinction is made in this regard.

The egalitarian ethic adds a very strong spiritual dimension to Islam. Orthodoxy, however, discards this ethic by institutionalizing hierarchies and enforcing the authority of religious leaders, who are men with power. Islamic fundamentalism is no different than other fundamentalisms, secular and religious, all of which have gained enormous power in the past two decades. Islamic fundamentalism has a complex relationship with other fundamentalisms, specifically those dominating the West. It is more than a threat of terrorism. A closer look reveals that these other fundamentalisms have created, sustained and exploited Islamic fundamentalism (Ali 2002).

In the current geopolitical context, the spotlight on Islamic fundamentalism has helped in concealing these other fundamentalisms. For example, the impact of religious fundamentalism in the United States on the lives of women and minorities is, according to Chomsky (1999), no different than what is happening in countries like Iran. The expansion of U.S. imperialism and the corporate rule is made possible by repression, occupation and appropriation—the ingredients that constitute all fundamentalisms, including Islamic. The only difference is that God is replaced by profit.

Muslim women, like all women, are struggling worldwide to find openings, however small, for articulating their human rights. Muslim women's struggle is not different than the struggle of millions of women who are coping with the impact of globalization and other similar fundamentalisms. Many Muslim feminists turn to the egalitarian ethics of Islam in this struggle.

Binding Interpretations

Islamists' misleading interpretation of the concept of *jihad* has posed an unprecedented threat to Muslims and non-Muslims. Muslims who disagree with fundamentalists are harassed, persecuted and even executed in many Islamic countries. In this context, Muslim women are deprived of the space to initiate a debate on gender relations in which to articulate an autonomous position. They are often forced to represent Islamists' views as their own position and Islamists' practice as their self-determined choice. The case of Dr. Taslima Nasrin, a feminist writer of Bangladesh, illustrates the threat faced by Muslims who challenge orthodoxy. Although most of Nasrin's writing is ostensibly fiction, the theme of her stories is women's oppression legitimized by Islam. As a consequence of what she wrote, she was forced to take asylum in Europe from the *fatwa* (verdict) that charges her with blasphemy, as declared by the Islamists in her country. According to the *fatwa*, this charge of blasphemy "obligates" Muslims to kill Dr. Nasrin. If a Muslim kills her, the actions of the killer can be perceived as a *jihad* and he/she will be rewarded.

Sifting Islam out of fundamentalism may help bring into focus the real meaning of *jihad*. *Jihad* is not about killing innocent civilians, Muslim or non-Muslim, even though it is popularly misconceived and misrepresented in this way. According to the prophet Mohammad (Peace be upon Him), it stands for fighting for justice and equality. The concept of the *jihad* encompasses human rights (by making a reference to *haq*, which literally means rights of the individual). Fundamentalists at grassroots levels may make a reference to this in conceptualizing *jihad*, but fundamentalist regimes, however, are sure to avoid this interpretation because it poses a challenge to their power. Significantly, this power gets consolidated by inciting the citizens to fight others rather than the injustice inflicted by their own regime. The United States and other western countries have played a critical role in helping such regimes to ignore the real meaning of *jihad*. Repressing the voices of dissidents, fundamentalists and progressive activists allows the repressive regimes a stability which is useful to the U.S. Indeed, often such regimes survive because of U.S. support.

In making the argument for sifting Islam from fundamentalism, I do not want to undermine the complexity of the work required, or the risks. The complexity arises out of a hierarchical system of knowledge production that excludes debate and dissent, thereby enabling the fundamentalist discourses to claim authenticity. Challenging this claim or authenticity poses the risk of being seen as challenging the words of Allah. Sorting out what Allah commands from what Islamists want Allah to command, what is authentic and what's falsification, is a hard intellectual and emotional struggle. Furthermore, the personal risk is that I might see what does not exist and, in so doing, falsify a truth—a truth that I find painful—and want to alter. I have observed so many well-intended Muslims making this mistake. I am aware that what I offer might be viewed as a critical insider viewpoint. I am also afraid of a looming *fatwa*, declaring what I say here as blasphemy.

My nervousness, which I mentioned at the outset, is not only personal. My concern arises out of a legitimate fear of strengthening Islamophobia—or anti-Islamic hysteria—that has even more tightly gripped the world since the tragic fall of the World Trade towers in New York City. On the other hand, Islamophobia has a lengthy history in the Christian world and is not merely a response to that tragedy. It is rooted in many historic events, including the crusades and the colonization of the countries popularly defined as Islamic (Shaheed 1995). The OPEC (Organization of Petroleum Exporting Countries) oil crisis in the seventies also played a major role in fostering the twentieth-century version of this phobia. In 1973, OPEC decided to cut back the production of crude oil, which put limits on the oil supply to the West and resulted in an escalation of oil prices.

It would be a mistake to portray Islamic fundamentalism as separate from and inimical to the West; it is not an enemy that the West needs to subjugate. The relationship between Islamic fundamentalism and the West, specifically the United States, is not easy to grasp. Indeed, there is evidence to suggest that the notion of Islamic fundamentalism is useful in the ideology of the West and that, ironically, with its anti-western position, it could not exist without the blessing of the West. Each of the two has used the other to justify state and religious intervention against the threat, real and imagined, of outside enemies. The West portrays itself as the rational, civilized norm in comparison to an unpredictable, violent East. For the Islamic fundamentalist, the West is godless and corrupt. Western notions of superiority and Islamic fundamentalism have both gained in strength because of the support, in the form of oppositional positions, that each has received from the other.

According to E. Said (1979), "orientalism" provides the West with an ideology and conceptual tools to construct all Islam as fundamentalist and Muslims as the barbaric others. Western scholars in diverse disciplines have made entire careers as orientalists, enjoying status in western scholarship that is based on a notion of difference and non-synchrony between East and West. The Eurocentric view of orientals is produced through an exoticizing gaze that is ultimately Islamophobic. This view is difficult to challenge, especially when Islamophobia and orientalism are used to explain tragedies like the destruction of the World Trade towers.

Necessary Enemies: Who Needs Whom?

Considering the role Islamic fundamentalism has played in both promoting and resisting U.S. imperialism, it is fair to say that this imperialism has participated in the creation of Islamic fundamentalism both at grassroots and state levels. The following two cases illustrate.

The United States support for a despotic regime that happens to be deeply embedded in Islamic fundamentalism is nowhere more significant than in the example of Saudi Arabia. Historically, U.S. politicians have depended on this ally for its support during the presidential elections. The flows of Saudi capital and cheap oil into the United States have been crucial factors in the U.S. economy. During the Gulf War in 1990, Saudi soil offered a base for U.S. troops who, by the way, never left Saudi Arabia.

The strategic importance of Saudi Arabia for the interests of U.S. imperialism has helped make gross violations of human rights, specifically women's human rights, all but invisible. Saudi women live in a gender apartheid that severely restricts their lives. They are not allowed to leave home without the protection of their male relatives. They have to follow a strict dress code and the Islamic Shari'a laws which do not treat women as men's equal. These laws allow honour killing and inequalities in a broad spectrum of family laws. Any attempts by women to resist are brutally crushed by their government. Yet, despite its violations of human rights, Saudi Arabia enjoys the status of being a "most favoured trade partner" of the United States and many other western countries. The United States also supports other fundamentalist regimes in the Muslim world (Blum 2002); in fact, many of the dictators who head these regimes could not survive populist resistance in the absence of this support (Ali 2002).

In 1995, some Saudi women were able to organize a protest rally against the state prohibition of women driving. They were severely punished by their government. The whole world witnessed women being sentenced and flogged; but no one did anything to support these women, even the United Nations also chose to remain silent. The silence by the West cannot be explained or understood without also acknowledging how Islamic fundamentalism is used to explain and justify U.S. imperialism in the Middle East.

A second case, this time from Afghanistan, illustrates the role of the United States in breeding and fostering grassroots fundamentalism. In the conflict between Afghanistan and the Soviet Union in the seventies, the United States and its western allies created a grassroots fundamentalist movement (Ali 2002). Osama Bin Laden, then an ally of the United States and a Saudi citizen was recruited and trained to lead the Mujahideen—young Muslim fighters—to fight against the Soviet Union. Bin Laden's charisma and the passion for *jihad* against godless communism helped organize the Mujahideen to fight fearlessly against a superpower and play a critical role in its ultimate dismantling. After the withdrawal of the Soviet forces, the young Muslim soldiers and Bin Laden continued their *jihad*. But this time the enemy was not the godless communists but the United States, its Saudi allies and other dictators in the Middle East (Blum 2000).

As a symbol of Islam, women also became a target in this *jihad*. The whole world witnessed, silently, the atrocities committed by the Taliban Mujahideen, who killed and brutalized whomever they perceived as non-believers. They, like other fundamentalists, extended their *jihad* onto other fronts. For instance, if they perceived that certain women had failed in following their version of Islam, the Taliban felt it was their right and also religious responsibility to kill those women. Ironically, in the discourse on the brutality of Taliban, the role of those who trained them to fight is obscured. The silence about the foreign policies of the powerful countries that create such situations continues still.

Unfortunately, Afghan women are not the only example. Saudi Arabia, Pakistan and many other countries are stark testimonies of the failure of the U.S. to withdraw its support from regimes that shamefully violate women's human rights. The appalling images of the Afghani women's brutalization by the Taliban—that came to light after September 11, 2001—

had been kept invisible for years. Up until that time, the world pretended that those women's lives were without incident, or at least were of no concern outside their own countries. Consequently, no one did anything to intervene despite the strong plea of several courageous Afghan women for help. Afghanistan could not contain the Taliban's influence within its boundaries. It spilled over to Pakistan where Zia Ul Haq, a military dictator who received enormous support from the United States during the Soviet-Afghan armed conflict, also turned to Islamic fundamentalism to justify the repression of dissent and to consolidate power usurped from the democratically elected prime minister, who was later executed.

Zia's regime is described as "the darkest period" for democracy and women in the history of Pakistan (Khan 1995a). Although women were not treated as men's equal prior to Zia's "reign of terror" (Mumtaz and Shaheed 1987), they had enjoyed certain rights. In fact, the 1973 constitution guaranteed a substantial number of seats for women in the national assembly. Access to education and employment was widening for at least middle-class women. Zia tried to turn the wheel backward. Women's response to his regime was a surprise to Zia. He could not subdue them with his relentless brutality. Zia was never reprimanded by the West for his actions or for the brutality of his regime. On the contrary, the financial and military support continued to pour in from the West.

The Effects of Fundamentalism on Muslim Women

Ideologically, Islamic fundamentalism seduces Muslims on several levels. For instance, it attempts to offer simplistic explanations for complex problems, such as the negative effects of modernity, the inequities in wealth distribution and the restoration of the Islamic civilization that started to crumble with the decline of the Ottoman Empire. This seduction often blurs the vision one needs to differentiate between Islam and fundamentalism. Moreover, anti-U.S. sentiment—so pervasive in the so-called Islamic world—also hinders any efforts to distinguish Islam from the fundamentalist sentiments that oppose women's access to education and employment. The threat of U.S. foreign policy is used to justify extreme responses, and it is Muslim women who pay the price.

Historically, Islamic fundamentalism has used the position of women in Islamic society and a particular understanding of *jihad* as two salient symbols of Islam. Both are embedded in a discourse that usurps women of their autonomous existence and isolates *jihad* from the egalitarian ethic of Islam.

According to E. Apfelbaum's (1992) formulation, the social identities of both marginalized and dominated groups are strategically used to skew the power balance in favour of the dominant group. These identities divide groups into two categories, which portray the subordinate group as a binary opposite of the dominant group. This division imposes an otherness on the subordinate group that in simple terms can be described as absolute marginality. Women's marginality is legitimized by "branding, stigmatizing, labeling" (Apfelbaum 1992: 269).

Apfelbaum (1992) describes a process of "grouping" in which Muslim women are embedded in a contradictory discourse that is very difficult to challenge, as it labels women as subordinate and divine. This divine labeling facilitates the indoctrination of women through their own internalizing of the label. Of course, women do not all respond in the same way, and Apfelbaum contends that the marginalized group does not accept such labeling for very long. Ultimately some are able to regroup on their own terms and challenge the indoctrination suggested by the labeling process. The process of grouping and de-grouping illustrates women's rejection and/or acceptance of an identification that attempts to distinguish them as more or less authentic Muslim women.

Grouping, as a response to state and religious dictates, produces multiple layers of women's oppression. They are subjected to a constant fear, which often forces them to participate in their own oppression by acting in compliance with forms of patriarchy. Consequently, in extreme cases, we may find mothers playing a prominent role in the murder of their daughters who are accused of violating family honour. It is appalling to see mothers turning against their own daughters. Yet, I do not hesitate to say that I have no problem in understanding why they do it and how their motherly instinct gets so twisted.

One can find many problematic verses in the text of the Qur'an about women's equality. The discourse on the equality of all human beings makes no distinction between men and women, although the gendered interpretation clearly privileges men. Similarly, the stories in Islam about the creation of humans and their fall from paradise, based on the Bible, provide grounds for male supremacy. Muslim feminists argue that there is no evidence of these stories in the Qur'an's text. Yet the mainstream discourse in Islam has insisted on its authenticity. For instance, the creation of *Hawa* (Eve) from Adam's "crooked rib" has been used to construct an inherent flaw in women's nature. This flaw creates the need for protection. Adam's crooked rib as Hawa's origin is clearly reflected in the identity constructed for women. Moreover, the need for Hawa's creation puts her female offspring in a precarious position. Since she is assumed to have been created to be Adam's companion and not as an autonomous individual, the identity her offspring are supposed to adopt places them in a subservient role. Their value as human beings, therefore, is measured with a different yardstick.

The interpretation of a second problematic story—the fall from paradise—squarely puts the blame on Hawa, who was seduced by the serpent but was able to seduce Adam, painting Hawa as a mixture of *zauf* (weakness) and *fitna* (disruptive potential) (Hassan 1999). This combination in Hawa's nature is carefully woven into the identity of her female offspring. *Zauf* is seen as a logical ground for male protection, while *fitna* requires a vigilant restraint. The pulls and pushes of these contradictory traits of women's identity may be a huge psychological pain, which has yet to be explored by the Muslim feminists. The social and material implications, however, are clearly reflected in the reality of women.

Interestingly, both of these stories are found to be narrated in a very different way in the text of the Qur'an (Hassan 1996). A representative of the Islamic Institute of Iran at the Beijing Plus Five review (Islamic Women's Institute of Iran 2000) talked about how both of these stories are narrated differently in the Qur'an than the versions written in the Old Testament of the Christian Bible:

> A careful look into the two accounts of the story of creation reveals some essential differences in the Qur'an. Contrary to the Bible, Qur'an places equal blame on both Eve and Adam for their mistake. Nowhere in the Qur'an can one find even the slightest hint that Eve tempted Adam—Eve is no temptress, no seducer and no deceiver. (Sherif Mohammad 1996, cited in Islamic Women's Institute of Iran 2000: 3)

Both Hussan (1996) and the Islamic Institute of Iran have done extensive research on how Eve was created. Neither of these sources found evidence of Adam's crooked rib being the origin of Eve.

Despite the obvious falsehood in attributing these stories to the Qur'an, they have been consistently used in the ruling discourse in the construction of women's identity and the prescription of gender roles. Women are indoctrinated to embrace this identity in Muslim societies all across the globe and to confine themselves to their gender roles by the threat of punishment during life and after death. For instance, from an early stage of their psychological development, women are made aware of their male relatives' rights to punish them for transgressions. They know too well the consequences of stepping outside the bounds of their identity and gender role. Both their identity and gender roles are represented as Allah's command, which if not followed may lead them to hell. The imagery of hell as a burning inferno and the grave as a restricting dark hole festering with snakes and other creatures are also powerful tools for keeping women in their place. Then there are the issues of being ostracized or killed. From my own experience, I know that it is hard to escape this fear because of the conversations about it that take place in many settings, including women's get-togethers. These conversations have gained more legitimacy since the upsurge of fundamentalism in the 1980s in Pakistan. The *durs* (teaching of religion) formally organized by women, has gained enormous popularity in all regions of Pakistan.

The representation of prominent Muslim women is another powerful strategy for indoctrinating women to accept their subordination. References are frequently made to the wives of the prophet Mohammad (Peace be upon Him), who played a prominent role in his life and in the evolution of Islam. The prophet, whose father died before his birth, was raised by his mother and a wet nurse. His first wife was a prominent businesswoman. Prior to their marriage, the prophet had been one of her employees. She was also the first person to accept Islam. She supported him financially and emotionally, and her status helped him gain credibility. Many of his wives were accomplished scholars and autonomous women. Ai'Sha, his youngest and favourite wife, was a scholar, strategist and linguist. He acknowledged her impressive scholastic ability and told his followers to look to her for leadership in knowledge about Islam. She quoted more than two thousand *ahadeeth* (sayings, narrations of the prophet) (Ahmed 1992), yet her name is often missing from the list of Islamic scholars. The prophet himself turned to her for consultation, yet her contribution in building Islamic scholarship is erased from history and collective Muslim consciousness. Although other of his wives were also scholars, it is not their abilities and achievements in the male sphere that are portrayed but rather that they were obedient wives. Ironically, Ai'Sha is used as an example to encourage young girls to accept early marriages (Ai'sha was married to the prophet at age nine, when he was fifty-six). Especially in countries like Canada, where Muslims are living as a minority, her example is quoted in the legitimization of under-age marriages of Muslim girls.

The acceptance of a constrictive identity may appear to suggest a weakness in Muslim women and can lead to many misleading assumptions about them. Therefore, it is important to understand the reasons for such acceptance. There is no question about the protection this acceptance offers to women. It saves them from hell both during and after life. They are promised paradise after death and safety during life only when they accept the prescription of their social identity. However, despite the pressures and temptations to accept this identity, one can find significant differences in the way Muslim women live this identity in many Muslim societies.

The representation of Islam as a homogeneous ideology and the *umma* as a unified community is filled with holes. The *umma* is as fragmented as are other faith communities. There are two major Muslim factions, Sunnis and Shi'ites, as well as further divisions within Sunnis and Shi'ites (Ahmed 1992). Moreover, more than one billion Muslims living all over the world are deeply influenced by their indigenous cultures and constantly struggle to negotiate the tensions between their cultural and religious identities. This tension is exacerbated in countries such as Canada where Muslims live as a minority. The threat of assimilation into the dominant culture may lead the Muslim community to put more pressure on individuals to repress their ethnicity over their religion. This has special implications for women, as their subjugation serves as a symbol of Islam.

The representation of worldwide Islam as monolithic is a strategy used to portray women as a subordinate group in all Muslim societies, whether it is true or not. Muslim women who chose to live the identity inscribed by their faith further reinforced this perception (Khan 1995b; 2000). Identifying as a faithful Muslim gives women a space where they belong and feel protected, a place where they can assert their cultural and religious specificity. In the racist context that has intensified Islamophobia in Canada and the United States, this space seems to offer what is lacking outside. Moreover, the majority of Muslim women usually have few other choices but to quietly accept seclusion, segregation and subordination.

The gendered interpretation of fairness and justice creates two separate yardsticks, one for Muslim men and the other for women and minorities (Ahmed 1992). Muslim feminists are posing a challenge to this yardstick by researching, reinterpreting and rewriting the text (Shaheed 1995). These ongoing engagements have a long history.[2] In 1975 Mernissi's ground-breaking book, *Beyond the Veil,* initiated the process. Dr. Nawal El Saadawi, an internationally known Egyptian feminist writer (and psychiatrist), points out stark similarities between Islam and the cultural traditions of Arab society. She raises serious doubts about the originality of the content of Islam. She states:

> The most restrictive elements towards women can be found first in Judaism in the Old Testament, then in Christianity and then in Qur'an. All religions are patriarchal societies—veiling of women is not a specifically Islamic practice but an ancient cultural heritage. (cited in Dyer 1990: A-13)

Despite the strict vigilance of Islamic clerics and leaders, many Muslim women throughout the history of Islam have steadfastly produced their own version of Islamic truth (Mernissi 1995). There are Muslim women who assertively claim the rights their faith has given them. They are seriously engaged in scholarly explorations of the text and its interpretation. For instance, Indonesian, Malaysian and Iranian women are looking into the text through gender lenses to identify the commonalities between CEDAW (the Convention for the Elimination of Discrimination Against Women) and Shari'a.

Despite the pressures of orthodoxy to dictate a monolithic way of living, many women have made different choices. They have managed to step outside the bounds of their role. Some Muslim women have succeeded in becoming heads of states in the past and in recent times. However, stories of the women whose achievements cross the prescribed bounds are rarely, if ever, told to Muslim children.

The Challenge of Regrouping

Building solidarity and speaking out against the unfair distribution of power are important elements of regrouping. It is hard to convince those who are negatively influenced by orientalism and the western portrayal of Islam that Muslim women have always been engaged in resistance and regrouping. The attempts of Muslim women to give legitimacy to this resistance are complicated by orientalism. The template of the passive and subjugated Muslim woman "cognitively incapacitates" us (Goldberg 1990) in our own struggle. The temptation to use the orientalist lens is irresistible for many western onlookers as they continue to treat the resistance of Muslim women as an oxymoron. This uncritical approach benefits fundamentalists because it engenders a huge gulf between Muslim women and western feminists.

I have often felt this gulf, such as when I participated in the Fourth International Conference of Women in Beijing in 1995 and its follow up review in 2000. Muslim women, with a few exceptions, such as the Afghan women struggling against the Taliban, were not offered solidarity by other women. In fact, the legitimacy of their voice was often doubted. Similarly, the position of the representatives of the Islamic countries in the debate about women's rights was portrayed as "hard-line," while representatives of countries like the United States, who usually foreclose this debate, were spared such labels. In order to build the solidarity necessary to fight the fundamentalists' supremacy, we need to discard orientalism and the ensuing ignorance of Muslim women's participation in resistance movements.

Challenging the orthodox interpretation of Islam and the assumption of the text's purity (as God's word) constitutes the very foundation of Muslim women's resistance movements. Narrow interpretations of Islam focus on formalism and rituals, obscuring the egalitarian ethic that is also present. The broader spiritual message of Islam intertwined with the principle of fairness is thus veiled.

Muslim women's networks, such as Women Living Under Muslim Laws, are undertaking impressive projects to resist the repressive Shari'a laws. Their connection with other women's movements, such as Sisterhood is Global, helps in shrinking the gulf that sets them apart from Jewish and other women. Of course, a huge majority of women live under abject poverty, and their struggle is confined to survival. They are silenced not only by their faith but also by poverty. The women who are stoned to death in the Muslim countries are usually poor women. They struggle on so many levels, including the struggle to avoid the sexual violence often perpetrated by the fundamentalists. The plight of the Afghan women during the Taliban regime attests to this. The current engagement of Muslim feminists has a history—it is following the tradition set by Sufi women who crossed over the prescribed borders of their gender role and attained respectable positions in society as scholars and spiritual leaders.

Postscript

At the beginning of this chapter, I indicated that I could not openly question the tenets of my faith because I was afraid. Although my fear has taken a different turn since I moved to Canada, I still hesitated to continue my struggle to uncover the truth, as I needed a safe space for explorations. I have not yet found that space. Even the feminist discourse on inclusion denies the space I am looking for, because I find subtle Islamophobia, which blurs the much-needed distinction between Islamic fundamentalism and terrorism, and Islam.

I remember an interview just after the destruction of the World Trade Towers in New York City with a reporter who asked me to comment on how it was linked with *jihad*. I told her *jihad* is not what the fundamentalists think it is. It is the fight for justice and equality, and this fight is supposed to be guided by ethical principles that prohibit the killing of civilians and the destruction of the environment. Moreover, Islam prohibits suicide. The journalist lost interest and abruptly cut me off, ending the interview. Her sudden lack of interest triggered other memories of times when feminist friends have doubted me openly about my feminism. They have often asked me, "How can you be a feminist, aren't you Muslim?"

The assumption that a Muslim woman cannot be a feminist is branding us, no different than the branding done by Islamic fundamentalists. Interrogating assumptions about Muslim women is, therefore, important work in honouring our resistance to patriarchy, which is the ground on which fundamentalism is erected. Sifting Islam from fundamentalism is a hard journey on a slippery and steep terrain. Muslim feminists must not walk on the terrain all by themselves. They need the solidarity of the global sisterhood. Their work will become much easier when their feminist sisters from the global north join their struggle by exposing the ongoing support of their countries to the despotic regimes and other fundamentalist forces in the so-called Islamic world. Muslim feminists are engaged in this struggle to free themselves and other minorities from subjugation by opening a space within Islam for articulating the fullness of their human rights. Failing to understand or deliberately ignoring the distinction between Islam and fundamentalism allows both the East and the West, including feminists in the West, to contribute to the oppression of Muslim women, not only in Muslim countries but also in Muslim communities in the West.

Notes

1. It is a religious requirement to add "Peace be upon Him" whenever the name of the prophet is mentioned.
2. In the contemporary context, the names of Ahmed (1992), Hussan (1996; 1999), Mernissi (1975; 1995) and Shaheed (1995) stand out for their contribution in all three of these areas.

References

Ahmed, L. 1992. *Women and Gender in Islam: The Historical Roots of a Modern Debate*. New Haven, CT: Yale University Press.

Ali, T. 2002. *The Clashes of Fundamentalisms: Crusades, Jihad and Modernity*. London; New York: Verso.

Apfelbaum, E. 1992. "Relations of Domination and Moments for Liberation: An Analysis of Power Between Groups." *Feminism and Psychology* 9.

Blum, W. 2002. *West-bloc Dissident: A Cold War Political Memoir*. NY: Soft Skull Press.

_____. 2000. *Rogue State: A Guide to the World's Only Superpower*. Monroe, Maine: Common Courage Press.

Chomsky, N. 1999. *Fateful Triangle: The United States, Israel, and the Palestinians*. Cambridge, MA: South End Press.

Dyer, G. 1990. "Islam isn't alone in patriarchal doctrines." *Toronto Star*, July 3.

Goldberg, D.T. 1990. "The Social Formation of Racist Discourse." In D.T. Goldberg (ed.), *Anatomy of Racism*. Minneapolis, MN: University of Minnesota Press.

Hassan, R. 1999. "Feminism in Islam." In A. Sharma and K. Young (eds.), *Feminism and World Religions*. New York: State University of New York Press.

_____. 1996. "Are Women and Men Equal before Allah? The Issue of Gender Justice in Islam." In E. Friedlander (ed.), *Look at the World Through Women's Eyes: Plenary Speeches from the NGO Forum on Women, Beijing '95*. New York: Women Ink.

Islamic Women's Institute of Iran. 2000. A paper presented at the NGO Forum of the 23rd Special Session of the General Assembly of UN, June, New York, NY.

Khan, S. 2000. *Muslim Women: Crafting a North American Identity*. Gainesville, FL: University Press of Florida.

_____. 1995a. "Race, Gender, and Orientalism: Muta and the Canadian Legal System." *Canadian Journal of Women and the Law* 8.

_____. 1995b. "The Veil as a Site of Struggle: The Hejab in Quebec." *Canadian Women's Studies* 5.

Mernissi, F. 1995. "Arab Women's Rights and the Muslim State in the Twenty-First Century: Reflections on Islam as Religion and State." In M. Afkhami (ed.), *Faith and Freedom: Women's Human Rights in the Muslim World*. Syracause: Syracause University Press.

_____. 1975. *Beyond the Veil: Male-Female Dynamics in a Modern Muslim Society*. Cambridge: Schenkman.

Mumtaz, K., and F. Shaheed. 1987. *Women of Pakistan: One Step Forward, Two Steps Back?* London: Zed Books.

Mohammad, Sherif. 1996. *Women in Islam Versus Judaeo-Christian Tradition: Myth and Reality*. Available October 14, 2003, from Jamiatul Ulama Transvaal www.islamsa.org.za/library/pamphlets_women_islam_judaeo

_xtian_tradition.html
Said, E. 1979. *Orientalism*. Toronto: Fitzhenry and Whiteside.
Shaheed, F. 1995. "Linking Dreams: The Network of Women Living Under Muslim Laws." In M. Schuler (ed.), *From Basic Needs to Basic Rights: Women's Claim to Human Rights*, Washington, DC: Women, Law and Development International.

Chapter Seven

Lean and Mean

Hegemonic Masculinity as Fundamentalism

Murray Knuttila

I begin with a basic, dare I say, fundamental question: Is it legitimate to consider the issue of masculinity in a forum dedicated to understanding contemporary fundamentalism? Our answer depends on how we define both masculinity and fundamentalism. If we begin with nominal definitions of fundamentalism, we notice a pattern. Most of these definitions focus on reference to literal or to strict Protestant/Christian interpretations of the Bible. For example, the *Oxford Compact English Dictionary* definition is "the strict maintenance of the ancient or fundamental doctrines of any religion or ideology" (2000: 446). The Merriam-Webster on-line dictionary also makes reference to literal interpretations of the Bible, with a second option: "a movement or attitude stressing strict and literal adherence to a set of basic principles." The *Dictionary of Sociology* places the word "religious" behind fundamentalism, then defines the phenomenon as "a movement or belief calling for return to the basic texts or 'fundamentals' of revealed religion." This definition notes that fundamentalism can be linked to a project of social reform or political power (Marshall 1994: 192).

If we understand fundamentalism as referring to a set of ideas, a doctrine, an ideology or a set of principles that could be secular and that can inform a social movement, then it is possible to argue that some forms of masculinity can be understood as being fundamentalist. Besides the definitional issues, for social scientists there is another set of important questions relating to the matter of why at certain historical moments fundamentalisms become social and political. Who promotes, articulates and benefits from the existence of fundamentalist beliefs and ideologies? Surely an understanding of the role of fundamentalism requires attention not only to what fundamentalism is, but why it exists or has come into existence. In this chapter I delve into these issues with respect to hegemonic masculinity.

Hegemonic Masculinity

The term "masculinity" is difficult to define because its usage is fluid, complex and politically loaded. The standard social science approach has been to use the concept of masculinity, along with femininity, as connoting gender. In this common usage, gender is understood as a cultural, historical, variable and contingent attribute associated with biologically based sex differences. Masculine refers to those traits that, in a particular culture, at a particular moment in time, are associated with the biological sex category male. There are a number of problems with this approach to defining gender, not the least of which are Anne Fausto-Sterling's (2000) questions regarding the assumptions surrounding the simple dichotomized female/male distinction. R.W. Connell warns of the tendency to assume that "cultural patterns simply express bodily difference"(2002: 9), because this draws our attention away from understanding gender as an essential element of our social relations and practices. Such an error is to fail to understand, as Harry Brod notes, that "gender is not an attribute of individuals, but a relational category" (2002: 165).

If gender is an inherently relational concept, how do we define masculinity? "Masculinity," Connell states, to the extent the term can be defined at all, "is simultaneously a *place* in gender *relations*, the *practices* through which men and women engage that place in gender, and the *effects* of these practices in bodily experience, personality and culture" (1995: 71, emphasis added). What is important about this definition is its explicit rejection of masculinity as just a trait or characteristic. Connell forces us to think about gender, in this case masculinity, as a social relation and a social practice that affects us in several dimensions of our existence. It affects us as individual persons, but it also affects the cultures and social structures that we, as social actors or agents, create. Connell's definition is more complex than many others, including that of Stephen Whitehead and Frank Barrett, who note that "masculinities are those behaviours, languages and practices, existing in specific cultural and organizational locations, which are commonly associated with males and thus culturally defined as not feminine" (2001: 15–16). The advantage of Connell's definition is that by explicitly including notions of place, practice and effect, we are forced to consider masculinity as a social process involving complex power and other social relationships between and among women and men.

The problem with nominal definitions is that words beget words, so rather than getting caught up in endless semantics, it is time to return to the issue at hand. Can we use the word masculinity to refer to one component of fundamentalism identified above, that is, strict adherence to an ideology or a set of basic principles? The strict answer is "no," because there is no such thing as a singular or essential masculinity. (Gardiner 2002; Connell 1995, 2000, 2002; Whitehead 2002; Whitehead and Barrett 2001). The very title of Connell's groundbreaking 1995 volume, *Masculinities*, summarizes the point. Judith Kegan Gardiner argues that what she calls "feminist infected masculinity studies" have reached consensus on several points including:

> that masculinity is not monolithic, not one static thing, but a confluence of multiple processes and relationships with variable results for differing individuals, groups, institutions and societies. Although dominant or hegemonic forms of masculinity work constantly to maintain the appearance of permanence, stability and naturalness, the numerous masculinities in every society are contingent, fluid, socially and historically constructed, changeable and constantly changing, variously institutionalized and recreated through media representations and individual and collective performances. (2002: 11)

Gardiner refers to a concept that I argue is potentially useful as we make our way through multiple masculinities—hegemonic masculinity. This is, of course, not a new concept, given that Connell has been using it for nearly twenty years (1987). It is, however, a concept that offers us an opportunity to return to the issue of fundamentalism. In so doing, we will take the advice of Anthony Giddens and locate our analysis in time and space. For our purposes here, I explicitly refine the notion of hegemonic masculinity to mean contemporary western hegemonic masculinity. The question now becomes: Is contemporary, western, hegemonic masculinity a form of fundamentalism?

Once again we are faced with a definitional issue. What do we mean by western hegemonic masculinity? It is important to note that the theoretical, empirical and political value of the very concept has been called into question. In his provocatively titled, *The End of Masculinity*, John MacInnes incorrectly notes that despite Connell's widespread use of the concept, he does not attempt an empirical definition. MacInnes (1998) suggests that this may be because in defining hegemonic or dominant masculinity, one usually ends up producing lists of stereotypical attributes (toughness, strength, unemotional, aggressive) that do not conform to any actually existing male. Stephen Whitehead is even more critical of the concept, arguing that it is typically associated with a theoretical tradition that places too much emphasis on conflicts over material advantage. Whitehead (2002) also argues that the concept is too "slippery," that it lacks substance, is reductionist and tends to be excessively structuralist, thus removing agency and the possibility of resistance. According to Whitehead, the concept is deterministic because the subject, men, are made marginal to the deterministic power dynamics of their so-called hegemonic masculinity, rendering them incapable of resistance or alternative behaviours.

These concerns notwithstanding, I argue that the concept of hegemonic masculinity is useful and necessary if we are to understand the mostly unabated prevalence of male domination at this point in world history. I say unabated even in the face of the obvious important gains that the various phases of feminism and the women's movement have brought, because men still enjoy many personal, social and economic benefits—the patriarchal dividend. As for the criticisms noted above, it seems clear that the concept is typically used in a manner closer to an ideal type as used by Max Weber than as an empirical description of actual men.

Perhaps a very brief methodological digression will make the point clear. Ideal types can be, as Weber (1949) argues, useful analytical tools when dealing with complex issues and phenomena. Indeed, he suggests that the use of ideal types "can be indispensable for heuristic as well as expository purposes." Such constructs, Weber explains, are "formed by the one-sided *accentuation* of one or more points of view and by the synthesis of a great many diffuse, discrete, more or less present and occasionally absent *concrete individual* phenomena, which are arranged according to those one-sidedly emphasized viewpoints into a unified *analytical* construct." Finally, he states, "In its conceptual purity, this mental construct cannot be found anywhere in reality" (1949: 90, emphasis in original). In short, it is an entirely legitimate intellectual approach to use abstract representations of the issues or phenomena we are examining in order to draw out some essential features that will enhance our understanding or facilitate comparative and/or empirical analyses.

Connell provides a concise definition of the concept of hegemonic masculinity: "Hegemonic masculinity can be defined as the configuration of gender practice that embodies the currently acceptable answer to the problem of the legitimacy of patriarchy, which guarantees (or is taken to guarantee) the dominant positions of men and the subordination of women" (1995: 77). Patriarchal systems are, however, never free-floating; that is to say, they are part and parcel of a larger system of productive and other social relations. Western patriarchy and capitalist market societies have developed together in a truly symbiotic manner. It is not necessarily the case that capitalism could only survive as a patriarchal system, and we know that patriarchal systems are compatible with non-capitalist economic relations. But it is the case that capitalism and patriarchy clearly exhibit elective affinity, to again borrow from Weber.

If we work from these assumptions, we must address the question of what sorts of gender practices are currently employed to legitimate patriarchy and support the dominant positions of men within a capitalist, market-based social system. In answering this question we must confront the issue of what we mean by hegemonic masculinity at a more empirical level and attempt to specify some of the content of our ideal type. Such an undertaking is difficult because, as Carrigan, Connell and Lee pointed out when they began to map the notion, hegemonic masculinity is not a syndrome or condition identifiable with certain symptoms. As they note, it is "a question of how particular groups of men inhabit positions of power and wealth, and how they legitimate and reproduce the social relationships that generate their dominance" (1987: 92). At the risk of articulating stereotypes, let us explore some possible features.

In her important essay on men and masculinity, Sally Robinson uses the term dominant masculinity, noting that it is typically conceived of as "straight, white, middle-class masculinity" (2002: 147). In their book, which tends to be in the "masculinity in crisis" genre, Ronald Levant and Gini Kopecky provide a more traditional view of masculinity, although they never use the word hegemony. They list several traditional masculine norms: "(1) avoidance of femininity; (2) restricted emotions; (3) sex disconnected from intimacy; (4) pursuit of achievement; (5) self-reliance; (6) strength and aggression; and (7) homophobia" (1995: 9). Michael Kimmel uses four phrases from Robert Brannon to summarize manhood: "No Sissy Stuff," "Be a Big Wheel," "Be a Sturdy Oak" and "Give 'em Hell" (1994: 127). In their essay "Weekend Warriors: The New Men's Movement," Kimmel and Michael Kaufman note that hegemonic masculinity can be defined as partly "a flight from femininity and its attendant emotional elements, particularly compassion, nurturance, affection and dependence," with emphasis on "independence, aggression, competition, and the capacity to control and dominate" (1994: 271). Many men and women will recognize elements in these descriptions that represent a specific form of masculinity that we are familiar with, have encountered or for some of us even practised. In his recent study, *The Men and the Boys*, Connell notes: "To say that a particular form of masculinity is hegemonic means that it is culturally exalted and that this exaltation stabilizes the gender order as a whole" (2000: 84).

The Patriarchal Dividend

We now turn to the issue of how all this works out in our lives and our societies. I argue that hegemonic masculinity can be understood as a range of traits, behaviours, practices and relations that serve to legitimate, reinforce, naturalize, support and generally maintain patriarchal society. These traits, behaviours, practices and relations are promulgated, articulated, promoted and reinforced across and through virtually every social institution. Varda Burstyn's *The Rites of Men: Manhood, Politics and the Culture of Sports* and Suzanne E. Hatty's *Masculinities, Violence and Culture* illustrate this point particularly well with regard to the intersection of the interests of some sectors of capital, the media and professional sports. But we might ask why this particular masculinity is able to maintain its hegemony?

The answer is a bit tough for men because men, whether we want to admit it or not, have a collective interest in our patriarchal social order. Connell uses the concept of a patriarchal dividend to explain. He has examined the income differentials between men and women, using a slightly different tact, focused not on the difference as representing a deficit for women, but as a surplus for men. He explains:

> I call this surplus the patriarchal dividend: the advantage to men as [a] group from maintaining an unequal gender order. The patriarchal dividend is reduced as gender equality grows. Monetary benefits are not the only kind of benefit. Others are authority, respect, service, safety, housing, access to institutional power, and control over one's own life. (2002: 142)

There are several empirical manifestations or indicators of the patriarchal dividend, including income. Comparative income data is often presented in terms of women's income as a percentage of men's income, typically a lesser percentage. Given that we are considering a dividend that accrues to men, I report the positive difference between men and women's incomes as a monetary form of the patriarchal dividend. According to Statistics Canada, in 2001, the average full-year, full-time male worker in Canada earned $49,250, compared to $35,258 for women in the same category. This represents a patriarchal dividend of 28.4 percent. Stated differently, 28.4 percent of men's incomes can be deemed to have accrued to them because they are men. The equivalent figures of all income earners were $24,688 for women and $38,431 for men, with men earning a patriarchal dividend of 35.8 percent.

The fact that men are able, perhaps unconsciously, to reap this benefit is all the more astounding when you consider that they typically work fewer hours. The *Globe and Mail* (March 13, 2001) reported on a Statistics Canada study that demonstrated that, of those in the paid labour force, on average women work more hours each day than men to the tune of an additional eighty hours annually. The study determined that much of this work was in fact unpaid domestic work in the home, work that is directly in the service of other family members, including men. Data collected for the Federal/Provincial/Territorial Ministers Responsible for the Status of Women provide another illustration of the benefits of being male. Their report, *Economic Gender Equity Indicators* (1997), establishes a series of gender equity indices. One of the most startling concrete illustrations of the advantage of being male is found in the data on paid and unpaid work patterns in families with no children. The data is presented in a format that represents a household with equal male and female workloads as one (*Economic Gender Equity Indicators* 1997: 31). The data reveals an index for gender equity in relationships such as 1.83 for women in the unpaid labour category and 0.89 in the paid category, meaning that while women do less paid work, they do much more unpaid work in the household, work that needless to say benefits male members of the household as well.

Other forms of the patriarchal dividend can be seen in the easier access men have to positions of political power. According to a story in the March 7, 2003, *Globe and Mail*, only 20.6 percent of the members of the House of Commons were women, ranking Canada thirty-sixth out of 182 nations in a recent study. It is not clear how this number could be cast as a precise measure of the dividend; however, it is clear that when men compose 79.4 percent of the members of the House, this must reflect in some way the fact that men have easier access to positions of power in major institutions, clearly another aspect of the patriarchal dividend.

Joni Seager's atlas of women in the world illustrates the international character of the patriarchal dividend as manifest in, to mention only a few dimensions, work relationships and property relations, as well as access to economic resources, education and healthcare (Seager 2003). Other of Seager's data relates to access to power and benefits associated with this access. One aspect of power that she does not directly address is corporate power. This lacuna has been addressed by others, including Marion Lynn and Milana Todoroff (1995) and S.J. Wilson (1996). Lynn and Todoroff document the segregation of women into five major occupations: "clerical, teaching, nursing, or other health related occupations, sales and service" (253). Wilson (1996) presents other evidence to make a similar point: there tends to be far fewer women than men in positions of power and control in our major economic activities. Business and enterprise are indeed male domains, and thus men predominately benefit from the wealth, power and status associated with these institutional positions.

The "men in crisis" literature notwithstanding, it seems clear that many, if not most, men in patriarchal society benefit from its social structures, relations and practices. You might say that benefit accrues to men as a group, although the hegemonic male referred to above might represent an ideal that many men would personally reject or find impossible to attain.

Patriarchy and Capitalism

As was noted above, we live in a patriarchal society that is embedded in a capitalist or market-based economic system. Like every other human creation, the market system operates at an optimum level when certain prerequisite conditions are in place. Among the essential preconditions for the effective operation of a market system are individuals who are prepared to engage in behaviour that is impersonal, competitive, self-seeking, aggressive, non-emotive, rational and calculating in terms of fiscal ends. Workers who are unencumbered by domestic responsibilities and other concerns not related to work are also valuable. Robert Presthus (1962) examined the kind of personality best suited for the competitive and bureaucratic milieu in his classic analysis of the relationship between work environment and human personality. Borrowing from the work of T. Adorno, Presthus argued that the ideal type personality for a competitive enterprise was someone who: holds conventional beliefs (including those relating to sex and family matters); exhibits authoritarian submission to those above and displays aggression to those below; accepts stereotypes; admires power and toughness; is cynical; and is anti-introspective (1962: 122–26).

If we return for a moment to the sorts of behaviours and interactions that are required to make an international competitive capitalist market economy operational, it is clear that a form of elective affinity is at work here. Success, indeed survival, demands managers who are capable of making tough and sometimes ruthless decisions. If the company's bottom line and thus its survival is in jeopardy, decisions that affect the employment and welfare of thousands of individuals and families, not to mention entire communities and regions, might have to be made. In such a circumstance the corporation's well-being requires the capacity to be unemotional about closing plants, relocating investment and downsizing in the interests of the company. The ability to wield power ruthlessly and exercise strength and domination are essential. Connell (2002) examined the gendered nature of the corporation, noting that: "The new-model executive, according to the textbooks, is a person with few permanent commitments but a driving interest in profit opportunities for his firm and himself" (101). To be in control, to feel in control and to be seen to be in control are decisive when competitors square off in a winner-take-all situation. An abiding faith in western science with its well-known masculine-domain assumptions of manipulation, control and mastery can provide the rationale for corporate behaviour (Smith 1987, Harding 1986). The necessity of working in a hierarchy and understanding one's place, even while entertaining aspirations for mobility, is necessary in the quasi-military world of international corporate competition. I say quasi-military not just because of the international dimensions but also the use of military tactics and language (such as "industrial espionage") to secure technical and business advantages. The much-practised movement of personnel between the military and corporate sectors adds to the tendency to value behaviour oriented towards power, control, ruthlessness and conquest.

It is thus clear that Weber's concept of elective affinity is useful here. There is a definite correspondence between the ideal type construct of the personality best suited for organizational life in market society and the characteristics of hegemonic masculinity. We have already identified men, collectively, as the primary beneficiaries of the patriarchal order, so we must now ask: Who benefits from the behaviours and actions of the market-oriented organizational personality? Capitalist, market-based societies are characterized by the existence of a fairly entrenched class system. Most social observers acknowledge the existence of substantial social inequalities whose genesis is somehow related to the operation of the market as a distributive mechanism. Those who come to the market with capital in hand and who receive financial rewards as a result typically require the assistance of a salaried or wage-earning labour force to operate their enterprises (Knuttila 2002). Given that the market is necessarily and inherently competitive, we can understand why those with capital benefit from the behaviours described by Presthus, behaviours that are clearly related to those associated with hegemonic masculinity.

Patriarchy, Capitalism and Fundamentalist Masculinity

I now bring together some seemingly disparate claims by first summarizing some of the claims already made. I have argued that capitalist, market-based systems require individuals to operate its major institutions who are capable of behaving in an impersonal, competitive, self-seeking, aggressive, non-emotive, rational and calculating manner. Such individuals must be capable of viewing the world in terms of fiscal ends and not be excessively encumbered by responsibilities and concerns not related to work. Brannon's representation of ideal manhood, encapsulated in the four dictates: "No Sissy Stuff," "Be a Big Wheel," "Be a Sturdy Oak" and "Give 'em Hell" has salience and authenticity. Connell's argument that masculinity is about place, relations, practices and effects and not merely personality traits is important. I have argued that the agents who organize, operate and sometimes dominate the major economic enterprises in capitalist societies are typically male. In a patriarchal society various benefits accrue to men collectively. Those in possession of capital accumulate significant material advantages in a market society. But how do we draw these threads together to in a manner that allows us to determine if fundamentalism is an appropriate concept to inform our understanding? Perhaps a slight ontological diversion will assist.

As social creatures, humans develop and engage in social practices that become regularized, routinized, patterned and structured or—in the language of sociology—institutionalized as a mode or way of doing things. As we deal with our individual and species needs and problems, we also develop stocks of knowledge and modes of understanding, some of which constitutes common sense, others of which are systematic, scientific and even religious. Such knowledge, ideas, belief systems and consciousness become a part of the social environment. An integral part of this process is the codification, storage and transmission of this knowledge. As human beings we produce our social structures. However, once these structures develop and emerge, they in turn become the central determinants of subsequent behaviours. Anthony Giddens (1984) refers to the fact that we are simultaneously the product and producer of our social structures as the duality of structure. But what sorts of practices do we engage in?

If human beings are to survive as individuals and as a species, we must deal with two basic problems. First, we must provide ourselves with the necessary material basis of our physical existence: food, clothing and shelter. In addition, because the future of any species is contingent on biological reproduction, we must somehow organize ourselves in terms of sexual and child-rearing practices. Besides being necessary for individual and species survival, these practices also seem to be central factors in influencing the general structures of the entire society. The organization of material production and biological reproduction has a profound impact on the entire range of institutionalized practices and structures that exist in a particular society. These key practices represent a kind of social basis or core around which other activities emerge and revolve.

The relationship between our biological reproductive and our material productive practices and the larger social structure is complex. All institutions in a social structure are part of a larger whole or totality, and as such they are connected through a complicated reciprocal set of relationships. The practices we commonly associate with the economic order, the family, the polity, religion and the educational order are each characterized by sets of ideas, stocks of knowledge and ideologies. Each of them has its own internal structures, patterns of organization and relationships with other institutional orders; however, each is affected in some manner by the modes of production and reproduction.

Material production in a capitalist society is organized around a systematic set of class relations, while biological reproduction obviously involves relationships between the sexes and matters of gender. We know that key aspects of the organization of social relations are the various stocks of knowledge, ideas and ideologies that emerge as these activities occur in time and space. Over the past five hundred years or more, we have seen the emergence of definitive notions about being female, male, femininity and masculinity in western society. Over the same time we have developed definitive notions and ideas about human nature, competitiveness, the role of self-interest and aggression. The fact that these systems of ideas developed simultaneously, if not in concert, has resulted in a classic case of elective affinity, both of capitalism and patriarchy and hegemonic masculinity and the type of behaviour appropriate in a market situation.

We now come to two critical questions: 1) Does the fact that the power practices associated with hegemonic masculinity are operative in both patriarchy and capitalism mean they can be characterized as a form of fundamentalism? 2) What is the value, heuristically and/or pedagogically, for declaring that there is such a thing as a hegemonic masculinity and that it is indeed a form of fundamentalism?

The key to addressing the issue of whether the gendered power practices that characterize much male behaviour in patriarchy and capitalism are a form of fundamentalism lies in our definition of fundamentalism. This chapter has been developed on the premise that fundamentalism need not be religious as long as the social practices of its adherents are guided by a relatively strict set of principles and ideas or an ideology that includes identifiable axioms that inform social practices. To the extent to which fundamentalism represents both a set of ideas and real social practices, hegemonic masculinity is a form of fundamentalism. The notion that male supremacy and domination are natural, inevitable, desirable, historically constant and therefore immune to challenge underpins what we are describing as hegemonic masculinity. These could be deemed to be the fundamental tenets of political activities and social relations upon which patriarchy is predicated. To the extent that adherents of these principles deem them to be obvious, unquestionable and legitimate to any person with a "lick of common sense," they are an excellent basis for fundamentalist social practice.

As for the second, partly rhetorical question, there are many answers, but one surely revolves around the issue of drawing men's attention to the fact that there is not a single masculinity. In her discussion of the role of men's studies, Sally Robinson explains why the notion of multiple masculinities is important. She notes not only that "masculinity must be deconstructed as a cultural construct but that men, too, must be convinced to distance themselves from the dominant fictions of masculinity that do, more often than not, procure rewards within patriarchal culture" (2002: 154). If we firmly grasp the notion of multiple masculinities, it is easier to keep reminding ourselves that all masculinities, including what we are calling hegemonic masculinity, are historically contingent relations of power. They are the beliefs and practices of social agents within a historical context, place, time and space, and as such, there is nothing essentialist about them. They are subject to critical analysis and open to political change, provided we are committed to egalitarian social relations.

A related pedagogical advantage might lie in the fact that understanding the limitations of an abstract ideal type construction will require us to enhance our understanding of the concept by focusing on research and analysis at a lower level of abstraction. In making this argument, I am acknowledging an important critique of the type of argument I have been developing here. In an important essay, "What Is Problematic about Masculinities?" Kenneth Clatterbaugh (1998) provides an overview of many of the uses and meanings that have developed around the notion of masculinity and masculinities. Despite his serious concerns, he does not argue that we stop examining and trying to understand the power relations inherent in the concept of masculinity, but rather that we be clear what the discourse on masculinities is about. He writes: "We should be reasonably clear that we are not talking about men when we are talking about images, stereotypes, or norms, and that we are not talking about images when we talk about men, male behaviours, privileges and attitudes" (42). It is important to keep in mind that the essential purpose of an ideal type is to assist in the explanation and understanding of individual cases. Karen

Pyke (1996) demonstrates how what I have been referring to as hegemonic masculinity actually plays itself out in the context of the behaviour and actions of men in their concrete day-to-day lives and actions. She documents how the ideology of hegemonic or dominant masculinity manifests itself in very different ways in different social classes. What is common in all the relationships is the notion that males do and should have power over others, including females; however, depending on the class position of the male, the actual relationships at work and home vary.

What is valuable about understanding the notion of hegemonic masculinity as a form of fundamentalism is the manner in which it can direct our attention to some of the abstract ideas and worldviews that inform the lives of men and women in patriarchal and capitalist society. It can also inform our efforts to understand the actual lives of men and women if we are prepared to use the concept not as an end but as a beginning. When used to inform empirical and historical research and analysis, it has the potential to assist our understanding of how the ideas and practices associated with hegemonic masculinity play out in actual social and historical situations. What we need if we are to work towards changing men is a better understanding of how they actually live out their lives in interaction with each other and with women. If we engage in more actual research, such as that reported by Karen Pyke above, we have a chance of knowing ourselves better.

It is important that individual men come to understand the social construction of their masculinities because, despite the structuralist tone of some of my comments, I do entertain some form of a post-structuralist ontology. What I mean by this is I understand that we are self-reflective, somewhat self-constituting beings whose existence is framed and formed by multiple positions. As such we are capable of critical engagement with our selves and history, and although we are constrained by that history, we also actively shape it.

References

Adorno, T.W. 1950. *The Authoritarian Personality*. New York: Norton.

Brod, Harry. 2002. "Studying Masculinities as Superordinate Studies." In J. Kegan Gardiner (ed.), *Masculinity Studies and Feminist Theory: New Directions*. New York: Columbia University Press.

Brod, Harry, and Michael Kaufman, eds.1994. *Theorizing Masculinities*. Thousand Oaks, CA: Sage Publications.

Burstyn, Varda. 1999. *The Rites of Men*. Toronto: University of Toronto Press.

Carrigan, Tim, Bob Connell and John Lee. 1987. "Toward a New Sociology of Masculinity." In H. Brod (ed.), *The Making of Masculinities*. New York: Routledge.

Clatterbaugh, Kenneth. 1998. "What Is Problematic about Masculinities?" *Men and Masculinities* 1, 1. July.

Connell, R.W. 2002. *Gender*. Cambridge, UK: Polity.

_____. 2000. *The Men and the Boys*. Berkeley: University of California Press.
_____. 1995. *Masculinities*. Berkley: University of California Press.
_____. 1987. *Gender and Power: Society, the Person and Sexual Politics*. Sydney: Allen and Unwin.
Economic Gender Equity Indicators.1997. Report for Federal/Provincial/Territorial Ministers Responsible for the Status of Women. Ottawa: Analytical Studies Branch, Statistics Canada.
Fausto-Sterling, Anne. 2000. *Sexing the Body: Gender Politics and the Construction of Sexuality*. New York: Basic Books.
Gardiner, Judith Kegan. 2002. "Introduction." In J. Kegan Gardiner (ed.), *Masculinity Studies and Feminist Theory: New Directions*. New York: Columbia University Press.
Giddens, Anthony. 1984. *The Constitution of Society*. Cambridge: Polity.
Harding, Sandra.1986. *The Science Question in Feminism*. Ithaca: Cornell University Press.
Hatty, Suzanne E. 2000. *Masculinities, Violence and Culture*. Thousand Oaks, CA: Sage Publications.
Kimmel, Michael, and Michael Kaufman. 1994. "Weekend Warriors: The New Men's Movement." In Brod and Kaufman.
Kimmel, Michael. 1994. "Masculinity as Homophobia." In Brod and Kaufman.
Knuttila, Murray. 2002. *Introducing Sociology: A Critical Perspective*. Toronto: Oxford University Press.
Levant, Ronald, and Gini Kopecky. 1995. *Masculinity Reconstructed: Changing the Rules of Manhood—at Work, in Relationships and in Family Life*. New York: Dutton Books.
Lynn, Marion, and Milana Todoroff. 1995. "Women's Work and Family Lives." In N. Mandell (ed.), *Feminist Issues: Race, Class and Sexuality*. Scarborough: Prentice Hall.
MacInnes, John. 1998. *The End of Masculinity*. Buckingham: Open University Press.
Marshall, Gordon, ed.1994. *The Concise Oxford Dictionary of Sociology*. Oxford: Oxford University Press.
Merriam-Webster On-line Dictionary. Available at www.m-w.com/cgi-bin/dictionary.
Oxford Compact English Dictionary. 2000. Oxford: Oxford University Press.
Presthus, Robert. 1962. *The Organizational Society*. New York: Vintage Books.
Pyke, Karen. 1996. "Class Based Masculinities: The Interpretation of Gender, Class and Interpersonal Power." *Gender and Society* 10, 5 (October).
Robinson, Sally. 2002 "Pedagogy of the Opaque: Teaching Masculinity Studies." In J. Kegan Gardiner.
Seager, Joni. 2003. *The Penguin Atlas of Women in the World*. New York: Penguin Books.
Smith, Dorothy. 1987. *The Everyday World as Problematic: A Feminist Sociology*. Toronto: University of Toronto Press.
Statistics Canada. "Earnings of Canadians." Available on October13/03 at: www12.statcan.ca/english/census01/products/highlight/Earnings/Page.cfm?Lang=E&Geo=PR&View=1a&Code=0&Table=2a&StartRec=1&Sort=2&B1=Both&B2=Full.
Weber, Max. 1949. *The Methodology of the Social Sciences*. New York: Free Press.
Whitehead, Stephen, and Frank Barrett, eds. 2001. *The Masculinities Reader*.

Cambridge: Polity Press.
Whitehead, Stephen. 2002. *Men and Masculinities: Key Themes and New Directions*. Cambridge. Polity.
Wilson, S.J. 1996. *Women, Families and Work*. Toronto: McGraw Hill Ryerson.

Chapter Eight

With Us or With the Terrorists

American Hyperpatriotism as Fundamentalism

JoAnn Jaffe

I am writing this after September 11, 2001, and at the end of the second Gulf War, Operation Iraqi Freedom,[1] whose unpredictable consequences are only now beginning to unfold. During this time, the public stage has been monopolized by the symbiotic conflict between two great fundamentalisms. The right-wing Christian United States President George Bush and the leader of the Islamic Al Qu'eda movement, Saudi Arabian Osama Bin Laden, have been each other's best friends. The terrible destruction of the World Trade Towers in New York, apparently planned and carried out by Al Qu'eda, has given Bush the catalyst he wanted to pursue his dual project of protecting "the American oligarchy from American democracy" at home (Lapham 2003) and furthering the aims of American imperialism abroad. Bin Laden has emerged victorious, as the might of the U.S. military failed to kill him in Afghanistan, and now promises to fill his camps with recruits as the United States plays out Operation Enduring Freedom[2] to the end. From the standpoint of the United States, the story that has been told about this conflict has drawn upon a deep imagery with both religious and civil overtones, as shown even in the names of the military operations deemed necessary to root out those responsible for the tragedy.

The United States rushes to capitalize on its military dominance, while its status as a capitalist world power wanes (Wallerstein 2002). Its economy is in decline as evidenced by high levels of foreign debt, its reliance on imports of foreign-produced industrial and capital goods, the rise and fall of its speculative trading regime, and widespread corruption in U.S. firms (Melman 2003). Levels of inequality are the highest in the industrialized world. Rates of unemployment have recently been estimated to be 6 percent of the United States population, with long-term unemployment making up one-quarter of the total.[3] An additional 1 percent are marginally attached workers without the immediate prospect of work and are therefore not counted in the unemployment statistics (United States Department of Labor 2003). It is estimated that the jobless rate would be at least 12 percent if it counted the millions of workers who have left the labour force with no hope of ever finding a job again (Melman 2003). The United States economy is on a permanent war footing as government finances every manner of weapons system but leaves basic services such as education, health care and housing going begging (Melman 2003).

Moreover, with the decline of the Soviet Union, the United States is increasingly unable to command political hegemony over its traditional allies (Wallerstein 2002). We are witnessing a return to intercapitalist rivalries such as characterized the period preceding World War I. The United States appears increasingly willing to abandon a multilateral approach to global governance and to attempt to regain its former strength through the unilateral military imposition of order.

I argue here that this shift in the U.S. political stance also involves an intensification and shift in U.S. ideologies and identities. These have an increasingly fundamentalist character as patriotism and the U.S.'s story about itself have evolved along side neoliberalism, rising immigration from non-European nations, economic decline and threats to its economic and political hegemony. The United States today employs an increasingly absolutist discourse to define what is truly "American," who is in the family and what range of beliefs count as loyal and acceptable.[4]

Fundamentalism

As used here, fundamentalism is a complex social phenomenon that can be approached from a variety of directions. Fundamentalism in one commonly accepted sense means a literal reading, an approach to core texts that says that meaning is transparent, that there is no problem of interpretation, translation or metaphor. It suggests that one can find a determinate reading that can endure throughout history (Pelikan 1990). Fundamentalism can also mean an emphasis on the traditional or fundamental. Left unproblematized is the question of whose understanding of tradition, whose judgment as to what is fundamental is allowed to be decisive. In this sense, fundamentalism implies an approach to the past—an imagined past—that is nostalgic and simplified (Jameson 1992). Reality presents itself whole. There is no struggle or negotiation.

Yet, what is traditional or fundamental is political, a question of power—whose reading or interpretation is given weight or credence? Fundamentalism, thus, needs hierarchy in order to exist. It also may need insecurity to thrive, as people grasp their privilege—or simply try to stabilize or defend their position—by freezing (or rolling back) social relations where they might. Fundamentalism is an absolutist impulse and set of social practices that are most about defining and controlling relations amongst people. It is totalizing in its approach to past, present and future society. It is against creativity and anti-democratic. It defines identities of in and out: priest/expert, saint/hero, and sinner/transgressor. Fundamentalism is reactive and reactionary.

Fundamentalism appears to get considerable energy from social changes that threaten privilege or conversely destabilize the status of those already in a dominated position. As such, it appears to have particular appeal as a strategy to secure, for example, patriarchal power when it appears to be under threat.[5] Fundamentalism, thus, often has a component that is about exerting/heightening control over women. This assertion/extension of patriarchy follows, because it is intimately tied into the control and domination that men exert over each other in hierarchical societies.

This is not to argue that class hierarchy precedes gender domination but rather to claim that both materialize as elements in the structure of domination and that this relation is particularly easy to see in processes of fundamentalist emergence. Patriarchy uses women as compensations or rewards for being dominated—you may be a poor worker, a soldier, indentured or a slave, but you still get to boss or be superior to your woman. If you are at the top of the hierarchy, you may acquire a status woman. Moreover, competition amongst men is partly based upon how well their women are able to take care of them, their households and their work. It follows then that in times of increasing competition and insecurity, men will seek to increase their control over women; fundamentalist strategies provide a means to do that. Women, on the other hand, may be attracted to fundamentalist discourses as they seek to promote and defend their situation, because they stand to lose so much in its destabilization.

Fundamentalism has also been described as a reaction to modernism (or modernization as the core project of development) or westernization (Barber 1995). Modernism may bring with it secularism, totalizing universalism or the social breakdown that often accompanies the pervasive generalization of market values. Fundamentalism may be about a reassertion of meaning or spiritual values, a reclaiming of local culture or a reaction to the loss of community or social order. As such, it is as much a part of modernity as is the proliferation of "instrumental rationality," means–ends calculations based on self-interest. Economic growth and marketization have remade the world, leaving whole regions behind and widening inequality in its wake.

U.S. Civil Religion and its Relation to Fundamentalism

In the case of the United States, the central fundamentalist identity today revolves around the tightly woven together religions of right-wing Protestantism and the patriotic American civil religion. The U.S. identity has long been recognized to have religious overtones (Fitzgerald 1987; Wilson 1971). Many immigrants came to the United States seeking to establish "the new Jerusalem." For centuries, U.S. citizens sought to establish "cities on the hill"[6]—pure, new communities, reflecting both a prophetic impulse and the desire to shake off any vestiges of the old. Such patriotism came to function as a civil religion, with the founding fathers representing the secular pantheon. Elements of Protestantism, frontierism and radical individualism, along with iconic ideas such as voluntary association and self-reliance, came to be incorporated into this religio-cultural system. Archetypes such as the cowboy, family farmer and rags-to-riches entrepreneur captured the public's imagination and remain central mythic figures in this civil religion.

According to Robert Bellah (1967:1), the U.S. civil religion contains:

> Certain common elements of religious orientation that the great majority of Americans share.... This public religious dimension is espoused in a set of beliefs, symbols, and rituals that I am calling the American civil religion.... The basic belief was that the United States of America had been chosen by God to be a model to the world of economic and political liberty and equal justice for all. Its destiny was one of defending these ideals and extending them where possible to other nations.

This discourse of "American exceptionalism" is a central feature of U.S. culture and politics and provides the fabric from which foreign relations are cut. U.S. citizens have a messianic image of themselves and their country, truly believing that the United States is special, that they are morally superior.[7] In the words of President Woodrow Wilson, the U.S. is the best country in the world, a "redeemer nation" that has "the infinite privilege of fulfilling her destiny and saving the world."[8] George W. Bush said, "My administration has a job to do and we're going to do it. We will rid the world of evil-doers." According to the doctrine of American exceptionalism, the U.S. is not subject to the same limitations or laws of history as other nations. The United States can use means of statecraft that, if done by other nations, would lead to their condemnation. It can build nuclear arsenals, experiment with biological and chemical weapons, and intervene in the affairs of other states—but the discourse of American exceptionalism connotes that these are carried out using a higher morality.

American exceptionalism allows the U.S. to view itself as special, but with a universally valid way of life. In the late twentieth–early twenty-first century, this exceptionalism includes the notion that capitalist democracy is historically determined, the highest point of the evolutionary order—indeed, the end of history.

American exceptionalism serves as a bridge across disparate identities, history and cultures to constitute a new identity that is distinctly Protestant in cultural framework and that provides a narrative and set of values to orient the nation. Conversely, however, it has also been used to distinguish "real Americans" from "foreigners"—the exceptionalist current becomes particularly strong in times of heightened immigration.

The discourse of American exceptionalism implies that the U.S. nation is a chosen people, whose destiny is to remake the world in its image. That they are the new Hebrews, with a new covenant and unique historical mission, is a deep and abiding theme in U.S. culture and politics. The Virginia minister Alexander Whitaker preached in 1613, "God hath opened this passage unto us and led us by the hand to do this work" (Cherry 1971: 33). The settlers in Virginia were, leading colonist John Rolf said, "a peculiar people, marked and chosen by the finger of God" (Cherry 1971: 26). The Biblical theme of chosen-ness has repeated itself in a series of distinctively U.S. exodus stories. This includes the origin myth, the story of the Mayflower, in which the Puritans fled religious persecution in Europe. It is also echoed in the story of the difficult Mormon trek westward to escape persecution and find a new land.

The mythology of the chosen people was used to justify the elimination of the pre-existing peoples of the Americas. Just as the Israelites had conquered Canaan, so were European colonizers warranted in taking the land of the indigenous peoples. Similarly, the discourse known as Manifest Destiny regarded the entire region between the Atlantic and the Pacific oceans as the God-given land of the United States and justified violence, war and annexation of foreign territories to achieve it.

The symbols, rituals, hymns and ceremonies of the civil religion are a constant presence in U.S. life. The national motto, "In God We Trust," is written on each bill of currency. The U.S. flag is displayed widely; its presence is ubiquitous in public places such as schools, churches and auditoriums as well as private sites such as cars, houses and coat collars. The Pledge of Allegiance (including the words "one nation under God"[9]) is recited every morning in most schools across the nation. A wide spectrum of events from scout meetings to business seminars now begin with the singing of patriotic music that blends national themes with the worship of God—for example, "The Battle Hymn of the Republic" and "God Bless America."[10] Many public holidays, such as the Fourth of July (Independence Day), Memorial Day and Thanksgiving, combine God and the United States. Politicians increasingly use religious language deriving from a Christian evangelical perspective to talk about state policy and the mission of the United States: Ronald Reagan spoke about the Soviet Union as "the Evil Empire"; George W. Bush promised to deliver God's infinite justice and destroy the evil-doers.

Civil religion uses the religious imagination and its doctrinal, dogmatic application to legitimate politics. It is used by both conservatives and liberals to create a popular hegemonic discourse in support of the government. Criticism of the state is regarded as heresy/anti-patriotism by the socially conservative right. Although democracy is a treasured icon, criticism of anti-democratic practice is a violation of the accepted terms of patriotic discourse. Liberals and the libertarian right cite the signs of the republic and their desecration in their defence of the sacred treasures of the United States. They usually do not call upon the same rhetorical elements, however. Liberals name the Bill of Rights of the constitution—particularly the first amendment, the right to free speech and assembly—as the central representation of the republic. The libertarian right holds sacred those elements which signify liberty and property in U.S. iconography: the second amendment to the Bill of Rights (the right to bear arms), the American revolution of 1776 and the Declaration of Independence.

The U.S. civil religion imagines a past that justifies the present, that is, it captures an image of itself in the present and imposes itself upon the past, writing a past that is in service to the present.[11] This is the reason, for example, why most people in the United States think that the first Americans were Pilgrims. Abraham Lincoln established the national holiday of Thanksgiving in 1863 (during the Civil War) to encourage national unity, morality and a sense of godliness (Lincoln 1863), and the story of the Pilgrims was grafted onto it during the 1890s (Shenkman 1991). This was a period of intense non-Anglo immigration that inspired an upsurge in the civil religion, including a passionate preoccupation with the flag.

The civil religion rewrites the past in other ways as well. Slavery, the internment of citizens of Japanese descent, the conquest or colonization of Northern Mexico, Cuba, Puerto Rico, the Philippines, Guam and Hawaii among other places, and the overthrow or destabilization of elected governments in Chile, the Dominican Republic, Guatemala and Zaire are just some of the events minimized, reinterpreted or forgotten in the mythological history of the United States. Today, George W. Bush repeatedly citing Saddam Hussein's gassing of the Kurds in 1988 as a reason to go to war in 2003—in spite of the fact that his father when president "signed a top-secret National Security Decision directive ordering closer ties with Baghdad and opening the way for $1 billion in new aid in 1989" (Frantz and Waas 1992)—is evidence that this process continues. President Reagan also vetoed a bill to stop supplying Saddam Hussein with chemical weapons. U.S. civil religion does not acknowledge the wrongdoing of its practitioners, because part of its purpose is to allow those in power to do whatever they see fit.

One of the central tenets of the U.S. civil religion is that there are no social classes and, therefore, no class conflict. In an unintended sense Weber may have been right in his *Protestant Ethic and the Spirit of Capitalism* in claiming that Calvinism was key to the development of capitalism. Weber claimed that the Calvinist emphasis on a predetermined, but unidentifiable, elect led many individuals to live as though they were one of the chosen. Calvinism thus created a population of people who worked hard and behaved frugally, while delaying gratification and accumulating and reinvesting capital in their enterprises, all the while believing their efforts would signify that they were among those rewarded by God. One might posit that it was less the behavioural changes wrought by Protestantism than the legitimacy conveyed that was most important. Whereas previously, conspicuous accumulation was suspect in an economy in which one person's gain meant someone else's loss, with Calvinism, those who accumulated the most appeared to be the most worthy; they appeared to be the elect. This feature of Calvinist culture continues today as a central cultural theme of the United States.[12] It has in fact been strengthened by twenty years of neoliberal discourse that promotes ideas such as that greed is good and that those who are wealthy are more deserving of wealth and more virtuous. George W. Bush was able to label Al Gore as unpatriotic by accusing him of engaging in "class warfare" when, in the campaign for the 2000 U.S. presidential election, Gore pointed out the growing inequality and inequity of the United States economy.

Developments in patriotic discourse that have reinforced the familial aspects of nationhood allow U.S. elites to deny the existence of class and class conflict. The neoliberal discourse on "family values" is largely an attack on working women and racialized minorities. As this discourse has become increasingly fundamentalist in character, it has made views on abortion and welfare reform (with, not incidentally, favouring a strong military, being tough on crime, the death penalty and tax cuts for the wealthy) litmus tests for political office. These issues are seen as those which, via their supposed contribution to family breakdown, have led to social breakdown in the U.S. According to this discourse, social decay is largely seen as stemming from sexual promiscuity; mothers who are absent because they work (speaking of the white, middle class); and female-headed households in which the mothers are home, but welfare dependent (speaking of the working, lower class and of people of colour).

The discourse of family values has through an interesting inversion turned into rhetoric on the United States as family. Presidential debates about family values, for example, have become contests in which the candidate shows how he might rule the nation as a father rules over his family. This metaphor of the family is replete with the subtext of "natural hierarchies." It has not only supplanted the idea of antagonistic unions or oppositional political parties, but has even gone some distance in displacing the previous questionable—but more egalitarian—metaphor of community.

This idea of the nation as imagined family is promoted heavily by the military. Indeed, the motto of one branch of service is: "The Air Force. One Team, One Force, One Family." The nation/military as family was displayed most prominently during the recent Gulf War. One good example was the rescue of Private First Class Jessica Lynch, a U.S. prisoner of war held in an Iraqi hospital. U.S. news outlets portrayed the rescue with such fanfare and celebration as if the military were retrieving one of the family. The message was that the United States is all one family and there would be "no one left behind." Similarly, the loss of seven astronauts in each of the Challenger (1986) and Columbia (2003) space shuttle disasters on take-off and re-entry, respectively, was depicted as a national family tragedy in which all might mourn. The media helps in developing this mythology by personalizing some people—giving a wealth of details about their private lives that normally only family and close friends know, for example—and depersonalizing others.

The discourse of the American Dream is still key to the civil religion. This mythology of social mobility says that any individual can succeed and is responsible for her own success. It allows politicians and others "to fall prey to the convenient amnesia that permits so much self-righteous posturing about how the 'dependent poor' ought to have the self-reliance and independence that the 'rest of us' have shown" (Coontz 1992: 69). Blaming those individuals who have failed to make it on their own allows society to escape responsibility for racist and sexist social practices and attitudes. Social and political issues are thus individualized and made into private troubles. Today, this individualization can be seen clearly in the passion for psychological explanation, as well its obsession with celebrity (combined in successful magazines like *People*). Moving towards sainthood in the hierarchy of the civil religion—or at least becoming a new archetype—are the heroes battling terminal diseases like cancer.

This is not to deny the apparently growing importance of soldiers as heroes. The affirmation that one "supports the troops" has functioned as a catechistic exercise within public speech. As the United States has become increasingly explicit about Empire, about maintaining its dominance through military power, one sees the increasing centrality of militarism in the United States.[13] Unlike earlier presidents, such as Eisenhower and Kennedy, who were genuine war heroes, George W. Bush is photographed in military uniform with little public comment. This would have been politically untenable in years past, because the U.S. constitution makes the president commander-in-chief precisely so there will be civilian control of the military. That this is no longer deemed important is worrisome.

U.S. Civil Religion and Militarism

Militarism strengthens earlier tendencies in the U.S. civil religion to develop patriotism most thoroughly through conflict with an enemy. During the Cold War, the enemy was the Soviet Union and godless communism. Today, the clash is with the terrorist. Since September 11, 2001, the United States has been able to deepen this us/them patriotism with adoption of the victim pose of noble, blameless suffering. This victim position has given the United States further fuel. Thus, George W. Bush can say, "You are either with us or against us," and this Manichean logic is accepted as the rightful condition demanded by absolute innocence.

When civil religion is combined with absolute power, that very power appears to be evidence of divine blessing. The chosen-people mythology leads the nation to believe that it has a mission, in fact that it is particularly qualified to redeem humanity. Its divine mission turns to danger for others when the salvationist urge is tied to national power. That very power seems to indicate that God is on the U.S. side, which then justifies its use (Parenti 1993). It may not be going too far to say that under these conditions, war becomes a religious rite and a religious duty. If the United States is able to redeem the world, perhaps it has an obligation to do so, even if the only means possible is by force.

U.S. Civil Religion and Evangelical Christianity

Today, the United States president and his most influential advisors, Richard Chaney, Donald Rumsfeld and Condoleezza Rice among others, have fused the civil religion and doctrine with premillenial fundamentalist Christianity. Premillenial Christians believe that the second coming will follow a violent global cataclysm, after which Christ will rule the earth for a thousand years. This will be followed by the final judgment and the punishment of the wicked. Since the Reagan presidency, the Republican Party has become the home from which right-wing evangelical Christianity fights its culture wars. This concentration of power parallels the population and political shift to the southern United States (as what is conceptualized as the heartland has also shifted from the Midwest to the mid-Southwest). This Christianity has a conservative perspective on women, sexuality, culture and multiculturalism. "Women should be submissive to their husbands, Disney World should be boycotted because of its tacit support of homosexuality, and multiculturalism is the death knell for the American way of life, these culture warriors aver" (Hankins 2003: 41). It marries this view with an apocalyptic outlook on world history and the United States's role in it.

Evangelical Christianity has long been an important feature of the United States cultural landscape. In the early to mid-nineteenth century, evangelical Protestants were among the foremost abolitionists, temperance crusaders and women's rights advocates.

> After the [Civil] War, the changes in American society wrought by such powerful forces as urbanization and industrialization, along with new intellectual and theological developments began to diminish the power of evangelicalism within American culture. Likewise, this evangelical superiority was diminished in pure numeric terms with the influx of millions of non-Protestant immigrants in the latter nineteenth and early twentieth centuries. Nonetheless, evangelical Protestantism remained a powerful presence within American culture.... Going into the twentieth-

> century evangelicalism still held the status of an American "folk religion" in many sectors of the United States—particularly the South. (Institute for the Study of American Evangelicals 2003)

Not all evangelical Christianity was, or is, premillenial. During most of the nineteenth century, almost all U.S. evangelicals were optimistic gradualists or postmillenialists. They believed that the kingdom of God would come as Christians preached the Gospel and gradually redeemed the world in the context of a United States republican government, economic expansion and the unfolding of progress brought by the reform movements. Towards the end of the nineteenth century, many evangelicals began to doubt this path, however, in the presence of persistent problems brought by urbanization and industrialization such as economic and social dislocations, environmental pollution and rising rates of diseases of poverty and crowding, the failure of reconstruction after the Civil War, and the immigration of millions of non-Protestant immigrants (Institute for the Study of American Evangelicals 2003).

Many evangelicals were attracted by a new doctrine known as dispensational premillenialism. In contrast to the hopeful postmillenialism, dispensationalism has a darker view of the world. It sees a world in chaos and decline, with moral decay and secular culture both a renunciation of God's order and a fulfillment of the biblical prophesies related to Christ's return. Their view is that we are living in the end times, when all Jews will return to Zion, the anti-christ will come (who, according to Jerry Falwell, will be a Jew), the final battle—Armageddon—will be fought, Christians will be raptured into heaven, the left-behind will fight the final battles and the heathen will burn for all eternity. (Note that this scenario sees all Jews either converting to Christianity or going to hell.) Dispensationalists support the State of Israel, not out of any love for Jews, but because they see the ingathering of Jews to Israel and their subsequent destruction as necessary to fulfill Christian prophesy. It is almost commonplace in left-wing Jewish circles to trace the increasingly rightward drift of the U.S. Jewish establishment as it has made common cause with the dispensationalists. This branch of right-wing Christianity is the source of much of the power of the incorrectly named Jewish lobby (Plitnick 2003).

Interest in dispensationalism has waxed and waned but has become increasingly important with the founding of the State of Israel and the capture of Jerusalem in the Six Days War in June 1967. These events seemed to portend the immediate fulfillment of endtimes prophecy. As well, many of the most prominent and visible evangelicals, such as Billy Graham, Jerry Fallwell and Pat Robertson, are dispensationalists. Hal Lindsay's best-selling book of the 1970s, *The Late, Great Planet Earth,* and Tim LeHaye's and Jerry Jenkins' popular *Left Behind* series of endtime novels of the 1990s and 2000s show that interest in the apocalypse is a highly important aspect of the evangelical subculture.

This combination of a fundamentalist civil religion with the fundamentalist dispensationalism of the powerful may very well present the danger of fascism under current world historical conditions.[14] Indeed, many of the essential elements of fascism appear to be present in twenty-first-century United States. Certainly, widespread feelings of great vulnerability—the feeling of being "beset"—reinforced by constant terrorists warnings, combined with an invincible war machine, create a context in which fascism might take root. According to Mussolini (1932), "fascism should more appropriately be called corporatism because it is a merger of state and corporate power." Trotsky (1969) made a prescient statement in 1930 about the certainty that fascism was on the horizon in Germany, saying that fascism happens when capitalists are willing to exploit the condition that the middle class have given up on the possibility of democracy. Fascism also appears to require a romantic, sentimentalized ideology of the nation. It glorifies the state or collective at the expense of the individual (Griffin 1991). It does away with the power of checks and balances and reduces the influence of alternative institutions to the corporatized state. It is militaristic, expansionist and willing to use violence (Laqueur 1996). It is against liberal social philosophy and tends to be monolithic and hierarchical in its perspective on politics and culture. Although it is clear that the next time around fascism will not look like Nazism, it is far from certain that fascism with a U.S. face has not already arrived, wearing a mask of hyperpatriotism.

Conclusions

As we loosen fundamentalism from its moorings as a description of a particular brand of religious philosophy, we can begin to see its usefulness as a social analytic construct used to examine particular strategies of discourse and rhetoric. In this sense, fundamentalist practices can be seen as ways of exercising and realigning relations of power. Fundamentalism can advantage individuals and groups by remaking the "official story" and by redefining relations amongst people, both within and without the fundamentalist circle. Fundamentalist strategies appear to flourish during periods of social change that are destabilizing of relative privilege or status.

U.S. hyperpatriotism can be viewed as a fundamentalist discourse that derives its identities and meanings from the already interwoven religions of right-wing Protestantism and the civil religion. The symbols, rituals, hymns and ceremonies of the civil religion are a constant presence in U.S. life. The civil religion provides a vocabulary and story with which to legitimate politics. With its religious overtones, it provides a powerful and popular hegemonic discourse that supports the capitalist state. The discourse of U.S. exceptionalism, which has long maintained that the

United States has a special mission ordained by God, plays a central role in the formation of foreign relations. It promotes a messianic image of the United States and of its role in the world. Today in the U.S. we see a particularly potent mix of civil religion and right-wing Protestantism with the rise and domination of economically powerful endtimes Christians in the state.

Notes

1. The official date for the start of Operation Iraqi Freedom is March 19, 2003. Although the end of the military campaign was declared twenty-eight days later and the end of the mopping up campaign was announced twelve days after that, the situation is not stable.
2. Operation Enduring Freedom is the propagandistic name given to the military campaign to drive Al Qu'eda out of Afghanistan and to wrest control of the Afghani government from the Islamic fundamentalist Taliban.
3. This does not include the 2.8 million active and reserve forces in the United States military (United States Department of Defense 2003) and the over 2 million adults in United States prisons (United States Department of Justice 2002).
4. I am using discourse here to mean a set of open narratives and narrative positions that help to create or maintain social locations, positions of power, and relational identities. Discourse, thus, helps to create a terrain of power or struggle, and is also implicated in strategies that people and institutions employ to obtain advantages over others. I am also exploring the discourses of American patriotism within the context of "culture as framework," in which culture frameworks are able to structure interactions through a combination of scripts and improvisations/strategies.
5. It is possible to see similar processes as being part of the dynamic of domination through racialization.
6. This phrase derives from John Winthrop's admonition to the Pilgrim community that founded the Massachusetts Bay Colony, "We must consider that we shall be A City Upon a Hill, the eyes of all people upon us."
7. One can hear echoes of the French "mission civilatrice."
8. According to Arthur Schlesinger Jr., "(In the seventeenth century) the Calvinist mind pronounced America the redeemer nation; in the eighteenth century it was Jonathan Edward's theology of Providence; in the nineteenth century it was Josiah Strong's theology of expansion (Manifest Destiny); in the twentieth century it was Woodrow Wilson's gospel of world order and John Foster Dulles' summons to a holy war against godless communism."
9. The phrase "under God" was included in the Pledge of Allegiance during the Korean War at the behest of Senator Homer Ferguson (R-MI). His rationale was "We know that America cannot be defended by guns and ships alone. Appropriations and expenditures for defense will be of value only if the God under whom we live believes we are in the right. We now live in a world divided by two ideologies, one of which affirms its belief in God while the other does not."
10. Note that this is in addition to the national anthem, "The Star-spangled Banner," which is commonly sung at the start of sporting and other events.

11. As a relevant ruling-party slogan from George Orwell's *1984* put it, "Who controls the past controls the future. Who controls the present controls the past."
12. One important change has been the necessary loosening of Calvinist frugality in order to provide the required consumption for a dynamic capitalist market.
13. After the Vietnam War, the United States government ended the politically unpopular draft, and thus has negated a significant source of anti-war sentiment in the United States. At the same time, the military has increasingly become the only means of social mobility for poor and racialized minorities.
14. One must note here two important documents that are serving as blueprints for foreign policy in the early twenty-first century, Zbigniew Brzezinski's *The Grand Chessboard: American Primacy and Its Geostrategic Imperatives*, Basic Books, 1997 and Paul Wolfowitz's *Project for a New American Century*, 1992.

References

Barber, Benjamin R. 1995. *Jihad Vs. McWorld: How Globalism and Tribalism are Reshaping the World*. New York: Ballantine Books.

Bellah, Robert. 1967. "Civil Religion in America." *Daedalus* 96.

Cherry, Conrad, ed. 1971. *God's New Israel: Religious Interpretations of American Destiny*. Englewood Cliffs, NJ: Prentice Hall.

Cohen, Norman J., ed. 1990. *The Fundamentalist Phenomenon: A View from Within, A Response from Without*. Grand Rapids, MI: Wm. B. Erdmans Publishing.

Coontz, Stephanie. 1992. *The Way We Never Were: American Families and the Nostalgia Trap*. New York: Basic Books.

Fitzgerald, Frances. 1987. *Cities on a Hill*. New York: Simon and Shuster.

Frantz, Douglas, and Murray Waas. 1992. "Bush secret effort helped Iraq build its war machine." *Los Angeles Times*. February 23.

Griffin, Roger. 1991. *The Nature of Fascism*. New York: St. Martin's Press.

Hankins, Barry. 2003. *Uneasy in Babylon: Southern Baptist Conservatives and American Culture*. Tuscaloosa, AL: University of Alabama Press.

Institute for the Study of American Evangelicals. 2003. *Defining Evangelicalism*. Wheaton, IL: Wheaton College. Available at www.wheaton.edu/isae/defining_evangelicalism.html [accessed June 25, 2003].

Jameson, Frederic. 1992. *Postmodernism, Or, the Cultural Logic of Late Capitalism*. Durham, NC: Duke University Press.

Lapham, Lewis. 2003. "Light in the Window." *Harper's Magazine*. March.

Laqueur, Walter. 1996. *Fascism: Past, Present, Future*. New York, Oxford: Oxford University Press.

Lincoln, Abraham. 1863. *Thanksgiving Proclamation*. Lincoln's papers in the Library of America series, Vol. II: 520–21.

Marsden, George. 1990. "Defining American Fundamentalism." In Cohen.

Melman, Seymour. 2003. "In the Grip of a Permanent War Economy." *Counterpunch*. March 15.

Mussolini, Benito. 1932. "What is Fascism?" In Paul Halsall (ed.), *Modern History SourceBook*. New York: Fordham University. Available at www.fordham.edu/halsall/mod/mussolini-fascism.html [accessed June 24, 2003].

Parenti, Michael. 1993. *Land of Idols: Political Mythology in America*. New York: St. Martin's Press.

Pelikan, Jaroslav. 1990. "Fundamentalism and/or Orthodoxy? Toward an Understanding of the Fundamentalist Phenomenon." In Cohen.

Plitnick, Mitchell. 2003. "Reclaiming Anti-Semitism." Jewish Voice for Peace. Available at www.zmag.org/ZNET.htm [accessed February 22, 2003].

Shenkman, Richard. 1991. *Legends, Lies and Cherished Myths of American History*. New York: Perennial.

Trotsky, Leon. 1969 (1944). *Fascism: What It Is and How to Fight It*. Marx-Engels Internet Archive. Available at www.marxists.org/archive/trotsky/works/1944/1944-fas.htm [accessed June 24, 2003].

Tuveson, Ernest Lee. 1980. *Redeemer Nation*. Chicago: University of Chicago Press.

United States Department of Defense. 2003. *Defense Almanac*. Washington, DC: American Forces Information Service. Available at www.defenselink.mil/pubs/almanac/ [accessed May 5, 2003].

United States Department of Justice. 2002. *Bureau of Justice Statistics: At a Glance*. Washington, DC: Bureau of Justice Statistics. Available at www.ojp.usdoj.gov/bjs/pub/pdf/bjsg02.pdf [accessed May 5, 2003].

United States Department of Labor. 2003. *Employment Situation Summary*. Washington, DC: Bureau of Labor Statistics. Available at www.bls.gov/news.release/empsit.nr0.htm [accessed May 5, 2003].

Wallerstein, Immanuel. 2002. "The Eagle Has Crash Landed." *Foreign Policy* July/August.

Wilson, Edmund. 1971. *Upstate: Records and Recollections of Northern New York*. New York: Farrar, Straus, and Giroux.

Chapter Nine

The Market Will Make it Right

Neoliberalism as Market Fundamentalism

Don Mitchell

Fundamentalism is, by one definition, a simple belief system based on the strict and literal interpretation of traditional religious teachings such as the Bible. For believers, the teachings are infallible, above question and are interpreted and applied without compromise to any given social context. The teachings impose discipline and control on the faithful followers. Christian, Jewish and Islamic fundamentalisms are the best known examples. This same literal, self-righteous use of doctrine is characteristic of the disciples of modern capitalism as they have captured and dominated the global political agenda over the past thirty years.

Market fundamentalism is an apt term for the righteous blend of religious orthodoxy and *laissez-faire* free-market ideology preached and practised by its advocates, who are deeply embedded in all our major social institutions but most notably within government, universities, business schools and research institutes. They include teaching and practising neoliberal economists and business, political and religious leaders. Their deep belief in the sanctity of the so-called free market insulates them and their followers from challenge or debate. Facts that set out negative social realities regarding poverty and inequality are dismissed as distortions of society caused by interference with the market. There are always distortions because there is no example in the history of capitalism of a pure, unregulated market at work. The purely competitive free market within human society is, after all, a myth; a utopian dream of the business class.

The owners of corporate business and their political associates usually present themselves as struggling to fulfill the potential of the market for the benefit of the whole society. Yet. as part of that struggle, like some giant societal flesh-eating disease, they deny and destroy the community fabric in which the market is embedded. This is a central contradiction of the teachings.

The doctrine of market fundamentalism is embraced by the business class globally and applied by neoliberal political administrations at every level. It has been their weapon of persuasion, inviting ordinary people to suspend their critical judgment, accept a conversion and become cheerleaders for the profit system. This political-religious culture has in its most recent years of dominance reversed a half-century of social progress and inflicted immense damage on the planet and its people. Privatization, deregulation and the worldwide pattern of dismantling community services and public enterprise all flow logically and deliberately from the teachings of the market fundamentalists.

> It is the most vicious fundamentalism of our times because it cuts across all religions, cultures and geographical barriers ... it has its temples and churches ... its conflicting denominations in IMF [International Monetary Fund] and the World Bank. It even has its televangelists ... turn on any channel to hear them preach their gospel of growth and greed. It is fundamentalism of the most devastating kind and it has done more damage to human life than any other fundamentalism.... (Sainath 2001)

Non-believers (nationwide and globally) are deeply affected in their personal and political lives by this powerful religious-like movement, just as non-believers are affected when they are surrounded by a fundamentalist religious community. Those whose memory extends to political life and choices that existed before 1980 have a growing sense of loss over their current choices. They feel a loss of community and exhaustion after years of defensive struggles over basics such as community health and education or the right to remain part of a union. Citizens younger than forty have been increasingly alienated by a political process that has never really worked for or with them. As a generation, notwithstanding the recent anti-globalization movement, they have become increasingly more cynical and disengaged. Clinical depression is at epidemic levels among youth.

The proven danger of market fundamentalism is its proximity to real power—political, economic and military, especially in the United States. It can propel zealots into office as governors, senators or even presidents. It is an overriding theme in the politics of the most powerful militarized state in all of human history. U.S. political leaders reduce the complexities of world geopolitics to simple slogans about good versus evil and extol the benevolence of free-market capitalism for all humankind. They enforce it as a model for underdeveloped countries to a degree it has never been applied at home. U.S. political leaders have made it clear they will repeatedly engage in war as necessary to establish and maintain their dominance and control in all world regions.

What makes this ideology attractive to those beyond the self-interested business classes of industrial nations? The teachings of classical liberalism are attractive to Christian, conservative fundamentalists because they reaffirm private property rights and the model of the patriarchal family as the basis for security and welfare.[1] The promotion of "family values" and Christian charities are a huge part of the conservative appeal. Leaders such as George W. Bush present themselves as father figures to the nation in times of personal insecurity. This Christian paternal ideology has been integrated into current conservative political movements such as the U.S. Christian coalition in the Republican Party and the Christian Right in the Canadian Alliance Party. Private wealth accumulation through property and trade is a largely male domain and reinforces the patriarchal family model (notwithstanding the gender exception of Britain's former prime minister, Margaret Thatcher).

The belief system that has driven the neoliberal "common sense" revolution is quite simple. Two sets of core values are linked: conservative religious fundamentalism and classical liberal free-market ideology are married within a single social and political network. They identify and target common political enemies such as collectivism, big government, unions and the welfare state. They also share an evangelical sense of self-righteousness and moral high ground based on survival-of-the-fittest values such as rugged individualism and competitive markets. Although still distinct phenomena, each with its own text, Christian fundamentalism and classical liberalism have been blended by the right into a broad political strategy in the U.S., Britain and parts of western Europe. They embody a born-again political culture restored to the good old days of *laissez-faire,* as supposedly existed sometime before 1930. The attraction and dominance of this political culture over the past three decades is undeniable. In a world presented as "choked" by inflation, debts, deficits and the growth and complexity of government in the 1970s and 1980s, this ideology has offered simple choices. Margaret Thatcher and Ronald Reagan re-popularized an old belief system that Tony Blair and George W. Bush continue to cling to.

Market fundamentalism, then, is a religious-like phenomenon, applying classical liberal doctrine as a forced fit for every social and economic circumstance. It is also for many a religious-linked phenomenon, sourcing the Bible (the word of God) as the true origin of free-market doctrine. For believers within Christian or Jewish communities, this link adds to the infallibility of liberal market theory. It is the justifying religious ideology behind the political forces of neoliberal change. While the global influence of market fundamentalism may have peaked within its current cycle, its beliefs and assumptions remain a major component of liberal capitalism as espoused by the current president of the United States and many other political leaders.

It is shocking to think that advanced industrial societies have allowed the unleashed and unaccountable power of a so-called free market to increasingly determine the conditions of their lives and communities. From airline safety, to air and water quality, to public health care, if it doesn't register as profitable on the market, it slides as a priority. At the same time, the total discrediting of the limited democratic power and accountability of governments by governments is an even more staggering feature of modern politics.

The changes that have transpired since 1980 are bewildering for the average citizen who was part of the political culture that existed pre-1980. Entrenched values and traditions of responsive and democratic governments that shaped the politics of the 1950s, '60s and '70s have been cast aside. Political leaders and parties still appeal (at election time) to certain values, for example, improved public health care, but deliver the opposite as market and corporate priorities assert themselves. In clear recognition of the loss of democratic power and choice, citizen participation in the electoral system has declined sharply in North America. Fewer than 50 percent of U.S. citizens have voted in recent national elections. Yet the illusions of freedom and democracy are still promoted as ideals within the dominant ideology we are terming market fundamentalism. Those who have money, "vote" with it. They generate ever higher rates of consumption through their investments and consumption patterns. The system of corporate capitalism continues to grow and dominate all aspects of global society. The market is all powerful.

The Myth of the Market

"Market fundamentalism" is the belief in the supremacy and infallible wisdom of the unregulated market to determine the correct patterns of human production and distribution. The market will determine levels of wealth and poverty within capitalist societies and across the global population. Growing inequality, widespread poverty and starvation are generally ignored and rationalized as short-term consequences of distorting market activity that will correct itself over time. (For example, in the absence of government interference, the poor will be motivated to work harder.)

This doctrine assumes that a competitive marketplace actually exists within modern capitalism. The belief persists that the "invisible hand of the market," as first imagined by Adam Smith, will create maximum efficiency, establish fair prices and wages, and adjust currency values and conditions of trade that will benefit everyone. These utopian conditions within the capitalist marketplace probably never existed. They certainly don't exist today in the era of massive grain subsidies and import tariffs on steel, autos, lumber and a host of other products. But the myth persists as infallible truth through the teachings of the media, corporate think-tanks, business economists and neoliberal politicians. This doctrine teaches that greed and self-interest are good, and that the common interest will be best served if everybody follows their own self-interest. In this view, society does not exist. As British Prime Minister Margaret Thatcher once declared, "There's no such thing as society. There are individual men and women and there are families" (Thatcher 1987). According to market fundamentalism, nearly all social activities are the outcome of personal, rational choices. Accordingly, practically every human interaction can be seen as contract-based and valued in terms of money.

A major and damaging consequence of the doctrine of market fundamentalism is that all public service, or "government" (any and all collective expressions of democracy which relate to the economic sphere), is deemed inefficient and hostile to the pure competition of the marketplace. Community venture or public service activity must be avoided or quickly replaced by profitable enterprise, or it will cause the dominant corporate system of a given region or country to be uncompetitive in the era of globalization. Driven by that logic, public services have been under assault throughout the world. Privatization is funded and/or promoted by the holy trinity of the World Bank, the International Monetary Fund (IMF) and the World Trade Organization (WTO).

The invisible hand of the market is, in reality, the carefully guided hand of massive international corporations (Dobbin 1998). The lead players in every major sector in the market are now larger than most countries. Under current rules of free trade or investors' rights, corporations are accountable to no one except (in theory at least) their shareholders. Industry itself places massive restrictions on any notion of free trade through vertical integration and industry-wide corporate associations that promote self-regulation and control over particular markets. "All of these restrictions suggest that the last thing that capital wants for itself is competition or the 'free' market, except perhaps as a means of gaining access to the state sector or 'closed markets' or non-market economies" (Teeple 1995: 80).

Historically, we have seen how unregulated or under-regulated markets have failed, from the Great Depression of the 1930s, to the collapse of the Asian economies in 1997–98. More recent examples are the Enron scandal and other similar corporate frauds. After Enron's CEO promised that deregulation would save California $9 billion per year, the state's annual energy costs soared from $7 billion to $27 billion in a single year and consumer prices rose 266 percent. As a result, Enron's stock rose 40 percent in 1998, 58 percent in 1999 and 89 percent in 2000, and the CEO's stock options became a gold mine—just before the company collapsed (Kelley 2002). This example illustrates the folly of a relaxed and loosely regulated market. The breach of faith committed by Enron cost thousands of employees their jobs and millions of U.S. citizens a huge loss in their pension investment savings.

The deregulation of food, utility and transportation markets in favour of market-based systems of profits has also created major dislocations. For example, once self-reliant agricultural and food systems and sensitive natural ecosystems, such as rain forest regions and deserts, are quickly undermined by market demand among industrial consumers for timber, oil and agricultural exports. Transportation services for remote populations are abandoned or priced beyond the means of the people. Investments for market profit and structural adjustment loans from the International Monetary Fund and the World Bank force privatization and the increasing withdrawal of government control over the critical areas of public health and public education.

How Market Fundamentalism Was Reborn

From the 1880s to 1930, Market fundamentalism, or *laissez-faire*, was the dominant approach to governance in the industrial societies of Europe and North America. The experience of the Great Depression shook the confidence of business and governments and the general public in the reliability of the markets. The experience of Roosevelt's New Deal in the U.S., World War II, the influence of the British economist John Maynard Keynes and the Bretton Woods institutions of the World Bank and IMF all contributed to a mixed economy and "welfare state" model of government. This model extended for the period roughly from 1945 to 1975. It did not develop quickly or easily, and it existed only because there was a consensus among all power brokers at the time that unregulated capitalism could not work as it resulted in corporate dislocation and unacceptable levels of human suffering. Even the editors of *Fortune* magazine acknowledged, in a June 1938 editorial, that what failed in the Depression "was the doctrine of laissez-faire." They wrote, in language that would get a business editor fired today: "every businessman who is not kidding himself knows that, if left to its own devices, business would sooner or later run headlong into another 1930" (cited in Kelly 2002: 2).

Keynes's logic, which said that governments were necessary to correct the naturally occurring crises and failures of capitalism, was embraced by business, government and a broadly established movement of organized labour. Keynesianism, as it is now termed, was endorsed and accepted in all western democracies. Keynes's objectives were, after all, not to undermine or end capitalism, but to preserve it and to protect it from its own excesses, as illustrated by the Great Depression.

Whether intended or not, Keynesian economic reforms created openings for liberal and social democratic governments to expand the role of government. State-supported pension plans, unemployment insurance, social housing and public health care became features of all industrial societies. The Keynesian logic of government leadership and stimulation of the economy provided the legitimacy needed for such social democratic experiments. It fully rejected the classical liberal doctrine that had argued that free markets alone should shape society. Conservative orthodox economists were in full retreat. In 1944, economist Karl Polanyi held that, "To allow the market mechanism to be sole director of the fate of human beings and their natural environment ...

would result in the demolition of society" (Polanyi 1944: 73).

In this Keynesian Golden Age from 1945 to 1975, economic growth was steady and incomes and living conditions improved in all advanced industrial societies. Third World colonized regions struggled for and gained some nominal independence as fledgling states. Then a pattern of recession and inflation set in. High energy prices, stagnant economic growth and high inflation caused profits to fall and unemployment to rise. Government debts and deficits spiked as interest rates were allowed to float to double digits. Corporate leaders began to have doubts about the viability of the system and looked for scapegoats. The business lobbyists lined up for tax cuts, trade liberalization, deregulation and privatization. Conditions were ripe for discontent and right-wing ideologues moved in. They used the media and political party debates to capture popular support, most especially in Britain and North America.

What emerged was the return of an old belief—dominant in the period from the 1870s to the 1920—that an unregulated free market could more efficiently determine all the needs and wants of society. The environment, the decline of rural Canada, labour standards and poverty again became marginalized concerns beyond the reach or mandate of the primary economic model of consumer goods production for the free market. By the 1980s, business, think-tanks and the ascending neoliberal political leadership had again placed total faith in the market and unrestricted private ownership. The dominant political parties in Canada, the U.S. and Britain embraced free trade as the bedrock of international economic policy. Explicitly right-wing leadership came to power, adopting an agenda of dismantling the welfare state. They sold off, contracted out or deregulated the services and resources of public enterprise. In Britain, the U.S., New Zealand, Australia and Canada, governments enthusiastically adopted this neoliberal agenda. At the same time, the Soviet economic system collapsed, replaced in part by foreign investors and local mafia.

Saskatchewan, as an example, under the Conservative government led by Grant Devine, began to unravel a half-century of Keynesian public interventions. Devine, an orthodox economist, was an enthusiastic Margaret Thatcher fan when he was elected in 1982. He was further motivated after the collapse of the Soviet Union in 1989. According to Devine, "the whole world [was] opening up. If Mikhail Gorbachev was the premier of Saskatchewan, he'd be way out ahead of me" (Pitsula and Rasmussen 1991: 180).

In spite of active resistance by Saskatchewan workers and their communities, Devine sold off and contracted out major pieces of the public sector, including the Saskatchewan Potash Corporation, a major source of public revenues. As with most neoliberal governments, however, his was inconsistent. Like other right-wing politicians (Ronald

Reagan and more recently George W. Bush), Devine increased the public debt while cutting taxes and reducing the operations of government. In the U.S., Reagan's and G.W. Bush's huge military expenditures contradict any notion of an economy driven by a consumer free market. The U.S. national debt under Bush has now reached $6.8 trillion (Oct. 2003), and he recently announced the largest tax-cut in U.S. history.

In Saskatchewan, Grant Devine continued to apply spending strategies through public subsidies for large and small businesses and farmers. It was the social side of Keynesian incentives that was abandoned. Deficit spending continued and spiralled the province into huge debt.

By the late1980s, market fundamentalism had taken hold throughout Canadian politics. The Conservative government of Brian Mulroney committed Canada to the Canada–U.S. Free Trade Agreement, reversing a near one-hundred-year resistance to continental integration. Moves towards privatization by both levels of government resulted in the loss of subsidy supports to agriculture and transportation and in the reduction of public services. Canada and several Latin American trading satellites of the U.S. became target markets for U.S.-based multinational service industries. The trend of growing privatization of the Canadian public health system deepened as a "tightly bunched and tightly wound cluster of neoconservatives continue[d] to repeat the dirge-like mantra that public health care is hustling the nation into the poorhouse, that profit and efficiency are inextricably linked and that medicare somehow makes us less free" (Travers 2002: 4).

An understanding of the dramatic shift in values within a political culture is central to any analysis of market fundamentalism. Sociologist Paul Starr explains how people's loyalties and assumptions shift. He describes privatization as "a reordering of claims" (Starr 1988: 37).

> This reordering of claims ... shifts power to those who can more readily exercise power in the market. It may also shift income and wealth, depending on the specific form the privatization takes.... The same political forces that support privatization generally also support cutbacks in public spending for social welfare; the same arguments used about incentives and efficiency used in favour of privatizing public services are also cited by those who want to terminate public financing for the services altogether. (Starr 1988: 37)

As Starr states, this loss of community control and accountability is inherent in the shift from public service to private profit. Privatization, once it happens, represents a permanent shift in power and understanding. Once the "private market" is entrenched as the basis of logic for certain activities, it removes those activities from social obligations, accountability or debate. Privatization by intent and in results permanently changes political cultures.

> Privatization is not only a policy; it is also a signal about the competence and desirability of public provision. It reinforces the view that government cannot be expected to perform well.... Privatization advocates raise questions exclusively about the adequacy of the public sector; the comparable questions about the private sector do not receive the same attention.... The privatization debate puts the advocates of more generous public programs entirely on the defensive. (Starr 1988: 36)

There is no doubt that the ideology of neoliberalism in the 1980s created a lasting shift in the political culture wherever it took hold. This chilling effect on public enterprise initiatives was evident in Saskatchewan after Grant Devine, in Chile after Pinochet and in Britain after Margaret Thatcher. Roy Romanow in Saskatchewan and Tony Blair in Britain, both leading governing parties (NDP and Labour) that are ostensibly more Keynsian in their values, continued to use the language and concepts of neoliberalism to rationalize their policies and to confirm their acceptance of deregulation and privatization. With Romanow in 1991 there was no return to a Keynesian model of government. Threatened by the size of the provincial debt and under pressure from international lending agencies, the Romanow government took up the pattern of lean government, deregulation and privatization. Lost public services and enterprises, such as child dental care and the public ownership of the potash industry, were not restored. A generation of progress squandered by the neoliberals remains a painful loss to the people of Saskatchewan.

Back to the Bible

Despite failed promises of neoliberalism around the globe, its protagonists persist. Promoters of the revival of free-market doctrine range from think-tanks (e.g., the Fraser Institute in Canada, the Cato Institute in the United States and the Adam Smith Institute in Britain), classical liberal economists and religious practitioners from a variety of faiths. The last group presents a case that links religious morality with the principles of classical liberalism. A good illustration of this connection are the writings of Noah Nissani, a Jewish intellectual with a U.S. background, now teaching and writing in Israel.

An astrophysicist, Nissani follows the political philosophy of nationalist, militaristic, "revisionist Zionist" Ze'ev Jabotinsky. Nissani produced a primer on classical liberalism linking biblical and ancient Greek threads of liberalism to the liberal thinkers of the seventeenth to twentieth centuries. His efforts are significant because he is trying to establish that the laws of liberalism are universal in their application, a part of human nature, and of course sanctioned by God. Nissani views liberalism's rise to prominence as the golden age of all human history. "During the 18th and 19th centuries, a period characterized by unprecedented social change and progress, Liberalism was the prevalent ideology in Europe and America. The atmosphere of liberty and free enterprise led to rapid development of science, technology and industry" (Nissani 1996). The return of market fundamentalism in the late twentieth century rejuvenated his "born again" spirit after years of watching the waste and ruin of what he viewed as "Keynesian socialism." "Today, following the collapse of the anti-liberal ideologies that bloodied the 20th century, the world is turning its face to this old ideology, i.e., turning one century backward, in a return to a lost direction" (Nissani 1996).

The important link to the Bible and broad religious teachings is clearly established in his mind. Liberal ideology, summed up by Rousseau's slogan (liberty, equality, fraternity), also reflects the basic tenets of the Jewish-Christian-Muslim common heritage, which are constantly repeated throughout the Bible. For Nissani, a real strength of liberalism is that it totally rejects the concept of the welfare state. He sees any collective support system as totalitarian and inconsistent with biblical teachings:

> Liberal freedom entails individual responsibility for one's own welfare and for that of one's family. Totalitarians reject the liberal notion of liberty, asserting that for the poor it means the liberty to die of starvation. Real liberty, they say, is liberty from misery and need. Pretending to free them from need, they in fact transform the citizens into protected asylum-dwellers who depend on the authorities for the satisfaction of their needs. (Nissani 1996)

Nissani views the debate on society and the role of the individual versus the collective as being rooted in the Greek classics. He attributes a major role to Aristotle as a founding liberal thinker, with brilliant insights akin to those of Adam Smith:

> In his approach to the issue of common versus private ownership, Aristotle appears to be a precursor of Adam Smith. "Property should be in a certain sense common, but, as a general rule, private; for, when everyone has a distinct interest, men will not complain of one another, and they will make more progress, because every one will be attending to his own business. (Aristotle, cited in Nissani 1996)

Nissani's general effort to root free-market liberalism within biblical references has an equivalent among conservative Christians in the United States and Canada. References to biblical sources to defend patriarchy, exclusion of homosexuals from marriage or family, racial segregation and capital punishment are common wisdom for the political Right from which they never retreat.

Critics of Market Fundamentalism

In recent years, popular resistance to neoliberalism has been taken-up by youthful anti-globalization coalitions around the world. They seem to have no single ideology but promote broad common values of economic and environmental sustainability, participatory democracy and equality. They are critical of market fundamentalism, which they see as accelerating inequality, destroying eco-systems, increasing world hunger and expanding terrorism and insecurity. They are finding allies in the popular resistance movements of Third World countries, such as Argentina, Mexico, Brazil and India, victimized by neoliberal "structural adjustment" policies.

Also included among the critics of the system are those who endorse industrial market capitalism but reject the rigid orthodoxy of the market fundamentalist version. One such critic is George Soros, multi-billionaire, investment broker, philanthropist and self-styled, modern-day international Keynesian. In recent years Soros has been a credible and growing source of criticism about the failures and damage of free-market globalization. He heads an endowment fund supporting development projects for countries and individuals suffering under neoliberal policies. Soros foresaw the financial crises in Asia and Russia. He argues that rethinking the capitalist system has to begin with the recognition that financial markets are inherently unstable (Soros 1998). The global capitalist system has evolved with the belief that markets, if left to their own devices, are stable and efficient. But according to Soros, this view is false, and "financial markets have recently acted like a wrecking ball, knocking over one economy after another" (Soros 1998: 2).

Soros puts the current potential for global collapse in historical context, comparing it to the period of World War I and the 1920s:

> The nineteenth-century incarnation of the global capitalist system … was destroyed by the First World War. After the war, there was a feeble attempt to reconstruct it, which ended in the crash of 1929 and the subsequent Great Depression. It is likely … that the current version of global capitalism will also come to a bad end, given that the elements of stability that were present in the nineteenth century are now missing. "Market Fundamentalism" became dominant around 1980.… The globalization of financial markets was a market-fundamentalist project, and it made remark-

> able headway before its shortcomings were exposed.... It's a false and dangerous ideology. (Soros 2002)

Soros is not alone among inside critics. Eisuke Sakakibara, former Japanese Deputy Finance Minister, also draws parallels between current globalization patterns and the pre-World War I period of *laissez-faire* capitalism. He praises Keynes and Karl Polanyi as voices of sanity whose insights seventy-five years ago are still appropriate to the early twenty-first century. Eisuke Sakakibara fears for global capitalism and for the conditions of human society:

> Financial markets are inherently unstable and there are social needs that cannot be met by giving market forces free rein. It is market fundamentalism that has rendered the global capitalistic system unsound and unsustainable.... Market fundamentalism, the contemporary version of 19th century laissez-faire, has imposed the market mechanism upon the society of many countries and the malfunctioning of markets has started to cause various social and political problems particularly in countries in transition and emerging economies. (Sakakibara 2001)

What Karl Polanyi offered in the 1940s was the enduring insight that markets are sustainable only insofar as they are embedded in social and political institutions. These institutions serve important functions without which markets cannot survive.

> This is why every functioning society has regulatory bodies that prevent unfair competition and fraud, monetary and fiscal institutions that help smooth out the boom-bust cycle as well as social insurance schemes that help bring market outcomes into conformity with a society's preference regarding the distribution of risks and rewards. (Sakakibara 2001)

Voices from the Third World

A central reality about exclusive market determination over the distribution of wealth and income is that the wealthy in the advanced industrial nations gain further advantage over the majority population of the underdeveloped world. Colonized regions are losing, not gaining, control over their land, labour and resources, which increasingly are harnessed for exports of cheap food and manufactured goods to the industrial north. Greater poverty and inequality are the consistent result. Third World analysts are deeply angry about the undemocratic power and destructive impact of market fundamentalism. They point to the contradictions and double standard in market-based free trade development strategies.

A central contradiction is the view that Third World countries should not have the same access to the regulatory, tariff and development tools that were exercised by Europe, North America and Japan to protect their domestic production and broaden their industrial base. Another contradiction cited by Third World critics is the notion that all regulation of the market is political interference and that "free markets" are inherently democratic and lead to prosperity.

"There is no necessary connection … between democracy and free markets. On the contrary shifting power away from elected governments to unelected corporations is an obvious threat to democracy" (Pithouse 2001). Richard Pithouse, a South African philosopher, further argues that free markets never have existed, except for a short period in pre-industrial England. The industrial powers, each in turn, used regulation and protection of industry as an essential tool of growth.

> America certainly didn't industrialize by deregulating its market and forcing its industries to stand or fall unprotected. But this was demanded, in the name of freedom, of Africa, Asia, Eastern Europe and South America. And, from Tanzania to New Zealand, shifting power away from governments and towards the market resulted in the impoverishment of the poor, chronic insecurity for the middle class, many of whom found themselves working on contract or facing retrenchment, and massive wealth for a super rich elite. (Pithouse 2001)

The costs of this externally imposed, exploitive system are enormous, borne by Third World populations (as well as by the poor and minority populations in the heart of industrial capitalism).

> The forced imposition of free market fundamentalism has caused enormous suffering in the dominated countries. Spending on infrastructure, health and education has declined and whole industries have been decimated. In South Africa we have lost a million jobs since 1994. We've denied our people life-saving medication. We've endured the pain and never seen the promised gain. (Pithouse 2001)

Argentina, perhaps more than any single nation, represents the failed poster child of market fundamentalism. It suffered the consequences over two decades of externally forced structural adjustment, ideologically bound solutions imposed by the most powerful institutions of global capital, the IMF and World Bank. Jorge Carpio, an economist, sociologist, labour expert and business consultant in Argentina, describes the impact of service cuts and the widespread privatization of institutions and utilities.

> For Argentina, the adjustment program meant ... liquidation of all the advances achieved after more than a half century of struggles for the rights of working people and low-income groups. Argentina ... had achieved ... development, placing us among the primary countries in Latin America in terms of GDP and the principal indicators of general welfare—such as health, education, infant mortality ... a society with a high level of social integration and homogeneity. Twenty years of ... adjustment policies has transformed the country ... back to underdevelopment. In the decade of the eighties, the unemployment rate remained at an average of about six percent ... in 1999, this rate had grown to more than 15%. In 1980, the poverty rate was at seven percent of the population; in 1999, official statistics ... revealed that 37% of the population was living in poverty. [Note that a BBC Report, Oct. 16, 2002, indicated 56 percent of the population in poverty and 22 percent unemployed] ... 60% of the economically active population experience ... either open unemployment, underemployment, informal employment or employment in "trashy jobs"—that is, unstable jobs with low salaries and no benefits ... result of the adjustment program, indicators of poverty, unemployment, diminished consumption and reduced income levels, reflects the redistribution of wealth that these policies promote to the detriment of the middle strata and low-income groups. (Carpio 2000)

Some of the frustration around market fundamentalism is directed at the corporate mass media, which has totally bought into the ideology and accepted that the market is the news and all other human events are either secondary or to be ignored. Palagummi Sainath denounces the media messengers, who are self-absorbed and uncritical of the damage being done to people. They are, he says, particularly insensitive to the reality of poverty.

> A career in the media is conditional on one's acceptance of the notion that poverty is in no way the result of free market capitalism. Insinuate anything else and you don't have space as a journalist.... If the link between poverty and free market exists, it's because we aren't free market enough, or the reforms have not moved fast enough. In short, you may have some space for poverty, but in no way can you question the prevailing ethos of market fundamentalism. (Sainath 2001)

In accepting without comment the consequences of free-market impacts, such as widespread poverty, the media accept the logic of the system. It's like passively reporting on a natural disaster with death and destruction over which no human force has control or influence. But these human-made disasters, which could be prevented, receive even less recognition or publicity.

A Citizen's Agenda

The fundamentalist ideology discussed here briefly is the basis of a broad political reform movement of the Right, which swept unevenly across the globe in the 1980s and 1990s. The wave of free-market globalization included massive privatization of public services throughout the world. Subsequent failures of neoliberalism in Chile, Argentina, Russia, Eastern Europe, New Zealand and North America are exposing this reform experiment for what it is: the institutionalization of a fundamentalist ideology. People have begun to recognize that the unregulated free-market route to prosperity is a myth for all but the wealthy few. They see increasing poverty and unsustainability as the continuing inevitable result of current trends. It will take an alternative ideology and strategy to recapture the public imagination and significantly shift the direction of change.

The alternative of creating balanced and planned economic interventions through the democratic participation of civil society is being promoted by global anti-capitalist coalitions in many countries. In Canada much of the debate turns on key issues and sectors such as health care and public utilities. These were watershed issues in the recent Ontario election that saw citizens rejecting finally the excesses and destruction of the "common sense revolution" of neoliberal Mike Harris, the former premier.

Like any entrenched religious movement, neoliberal fundamentalism will not retreat or disappear. These fundamentalists believe too strongly, and they have the backing of wealth. They will only be contained by offering alternative visions and strategies that have been shown to work.

As George Soros points out, one problem we face is that we live in a global economy, but the political organization of our global society is totally inadequate. We cannot establish or preserve peace and we have no mechanism to counteract the excesses of the financial markets. Without such controls, the global economy will break down. A global society, he wrote,

> does not mean a global state. To abolish the existence of states is neither feasible nor desirable; but insofar as there are collective interests that transcend state boundaries, the sovereignty of states must be subordinated to international law and international institutions. (Soros 1998: 2)

Soros calls for a new internationalism but acknowledges that the greatest opposition to this idea is coming from the United States "which is unwilling to subordinate itself to any international authority" (Soros 1998: 2).

In a similar vein, Sakakibara's alternative vision is simply a regulated global economy "that inter-connects each region and country with their unique culture and socioeconomic regime … co-existence of diverse civilizations with global networking will create a much better world than the unilateral imposition of monolithic ideologies, such as market fundamentalism" (Sakakibara 1999).

Within nation states, citizens' movements are organizing from the community level up to reclaim their nation's agenda, which has been surrendered to the neoliberal ideology and forces of globalization. In Argentina, for example, Jorge Carpio describes their alternative coalition:

> We are mobilizing a range of social forces—trade unions, business associations, religious groups—to build a civil-society movement … to challenge adjustment policies and put forward alternatives that benefit the majority of the population and not merely the large transnational corporations. People are increasingly realizing that adjustment programs only benefit a few at the expense of the many … a development path which takes into account people's dignity and reclaims the values that were the patrimony of the country throughout its history, such as social wellbeing and the possibility of social integration and opportunities for all … only when there is commitment to true civil-society participation will it be possible to get out of the economic jam we are in. (Carpio 2000)

Globally and at the community level market fundamentalism is up against the citizens' agenda. In Canada, the 100,000-strong Council of Canadians along with coalition partners such as the Canadian Health Coalition and Canadian Labour Congress is promoting such a citizens' strategy.

The notion of "public domain" for certain areas of human activity is an historically validated and natural complement to liberal values of individual rights extended into collective rights. Preserving the "village commons" as a core value strictly limits the absolute preeminence of private property and private wealth in areas of public welfare. It leaves a glimmer of hope for future generations.

Notes

1. When exploring the internet under "market fundamentalism" the first connection I discovered was a literal linking of fundamentalist values to the capitalist market. The "Timothy Plan Family of Funds" is a mutual fund investment company for Christian fundamentalists.

References

Bidstrup, Scott. 2002. "Free Market Fundamentalism: Friedman, Pinochet and the 'Chilean Miracle'." Available at www.bidstrup.com/economics.htm [accessed March 15, 2003].

Brandord, Becky. 2002. "Hunger Follows Crisis in Argentina." BBC report carried on Internet. Oct 16. Available at www.bbc.co. uk [accessed March 15, 2003].

Buchan, James. 2000. "Saving the Soul of Classical Liberalism." *Wall Street Journal* Jan. 1.

Carpio, Jorge. 2000. "The Failure of Structural Adjustment in Argentina." Presentation, GAP Public Forum, U.S. Congress on World Bank and IMF Economic Policies. April 18.

Couch, Jim F., and William F. Shughart. 1998. *The Political Economy of the New Deal.* Northampton, MA: Edward Elgar.

Dobbin, Murray. 1998. *The Myth of the Good Corporate Citizen.* Toronto: Stoddart Publishing.

Dumble, Lynette. 2000. "Beyond Market Fundamentalism." *Hindu* Sept. 24.

Foldvary, Fred. 1994. "Public Goods and Private Communities: The Market Provision of Social Services." Available at www.cf.ac.uk/cplan/chris/gci/FoldvaryChapters.htm [accessed March 21, 2003].

Kasper, Wolfgang, and Manfred E. Streit. 1998. *Institutional Economics Social Order and Public Policy.* Fairfax, VA: The Locke Institute.

Kelly, Marjorie. 2002. "Waving Goodbye to the Invisible Hand: What Enron Teaches Us About Economic System Design." *Business Ethics* 16, 1 (January/February).

Meadows, Donella, Dennis Meadows and Jorgen Randers. 1992. *Beyond the Limits: Confronting Global Collapse, Envisioning a Sustainable Future.* South Burlington, VT: Chelsea Green Publishing.

Niskanen, William A. 1994. *Bureaucracy and Public Economics.* Northampton, MA: Edward Elgar.

Nissani, Noah. 1996. "Classical Liberalism." Available at www.liberal.org.il/democrac.htm [accessed March 21, 2003].

Pitsula, James, and Ken Rasmussen. 1991. *Privatizing a Province: The New Right in Saskatchewan.* Vancouver: New Star Books.

Polanyi, Karl. 1944. *The Great Transformation.* Boston, MA: Beacon.

Pithouse, Richard. 2001. "For Humanity and against Market Fundamentalism." Department of Philosophy, University of Durban-Westville, Durban, South Africa. August. Available at www.3rdearmusic.com/forum/marketfund.html [accessed March 10, 2003].

Progler, Yusef. 2000. "Economic Neo-liberalism: The Target of Popular Protests Against Global Capitalism." *Crescent International* May 1–15.

Rowley, Charles K. 1998. *Classical Liberalism and Civil Society.* Northampton, MA: Edward Elgar.

Rowley, Charles K., and Richard E. Wagner. 1995. *Trade Protection in the United States.* Northampton, MA: Edward Elgar.

Sainath, Palagummi. 2001. "Poverty, Market Fundamentalism and the Media." *AlterNet.* June 19. Available at www.alternet.com [accessed March 10, 2003].

Sakakibara, Eisuke. 1999. "The End of Market Fundamentalism." Paper presented at the Foreign Correspondents' Club, January 22. Available at iml.umkc.edu/

econ/economics/ Institutional/Readings/Eisuke/fundamentalism.html [accessed March 10, 2003].

Soros, George. 2002. "Why the Markets Can't Fix Themselves." *The New Republic* September 2.

_____.1998. *The Crisis of the Global Capitalism*. New York: Public Affairs.

Starr, Paul. 1988 "The Meaning of Privatization." *Yale Law and Policy Review* 6.

Teeple, Gary. 1995. *Globalization and the Decline of Social Reform*. Toronto: Garamond Press.

Thatcher, Margaret. 1987. Interview. *Women's Own Magazine*. October 3.

Travers, James. 2002. "Myth makers in full throat." *Moose Jaw Times herald,* December 6.

Chapter Ten

Equality Rights and Re-Privatized Public Services:

Religious Fundamentalism Meets the *Charter*

Ailsa M. Watkinson

Religious fundamentalism appears to be gaining strength worldwide and it is a matter that needs close examination and exposure by all equality-seeking groups. Religious fundamentalism (including that found within Christianity, Buddhism, Hinduism, Islam and Judaism) is a direct and powerful challenge to the equality rights of women, children, racialized people and sexual minorities.[1] By religious fundamentalist I mean a group that:

> believes that the group and society need to be rescued from the secular state; rejects Enlightenment norms, particularly individual rights and secularism; is committed to the authority of ancient scripture; holds a total worldview such that religious beliefs are inseparable from politics, law and culture, relies on an idealized past; is selective in drawing from the past for religious traditions and orthodox practice; centers that idealized past in a patriarchal framework mandating separate gender spheres and a pristine morality; rejects outsiders and the concept of pluralism; and is committed to activism and fighting for changed social, political and legal order. (Howland 1997: 277–78)

The term fundamentalist does not apply to all religions or religious groups. There are many denominations or sects within religions that are not fundamentalist. As such, many religious groups are not a threat to the rights of equality-seeking groups and, in fact, have taken the lead in promoting those rights. My concern is with those religious organizations that, under the guise of public service and religious freedom, promote and practice tenets that undermine our understanding and protection of human rights.

In Canada, religious organizations are re-establishing themselves in the sphere of public service delivery. Since public services must be provided in a manner that respects the equality rights and fundamental freedoms of the recipients, it is vital that we become familiar with the theology and practices of these organizations.

Canada has seen a growing industry in the development of faith-based public programs. For example, in the area of public education, there are a number of alternative education programs which bring with them religious practices and doctrine, such as independent schools, associate schools, charter schools and Logos programs (programs offered in some public schools designed to support Christian values and beliefs). In addition, faith-based public programming includes adoption services, pregnancy counselling, prison programming, extra judicial measures (often designed for youth in conflict with the law) and other such programs. In the United States, President George W. Bush has made it known that faith-based services will be a major part of his administration. As one writer reports, George W. Bush "has opened his policy offices to the views of fundamentalist Christians and has initiated policies that would allow religious groups to offer social programs" (Saunders 2001: A2).

Christian programming in Canadian prisons is well established and expanding. One chaplaincy, under the direction of Corrections Services Canada, provides programs in a women's prison with such titles as, "Lord Teach me to Pray," "Lord Heal my Hurts" and the "Christian Principles of Financial Planning." A prisoner's willingness to take part in prison programs bodes well for them in their attempts for parole and other release options. However, these types of programs are inviting only to prisoners who are Christian, thus limiting access to valuable programming for those who are not.

The increasing inclusion of faith-based organizations in the delivery of public services has been brought about, in part, by the restructuring of those services. In the 1980s and 1990s, provincial, federal and municipal governments in Canada used the perceived need to cut deficits as the rationale for cutbacks to social programs (Watkinson 2001). Many provinces cut social assistance benefits and placed more restrictions on eligibility criteria, leaving thousands of citizens in untenable situations. In addition, federal transfer payments were drastically cut, leaving the provinces with fewer resources to provide public services (Rice and Prince 2000). Religious-based organizations, among others, stepped into this public service breach.

We generally view practising a religion as a basic right under human rights laws. However, many religious fundamentalists promote ideas that are antithetical to equality-seeking groups. Are these religious organizations in need of protection under human rights law or do we need protection from them?

In this chapter I focus on Christian fundamentalist organizations, as Christianity is the religion of the majority in Canada. Statistics Canada reports that Roman Catholics and Protestants make up 72 percent of the total population (Statistics Canada 2003). Moreover, it is generally Christian organizations that play a prominent role in the delivery of public services. I also include fundamentalist religious groups that are sometimes referred to as merely "conservative religions." They are distinguished from fundamentalist religions because they are not considered "militant activists." However, as their ideologies often overlap, I make no distinction.

This chapter considers the role of human rights legislation in curtailing the influence of religious fundamentalism in the public arena. I argue that religious fundamentalism is a threat to the equality rights of women, children, sexual minorities and racialized people. The practices and teachings of religious fundamentalists often extend beyond the bounds of what is lawful in Canada and under international human rights laws. This is especially worrisome when we are witnessing, more and more, a religious intrusion into the realm of public services—an intrusion that is well orchestrated, well funded and, in many instances, invited.

Equality Rights and United Nations Documents

Canada's *Charter of Rights and Freedoms* has its genesis in the 1948 *Universal Declaration of Human Rights.* Canada, and most of its provinces, are signatories to the *Declaration* and other international human rights treaties including the *International Covenant on Civil and Political Rights,* the *International Covenant on Social, Economic and Political Rights,* the *Convention on the Elimination of All Forms of Racial Discrimination,* the *Convention on the Elimination of all Forms of Discrimination Against Women* and the *Convention on the Rights of the Child.*

These documents are a common benchmark by which to examine social policy and government action or inaction (Watkinson 2001). Their shared theme is the recognition of the dignity and worth of the human person and the promotion of equality and liberty rights of all people. For example, Article 5(a) of the *Convention on the Elimination of all Forms of Discrimination against Women* calls on state parties to:

> modify the social and cultural patterns of conduct of men and women, with a view to achieving the elimination of prejudices and customary and all other practices which are based on the idea of the inferiority or the superiority of either of the sexes or on stereotyped roles for men and women.

Courtney Howland (1997), in her discussion, "The Challenge of Religious Fundamentalism to the Liberty and Equality Rights of Women," illustrates how international human rights documents, specifically the *United Nations Charter* and the *Universal Declaration of Human Rights,* have been used to challenge racial discrimination supported by religious beliefs. The case she highlights is apartheid in South Africa.

The apartheid system in South Africa had it roots in the Afrikaners'

Calvinist beliefs. As Howland notes, "Afrikaners believed that they were the chosen people with a divine mission to rule over all others, and from this followed their belief in white supremacy and a policy of racial segregation and discrimination" (1997: 347). Their policy of apartheid was challenged before the International Court of Jurists in 1970.[2] It found that South Africa's racial discrimination policy of apartheid was a "flagrant" violation of the U.N. *Charter*, the founding document of the United Nations and all subsequent U.N. treaties and covenants. The U.N. *Charter* "reaffirms faith in fundamental rights, in the dignity and worth of the human person, in the equal rights of men and women and of nations large and small" (United Nations Charter 1945, Preamble) and promotes "respect for and observance of, human rights and fundamental freedoms for all without distinction as to race, sex, language or religion" (United Nations Charter 1945, Article 55).

The International Court was not persuaded that religious beliefs could justify apartheid. As Howland notes, "it is clear that international law should not now accept the freedom of religious belief as justification for systematic racial discrimination" (1997: 349).

A "comparison," Howland points out, "may be drawn between slavery on the basis of race as it has been justified under religious rhetoric and women's inferior position as it is currently justified under religious fundamentalist rhetoric"(1997: 362). Slavery has been defended by relying on "Genesis 9:24–25 where Noah awakens from his drunkenness and curses Ham, his youngest son, that Canaan (Ham's son) be a 'servant of servants' of his brethren and Leviticus 25:44–46 where God tells Moses that Hebrews should not sell their own brethren but should buy their slaves 'of the nations that surround you'" (Howland 1997, footnote 374). Women's inferiority has also been justified by a literal interpretation of the Christian Bible. For example, Ephesians 5: 22–24 states: "Wives, be subject to your husbands as to the Lord; for the man is the head of woman, just as Christ also is the head of the Church. Christ is, indeed, the Savior of the body; but just as the church is subject to Christ, so must women be to their husbands in everything." Even though it is estimated that Ephesians was written more than eleven hundred years ago and was not the literal transcript of Jesus's words (Spong 1991), this scripture and others are used by many fundamentalist organizations to justify women's submission and obedience to male leadership and control. Paul, the Apostle, in his letters to the Corinthians exhorted women to be silent in church: "If there is something they [women] want to know, they can ask their husbands at home. It is a shocking thing that a woman should address the congregation" (1 Corinthians 14: 34–35).

Similarly, beliefs regarding child rearing practices are often supported with reference to the Old Testament (Greven 1991; Straus 2001). For example, the use of corporal punishment on children is justified by reference to Proverbs, "Folly is deep-rooted in the heart of a boy; a good beating will drive it right out of him" (Proverbs 22:1). Discrimination against gays and lesbians is justified by Christian fundamentalists who rely on the book of Leviticus, written nearly three thousand years ago and three hundred years after Moses reportedly lived (Spong, 1991). It is especially replete in its condemnation of homosexuality. It says, "You shall not lie with a man as with a woman; that is an abomination" (Leviticus 18:22), and later, "If a man has intercourse with a man as with a woman, they both commit an abomination. They shall be put to death"(Leviticus 20:1).

A literal and selective interpretation of the Bible, such as those noted above, is clearly out of step with human rights laws. There are no allowances within the U.N. *Charter* for reservations on the basis of religion. Howland maintains that the wording of the U.N. *Charter* is such that no particular religious law is the source for human rights nor dictates international human rights standards (1997: 341). In other words, "systematic discrimination on the basis of sex under religious fundamentalist laws is not permissible as a manifestation of the freedom of religious belief under the [United Nation's] Charter any more than South Africa's system of apartheid was permissible. Both violate the [United Nation's] Charter" (Howland 1997: 349).

The *United Nations Universal Declaration*, as noted earlier, protects liberty rights and equality rights. It clearly conflicts with religious fundamentalist beliefs and practices that require women to submit to and obey their husbands. The consequences of these beliefs are both obvious and subtle.

> The differentiation places obvious burdens on women: submissive status, physical abuse, economic dependence, limitations on travel in their own community and abroad, and limitations on the ability to work and seek education. The [practices] place women in an inferior position to men and demand that women have less power than men, granting men the final say in all matters as the head of the family. (Howland 1997: 351)

Not only are the requirements of obedience and submission an affront to women's equality rights, they also impede the liberty rights of women, including women's democratic rights and practices.

Every state that is a signatory to these international laws has a duty to ensure that women's equality and liberty rights are upheld. In Canada, not only do we have international human rights laws to support the challenge of religious fundamentalism, but we also have the *Canadian Charter of Rights and Freedoms*. Canada's *Charter* clearly extends equality rights to children, sexual minorities, racialized groups and women. Therefore, we can make similar arguments, using the *Charter* and other human rights documents, to protect equality-seeking groups whose rights are made vulnerable by the move to include faith-based organizations in the delivery of public services.

Canadian *Charter of Rights and Freedoms*

Canada has included, in its constitution, a *Charter of Rights and Freedoms*. Many of the sections in the *Charter* were inspired by the *United Nations Declaration on Human Rights* and other relevant human rights documents. The *Charter's* place in Canada's constitution makes it part of Canada's supreme law (*Slaight Communications Inc.* 1989: 1078). The *Charter* came into effect over twenty years ago. The Supreme Court of Canada's interpretation of the *Charter*, including its application, the limits to be placed on rights and freedoms and the interpretation of equality rights have important implications for this discussion.

The *Charter of Rights and Freedoms* protects the equality and fundamental freedoms of all Canadian citizens. Section 15 of the *Charter*, often referred to as the "equality section" states:

> Every individual is equal before and under the law and has the right of equal protection and equal benefit of the law without discrimination and, in particular, without discrimination based on race, national or ethnic origin, colour, religion, sex, age or mental or physical disability.

Over the years, the Supreme Court has considered whether groups other than those listed are protected. They are. Added to the list are those discriminated against on the basis of citizenship (*Andrews* 1989), marital status (*Miron* 1995) and sexual orientation (*Vriend* 1998) and living on or off reserves (*Corbiere* 1991). The *Charter* also protects fundamental freedoms such as the freedom of conscience, religion, thought and association, and the right to life, liberty and security of the person.

Obviously, there is the potential for tension between freedom of religion and equality rights as outlined in the *Charter*. The dilemma for public policy development is where and how to draw the line, what rights take precedence.

Application of the *Charter*

Section 32 of the *Charter* states that it applies to Parliament and the legislature and government of each province and territory. The Supreme Court has ruled that its provisions extend to government legislation, decisions, actions and inactions, to agencies receiving public money and to agencies that provide a public service (Watkinson 1999). Thus, any governmental action is subject to *Charter* scrutiny. The common denominator is a governmental connection.

For example, the Supreme Court has found that the *Charter* obligations apply to a college's mandatory retirement policy because the Minister of Education, by statute, exercises a degree of control over the college (*Douglas/Kwantlin* 1990). It also applies to collective agreements arising from employers who are established by virtue of legislation (*Lavigne* 1991), independent administrative bodies established by government (*Blencoe* 2000) and services provided in hospitals through the legislation establishing the provision of medical services (*Eldridge* 1997).

The later case is of significance. The case of *Eldridge v. British Columbia (Attorney General)* examined whether a private entity can be held accountable under the *Charter*. The case was brought forward by deaf patients who argued successfully that the lack of sign language interpretation impaired their right to equal benefit of a social service—in this case, medicare. Health care in the province of British Columbia, as well as in other Canadian provinces, is governed by federal and provincial legislation. Hospitals play a major role in the provision of health care services and are considered private, that is, non-governmental institutions. In the case of *Eldridge* the hospital argued that since it was a private entity[3] it was beyond the reach of the *Charter*. The argument failed.

The Court ruled that private institutions were part of government when they perform tasks assigned to them under legislation. Hospitals provide medically necessary services and carry out a specific governmental objective. The *Hospital Insurance Act*, "provides for the delivery of a comprehensive social program" (*Eldridge* 1997: para. 50) and "hospitals are merely the vehicles the legislature has chosen to deliver this program" (para. 50). Thus, *Charter* rights, including the equality rights, apply to the delivery of services in hospitals.

In order for the *Charter* to apply to a private entity "it must be found to be implementing a specific governmental policy or program"(*Eldridge* 1997: para. 43). The question is no longer whether the entity is private or public but what is the nature of the activity at issue. Is the entity implementing a specific statutory scheme or government program? If it is, then it is subject to review under the *Charter*. After all, as the Court noted, "governments ... should not be allowed to evade their constitutional responsibilities by delegating the implementation of their policies and programs to private entities" (*Eldridge* 1997: para. 42).

The hospital was found to have discriminated against the Eldridges and other deaf people in that it did not provide sign language interpretation so that they could enjoy the same health care services as hearing persons. The Court said, "the provision of these services is not simply a matter of internal hospital management, it is an expression of government policy" (*Eldridge* 1997: para. 50).

This and other similar court decisions, then, are significant for those who are concerned with the intrusion of religious fundamentalism into the public realm. Considering the reasoning of the Supreme Court in regard to hospitals, it is reasonable to assume that the *Charter* rights and freedoms will apply to all human service agencies that fulfill a government policy. This would include social services, medical care and public education. By way of example, private schools that provide a public service, that is public education, must do so in a non-discriminatory manner. Their curriculum cannot in any way endorse views that are counter to the equality rights of equality-seeking groups. Disciplinary methods, dress codes and admission policies must also conform to the *Charter* provisions.

With the increasing erosion of public services and downloading of these services to community-based agencies, the decision of *Eldridge* takes on added weight. It assures us that any community-based agency providing a public service—one that is governed by legislation such as child protection, public education, corrections services, social assistance, health care and alternative measures or one that is funded by public money—must provide the service in a manner consistent with the *Charter's* provisions. For some faith-based organizations this can be a problem. Whether this will apply to internal employment practices is an unknown. But it seems reasonable to expect that governments will prevent an agency that discriminates in its hiring practices to deliver a public service.

It has been reported that, in the United States, for example, the Salvation Army was seeking an exemption from federal and state laws which prohibit discrimination on the basis of sexual orientation and require spousal benefits to same sex couples (Carney 2001). Vice President Dick Cheney supported the idea saying, "a key part of the President's faith-based initiative is to make certain that, in order to acquire or to participate in providing these social services with government funds, we not require fundamental changes in the underlying principles and organized and doctrines [sic], if you will, of the organizations that participate, and that's been a consistent policy throughout"(Carney 2001). A similar request made in Canada would come face to face with a public as well as a *Charter* challenge.

Margot Young believes that the wisdom arising from *Eldridge* is "about preventing the evasion of *Charter* commitments through a delegation of governmental responsibilities under the *Charter* [which] is apposite in the current political climate of government downsizing and privatization of traditional activities of the post-war state" (1998: 250).

Limitations of the *Charter*

Section 1 of the Charter allows for the limiting of rights and freedoms, it states:

> The *Canadian Charter or Rights and Freedoms* guarantees the

> rights and freedoms set out in it subject to such reasonable limits prescribed by law as can be demonstrably justified in a free and democratic society.

The *Charter's* purpose is to ensure that Canadian society is free and democratic and the same principles inherent in a free and democratic society are to be considered when limiting rights. The Supreme Court of Canada said that the values and principles of a free and democratic society include:

> Respect for the inherent dignity of the human person, commitment to social justice and equality, accommodation of a wide variety of beliefs, respect for cultural and group identity, and faith in social and political institutions which enhance the participation of individuals and groups in society. (*R. v. Oakes* 1986: 136)

The strain between respecting religious freedoms, equality rights and fundamental freedoms has been considered in a number of cases heard before the Supreme Court of Canada. For example, in a 1995 case, Jehovah's Witness parents argued that their right to religious freedom, as guaranteed under section 2 (a) of the *Charter*, was infringed when their premature baby was made a temporary ward of the state in order to allow for emergency blood transfusions (*B.(R.)* 1995). As Jehovah's Witnesses, the parents objected to blood transfusions for religious reasons. The Court said:

> freedom of religion is not absolute. While it is difficult to conceive of any limitations on religious *beliefs*, the same cannot be said of religious *practices*, notably when they impact on the fundamental rights and freedoms of others. (*B.(R.)* 1995: para. 106, emphasis added)

Allowing the parents to act upon their religious beliefs could impair the right to life and security of the child, who is also protected under section 7 of the *Charter*. While the Court agreed that the temporary wardship of the child did infringe the religious freedom rights of the parents, it ruled that limiting their religious freedom under section 1 of the *Charter* was reasonable and justifiable. A section 1 analysis allows the courts to consider each case in its context and determine whether it is appropriate to limit a right. As noted earlier, the process takes into account the values and principles of a free and democratic society, which includes respect for the dignity of the human person and a commitment to social justice and equality.

The Supreme Court had ruled that fundamental freedoms, including freedom of expression and freedom of religion, do not operate in a vacuum. Freedom is "subject to such limitations as are necessary to protect public safety, order, health, or morals or the fundamental rights and freedoms of others" (*R. v. Big M* 1985, para. 337). The court also noted that "although the freedom of belief may be broad, the freedom to act upon those beliefs is considerably narrower" (*B.(R.)* 1995, para. 226).

A year later the Court considered the case of *Ross v. School District #15*. The case involved a teacher, Mr. Ross, who had made racist and discriminatory statements in writing and on public television. He had also published four books outlining his beliefs. The thrust of his argument was that "Christian civilization was being undermined and destroyed by an international Jewish conspiracy" (*Ross* 1996: 836–37). A parent filed a complaint with the Nova Scotia Human Rights Commission. The complaint resulted in an order directing that Mr. Ross be removed from the classroom. Mr. Ross appealed the order to the Supreme Court (Watkinson 1999).

The Court was asked to consider whether the order to remove Mr. Ross from his teaching position infringed his fundamental freedoms of religion (section 2(a)) and expression (section 2(b)). In a unanimous decision the Court found that Mr. Ross's fundamental freedom rights had been infringed. However it also found that limiting Mr. Ross's fundamental freedoms was justified because of the context of the case. The Court said, "the objective of promoting equal opportunity unhindered by discriminatory practices based on race or religion (is) pressing and substantial" (*Ross* 1996: 879).[4] Another important consideration, the Court asserted, is Canada's commitment to international human rights documents. The Court referred to the international community's commitment to the eradication of discrimination. The commitment, it said, extends to prohibiting the dissemination of ideas based on racial or religious superiority.

As can be seen from the cases discussed above, the *Charter* allows for the limiting of rights and freedoms, such as religious freedoms, when they interfere with the equality or fundamental freedoms of others. Those who argue that their religious rights give them the entitlement to not only hold their beliefs but practise them in ways that lessen the dignity of others are not protected by the *Charter* nor other human rights documents.

Believing and Practising

The Supreme Court of Canada had noted the distinction between religious beliefs and religious practices. It reviewed the matter again in a 2001 decision. The case provides clear direction as to the types of evidence needed to argue that religious beliefs have become problematic.

The Court was asked to rule on a decision made by the British Columbia Teachers' Federation (BCTF) regarding the suitability of graduates from the Trinity Western University (TWU), a Christian-based teacher education program. The TWU applied to the British Columbia College of

Teachers (BCCT) for permission to assume full responsibility for the teacher education program, so as to have the entire program reflect its Christian worldview. Prior to the application, TWU students completed their final year of studies at Simon Fraser University. BCCT refused to approve the application because they were concerned that the institution appeared to follow discriminatory practices. The TWU Community Standards, which applied to faculty, staff and students, required them to refrain from practices that are biblically condemned. These practices included "sexual sins including ... homosexual behaviour" (*Trinity Western University* 2001: para. 4).

The Supreme Court ruled that it was beyond the jurisdiction of BCCT to make such a decision. The suitability or unsuitability of the graduates could only be determined with evidence, not based on their beliefs alone. The Court's concern was that the BCCT's decision was based on inference rather than any concrete evidence (*Trinity Western University* 2001: para. 32). The Courts said:

> the proper place to draw the line in cases like the one at bar is generally between belief and conduct. The freedom to hold beliefs is broader than the freedom to act on them. Absent concrete evidence that training teachers at TWU fosters discrimination in the public schools of B.C., the freedom of individuals to adhere to certain religious beliefs while at TWU should be respected. (*Trinity Western University* 2001: para. 36)

In order for the BCCT to have denied accreditation to TWU graduates, the Court said,

> it should have based its concerns on specific evidence. It could have asked for reports on student teachers, or opinions of school principals and superintendents. It could have examined discipline files involving TWU graduates and other teachers affiliated with a Christian school of that nature. Any concerns should go to risk, not general perceptions. (*Trinity Western University* 2001: para. 38)

When challenging the manifestations and practices of religious fundamentalism, clear evidence of the associated risks is required. What is needed, for example, is evidence that faith-based organizations limit the options available to women facing an unwanted pregnancy; evidence of religious beliefs influencing those coming to terms with their sexual identity; evidence regarding the support provided to women attempting to leave an abusive marriage; evidence of the impact of religious beliefs on the welfare of children; evidence of discriminatory practices in schools or other public institutions.

Conclusion

Currently a Christian religious organization, Prairie Hope Ministries, has set up an addiction recovery centre for teenage boys in Saskatchewan and is seeking operational funding in order to begin its work. They state that they will have space for eleven students, sixteen years and older. The length of stay is estimated to be between four to eighteen months. Since Prairie Hope Ministries is a Christian organization "the students will be expected to attend chapel and Bible studies" (Haight 2003: A3). According to the spokesperson for the organization:

> We're not saying that you can't come into our program if you're Muslim or Indian or Buddhist or agnostic. At the end of the day, if you decide you want to become a Christian, all right. But if at the end of the day you don't become a Christian and you just apply the morality and the ethics and the values that you learn and that's good enough for you, OK. (Haight 2003: A3)

The spokesperson said he is surprised "that Saskatchewan is the only jurisdiction in all of North America that does not have a faith-based addictions recovery program" (Haight 2003: A3). Some may see this proposal as a good idea and one that is long overdue. However, this is the type of program that needs our careful inspection, simply because it is offered by a religious organization. Will the centre undertake practices that uphold the rights and freedoms guaranteed in human rights laws? The analysis needs to first consider whether such a centre falls under the jurisdiction of human rights legislation, for example, the *Charter,* and if so, whether the actions and practices are consistent with *Charter* principles.

As long as the addiction recovery centre is run privately and youth volunteer to attend, the program does not fall under the *Charter's* gaze. However, once the centre receives government funding and/or youth elect to attend at the centre as an alternative to custody or some other judicial sanction, the centre is bound by the *Charter.* At either point—receiving public funding or providing a public service—the actions and practices of the centre must be in keeping with the equality rights and fundamental freedoms enunciated in the Charter. This means that if those in attendance at the proposed centre are required to attend chapel and study the Bible, the practices overtly contradict *Charter* principles. The centre is promoting Christian doctrine and thus discriminating against other religious believers and non-believers. Other areas of concern would be their hiring practices, their teachings concerning equality-seeking groups and their theology.

Human rights laws are important tools for us to use in curtailing the discriminatory practices of religious fundamentalism in public spaces. Familiarity with human rights documents provides us with the tools necessary to ferret out and articulate discriminatory practices. These documents and the decisions arising from them give citizens standing to oppose the transfer of public services to faith-based organizations and the right to question where funding comes from, where the authority to carry out specific programs comes from, who is to attend and what types of practices are carried out within a service.

The *Charter's* provisions, including the recognition of the equality rights of all Canadians, cast a wide net over the actions and inactions of all forms of government as well as private institutions that perform governmental duties. The effect is that private and public institutions that provide a government service or receive funding from the government must ensure that their practices respect the equality rights of those they serve.

Inequality and repression have, throughout history, flourished under the banner of freedom of religion. Today, the resurgence of religious fundamentalism finds history repeating itself. Governments may argue that allowing faith-based organizations to provide public services is cheaper and in some instances a more efficient way to provide public services. However, it may not meet the government's legal commitment to ensure that Canadian society reflects the values and principles of a free and democratic society, which the Supreme Court has interpreted to mean a society that demonstrates respect for equality and the inherent dignity of the human person (*R. v. Oakes* 1986: 136).

Notes

1. The term "sexual minorities" includes individuals who have traditionally been distinguished by societies because of their sexual orientation, inclination, behaviour, or nonconformity with gender roles or identity (Wilets 1997: footnote 1).
2. See Legal Consequences for States of the Continued Presence of South Africa in Namibia (South West Africa). Notwithstanding Security Council Resolution 276 (1970), 1971 I.C.J. para 131, at 57. There is a strong historical connection with slavery and the Bible (Noll 1993).
3. Hospitals are non-governmental entities, meaning that they are run independently from governments. Health care in British Columbia is governed by the *Medical and Health Care Services Act*, which sets up hospitals, and the *Hospital Insurance Act*, which set up the Medical Services Commission. All provinces have similar schemes. It is the connection to legislation and government policy that ties non-governmental entities such as hospitals to the *Charter*.
4. These comments were a reiteration of the former Chief Justice's comments in *Canada (Human Rights Commission) v. Taylor* (1990) and repeated with approval. The case dealt with hate messages.

References

Andrews v. Law Society of British Columbia. 1989. 1 Supreme Court Reports 143.

B.(R.) v. Children's Aid Society of Metropolitan Toronto. 1995. 1 Supreme Court Reports 315.

Blencoe v. British Columbia (Human Rights Commission). 2000. 2 Supreme Court Reports 307.

Board of Education Saskatoon School Division No. 13 Policy 1020.3.

Canada (Human Rights Commission) v. Taylor. 1990. 3 Supreme Court Reports 892.

Canadian Charter of Rights and Freedoms, Part 1 of the *Constitution Act*, 1982, being Schedule B to the *Canada Act* 1982 (U.K.), 1982, c. 11.

Carney, Timothy P. 2001. "Administration retreats on protecting Salvation Army." *Online Human Events: The National Conservative Weekly*. Available at www.humaneventsonline.com/articles/07-16-01/carney.html [accessed on June 6, 2002].

Convention on the Elimination of All Forms of Discrimination Against Women (CEDAW), G.A. Res. 34/180, U.N. GAOR, 34th Sess., Supp. No. 46, U.N. Doc. A34/46 (1979).

Corbiere v. Canada (Minister of Indian and Northern Affairs). 1999. 2 Supreme Court Reports 203.

Dobson, James. 1987. *Dare to Discipline*. Wheaton, IL: Tyndale House Publishers, Inc.

_____. 1986. *Love Must Be Tough*. Waco: Word.

Douglas/Kwantlen Faculty Assn. v. Douglas College. 1990. 3 Supreme Court Reports 177.

Eldridge v. British Columbia (Attorney General). 1997. 3 Supreme Court Reports 624.

Ellison, Christopher G. 1996. "Conservative protestantism and the corporal punishment of children." *Journal for the Scientific Study of Religion 35*.

Greven, Philip. 1991. *Spare the Child: The Religious Roots of Punishment and the Psychological Impact of Physical Abuse*. New York: Alfred A. Nephew.

Haight, Lana. 2003. "Groups seeks operating funds for teen addictions centre." *The Star Phoenix* Saskatoon. October 9.

Howland, Courtney W. 1997. "The challenge of religious fundamentalism to the liberty and equality rights of women: An analysis under the United Nations Charter." *Columbia Journal of Transnational Law* 35.

Lavigne v. Ontario Public Service Employees Union. 1991. 2 Supreme Court Reports 211.

Miron v. Trudel. 1995. 2 Supreme Court Reports 418.

Moore, Oliver. 2002. "Lawyers tune final arguments in crucial child hearing." *Globe and Mail* June 29.

Mullaly, Robert. 2002. *Challenging Oppression: A Critical Social Work Approach*. Toronto: Oxford University Press.

Noll, Mark A. 1993. "The Bible and Slavery." In Randall M. Miller, Harry S. Strout and Charles Reagan Wilson (eds.), *Religion and the American Civil War*. New York: Oxford University Press.

R. v. Big M Drug Mart Ltd. 1985. 1 Supreme Court Reports 295.

R. v. Oakes. 1986. 1 Supreme Court Reports 103.

Rice, James J., and Michael J. Prince. 2000. *Changing Politics of Canadian Social Policy*. Toronto: University of Toronto Press.

Ross v. School Board #15. 1996. 1 Supreme Court Reports 825.

Saunders, Doug. 2001. "U.S. got what it deserves, Falwell says." *Globe and Mail* September 15.

Slaight Communications Inc. v. Davidson. 1989. 1 Supreme Court Reports 1038.

Spong, John Shelby. 1991. *Rescuing the Bible from Fundamentalism: A Bishop Rethinks the Meaning of Scripture*. San Francisco: Harper Collins Publishing.

Statistics Canada. 2003. "Census of Population: Income of individuals, families and households; religion." The Daily, May 13. Available at www.statcan.ca/Daily [accessed on June 18, 2003].

Straus, Murray. 2001. *Beating the Devil out of Them; Corporal Punishment in American Families and its Effects on Children*. London: Transaction Publishers.

The Universal Declaration of Human Rights. 1948. G.A. Res 217 A (111), U.N. GAOR, 3rd. Sess., U.N. Doc. A/810.

Trinity Western University v. British Columbia College of Teachers. 2001. 1 Supreme Court Reports 772.

United Nations Charter. 1945. 59 Stat. 1031, T.S. No. 993, 3 Bevans 1153.

Vriend v. Alberta. 1998. 1 Supreme Court Reports 493.

Watkinson, Ailsa M. 2001. "Human rights laws as advocacy tools for a global civil society." *Canadian Social Work Review 18:2*.

_____. 1999. *Education, Student Rights and the Charter*. Saskatoon: Purich Publishing.

Wilets, James D. 1997. "Conceptualizing private violence against sexual minorities as gendered violence: An international and comparative law perspective." *Albany Law Review* 60.

Young, Margot. 1998. "Change at the margins: Eldridge v. British Columbia (A.G.) and Vriend *v. Alberta.*" *Canadian Journal of Women and the Law 10*.

Chapter Eleven

Slippery and Unstable:
School and Human Rights

Carol Schick

"Fundamentalism" is an imprecise term that defies neat boundaries. The term came to use in the United States during World War I among Protestant Christians who wanted to return the tenets of their faith to its fundamentals (Armstrong 2001; Bendroth 1999). While precise definition seems impossible and a matter of equivocation, van der Vyver suggests that "fundamentalism is associated with certain trends within a particular religious community" (1996: 1). Further, because fundamentalism can signify different things to different people, religious fundamentalism represents only one variant. While the term has been applied most frequently to religious groups, it also can also refer to national and social movements, described by Ghassan Hage (2001) as "national fundamentalism." All but the most militant movements do not necessarily acknowledge that their beliefs are what outsiders might call "fundamentalist." In spite of the many different aims and fervently held beliefs, however, movements termed fundamentalist bear a strong resemblance to each other.

Deciding who and what can be called fundamentalist is a challenge both of definition and identity. In spite of the fact that those described as fundamentalist do not necessarily name themselves as such, the effects of what they espouse can produce social identifications for themselves and those they oppose (or who oppose them). Not only is the term operationally imprecise, fundamentalism is also a social construction with the slippage and ambivalence that accompanies any category. While religious or political extremism might be easily observed, it is not separate from the social milieu against which it marks itself. This chapter argues that fundamentalism exists as a contradiction on many fronts, including its core values and principles and the notion of a fixed and unchanging social identification. These core values, which the world is said to need, are over and against other measures such as universal progress and human rights. Indeed, with a precisely defined exclusionary positioning, an exclusive fundamentalist identity can only recognize itself in relation to the presence of a highly visible, excluded outsider.

Fundamentalists are in an untenable and contradictory position when they call upon freedom of religion to justify their opposition to human rights legislation, from which designated minorities, including religious minorities, benefit. In spite of the contradictions, the language of victimhood used by fundamentalists is appealing to groups whose taken-for-granted privileges are being eroded through the language of human rights. Fundamentalism is produced, on the one hand, through eschewing universalism and human rights norms and, on the other hand, through a construction of otherness and alterity against which the insider fundamentalist can know herself. In the shifting nature of constructed social identities, the conflicting desire for both insider and outsider status renders the fundamentalist category unstable and ambiguous. It is important to pay attention to fundamentalist discourses for the ways language temporarily conceals distinctions, even to fundamentalists, between insider/outsider, oppressor/oppressed.

Even though the various types of fundamentalism make it difficult to define, fundamentalism can be said to include certain practices. First, it claims the authority of the past as an unchanging reality, while reinterpreting precepts in a way that is new and unprecedented. It is committed to basic principles believed to be eternal and immutable. The past is revered and glorified; the good old days are seen as superior to the present. Second, it separates itself from those not in the creed. Solidarity is promoted through a sense of self-sufficiency and self-righteousness. The third practice is the redefinition of the fundamentalist community with respect to non-adherents, as well as a narrowing of acceptable belief and behaviour among adherents. The tenets within the belief system, whether it is religious or otherwise, are said to have causal force and are sufficient unto themselves. Intolerance and condemnation of outside forces—as in national fundamentalism—are practices that are also conducive to xenophobia.

J.D. van der Vyver on Religious Fundamentalism

J.D. van der Vyver (1996) categorizes fundamentalist types based on their adherence to and departure from principles of universal human rights. He demonstrates the strength of human rights in adjudicating moral issues across political, economic or social conditions. In this context, van der Vyver (1996) describes three types of fundamentalism. First, "radical fundamentalism" refers to extremes of religious practice that result in criminal activity. These shocking examples are familiar because of their ability to make the news. They include the group suicide of followers of Jim Jones in Jonestown, Guyana, in 1978; the build up of firearms in anticipation of the end of the world followed by the fiery deaths of eighty-one members of the Branch Davidian compound in Waco, Texas, 1993; the cult of Supreme Truth in Tokyo which attacked the subway system with nerve gas in 1995, killing twelve people and injuring five thousand; the bombing of the World Trade Centre in 1993 and the collapse of the World Trade Towers on September 11, 2001. It is important to note that these examples are the fanatical fringe of any religion that they might profess.

Their radical actions are infused with an extremism that completely disregards human rights and the law.

The second type, "intransigent fundamentalism," is also at odds with human rights legislation. Its tenets and beliefs, which claim to predate the development of human rights thinking, can be traced to age-old revelations and ancient texts. Religious fundamentalists of Islamic, Jewish or Christian teaching adhere to their own religious doctrines in the event of a conflict with human rights laws. Each views the legislation as a relative good in so far as it is not held in contradistinction to their religious tenets. Religious fundamentalists are not the only jurisdiction that promotes its own laws over a strict adherence to human rights principles. Van der Vyver (1996) points out that the United States, as a secular entity, also promotes a relativism that insists its laws supercede those arrived at by international agreement over common value systems. Two examples are the use of capital punishment and that United States citizens are not subject to any court higher than that of their own country. For intransigent fundamentalism, human rights principles that cannot be accommodated are simply discarded.

The third type of fundamentalism, according to van der Vyver (1996), is "pro-active." At times this type of fundamentalism might use human rights as a tool to substantiate certain of their struggles or to condemn the actions of others. There would be selective use of human rights principles to coincide with certain religious points of doctrine. Conversely, when religion is used to protest violation of human rights, the actors can use selective religious texts to substantiate their claims. Fundamentalists are sometimes surprised to find themselves on the wrong side of the human rights law, because, as their motives and work are prompted by religious beliefs, they believe themselves to be intrinsically good. An example of pro-active fundamentalism is found in Christian missionary work, such as is carried on in Africa, which aims to care for the "physical as well as the spiritual well-being of its parishioners" (Richard Joseph, cited in van der Vyver 1996: 6). The effect has indeed been contradictory, as Christian churches in Africa at times participated in "blessing and legitimating the most corrupt regimes, and then again opposing repressive governments by affirming the rule of God" (Charles Villa-Vincencio, cited in van der Vyver 1996: 6).

The following example illustrates a pro-active fundamentalism in which the demands of human rights are discredited by religious attitudes and practices. This example involves conservative religious supporters who are not normally involved in political activism but who are moved to demonstrate publicly by fundamentalist aspects of their religious convictions.

In 1999, a Saskatchewan Human Rights Board of Inquiry heard the case of *Fancy v. Saskatoon School Division No. 13* concerning the use of the Lord's Prayer in public schools. A complaint was brought against the Saskatoon School Division, alleging that the practice of reciting the Lord's Prayer during school functions discriminated against the religious freedom of the complainants' children. Christian groups vigorously opposed the removal of the prayer in spite of the expectation and legal requirement that minority rights are protected in public schools. In other places, policies that promote the indoctrination of Christianity have been seen as contrary to human rights codes and the *Canadian Charter of Rights and Freedoms* (Watkinson 1999). Saskatoon is not an exception. The Board of Inquiry found in favour of the complainants that the recitation of the Christian prayer was, indeed, discriminatory.[1] This ruling of the Saskatchewan Human Rights Board of Inquiry was strongly contested in letters to the editor in the *Star Phoenix* in Saskatoon and in presentations to the Public Board of Education. Prayer advocates defend the discriminatory practice of reciting Christian prayers in public schools and justify their stand on their allegiance to God and country. They argue that benefits accruing to all children through reciting the prayer outweigh any discrimination or infringement on human rights that may occur.

I describe the position of the prayer advocates as fundamentalist with respect to religious and national discourses that advocates employ in public debates. Viewing the public discourses through the lens of fundamentalist practices sheds light on what is at stake for advocates and provides some explanation for the protracted nature of the debates, which continue still (see *Star Phoenix* 2003: A17). In this Saskatoon example, a combination of at least three separate moves suggests that the advocates' stand can be explained through a fundamentalist lens. The first instance is an expressed desire to establish a particular historical legacy of the nation—as Christian and white. This selective history, which emphasizes the qualities of hard work and sacrifice, is imbued with nostalgia for a society settled by white Europeans. Second, the claims of national belonging are narrowly defined through the discourses of a white settler society: 1) strict religious practices (the observance of the prayer is offered as evidence of why it should be retained); 2) skin colour (whiteness as the semiotic for Christianity); and 3) immigration status (having been part of the first wave of European settlement). Third, in spite of the attempt to proscribe school practice (Christian prayer must remain) in a restrictive way, there is a desire to influence public space as broadly as possible. In other words, Christian entitlement should not only be protected as the exclusive heritage of people who claim founding status; it should also be applied universally through schools in Saskatchewan (or at least Saskatoon). A conflict arises for prayer advocates in that they want to claim a separate and exclusive status as founders of the nation, yet, they wish to influence public policy broadly in a community that is re-examining its traditions in light of human rights legislation and changing socio-political conditions.

The prayer advocates continue to insist on their exclusive "history" and that their way of living be taken up as "the way of living" (Foucault 1990).

This is a moderate example of tensions between religious conviction and democratic human rights. In the emotionally charged debates, prayer advocates are positioning themselves as central to national (Canadian) identity even while the courts of Canada rule against them. This ruling shatters the positioning of religious conservatives and destabilizes their claims as representatives of God *and* country. In spite of the fact that fundamentalist positions are often seen as occupying clearly defined social spaces, this example illustrates that fundamentalists are ambiguously positioned as both insider and outsider. The shifting nature of fundamentalist identity is problematic for adherents in that they want to be exclusive and also widely influential. Fundamentalist identity can be described—perhaps contrary to the desire of fundamentalists—as a social construction and not as the unchanging fixture of moral and authentic reckoning. The disruption to public roles and identifications is, in part, a response to the shifting nature of fundamentalist influence and desire.

Constructed Identities

With respect to religious practice, just who is a fundamentalist? Although there are many definitions of fundamentalism, a precise definition of who might be designated as fundamentalist seems difficult to agree upon. Singling out certain trends of religious thought or action produces neither a definitive nor exclusive identification, especially as the range of fundamentalist action varies widely. On the one hand, there is extreme withdrawal from mainstream society and, on the other, a rigorous evangelical outreach. An editorial in the avowedly right-wing *Alberta Report* (Byfield and Byfield 2000) argues that there is very little agreement on what is meant by the term. It states that the identity known as a fundamentalist is ambiguous and that even politicians Stockwell Day and Preston Manning could not be defined as fundamentalist with any certainty. The interesting part of the equivocation is a reluctance on the part of this strongly pro-Christian periodical to apply the label fundamentalist, as if acknowledging the leaders as such were something to be avoided. As van der Vyver states with respect to religious practice throughout the twentieth century in North America, the term fundamentalism has "acquired a distinctly negative connotation" (1996: 1). The term is frequently used as a way of discrediting the beliefs or conduct of people seen to hold extreme or essentialist views. Not surprisingly, it is also a term used most often by those who are the object of fundamentalists' reproach. As noted in the *Alberta Report*, fundamentalism, as a derogatory term, is applied with "liberal abandon" (Byfield and Byfield 2000).

By definition, fundamentalists insist on "realist" interpretations of social, material, historical and religious events. Problems and ambiguities arising in the present are explained by fundamentalists as evidence that the truth or reality of the world has been covered up or not yet fully revealed. One reason for rejecting certain human rights legislation with which they disagree is that religious fundamentalists see their own tenets decreed by divine truth and not that of human beings, whose truths are changing. The attempt to align themselves with the immutable and unchanging will of God is a significant aim of Christian fundamentalist organizing. On matters of biblical interpretation, fundamentalists insist on the inerrancy and literalness of the Bible; they also stress a sudden and cataclysmic end of the earth in the Second Coming of Christ. Rising militancy among religious conservatives in North American society in the twentieth century does not simply represent a surge of religiosity or interest in religious matters. It is the increased secularization of society that spurs fundamentalists to a rejection of material ways, even while their own fortunes are rising with the times. Although fundamentalism appears to be a stand against outsiders, its efforts are more directly focused on those of the same faith (Armstrong 2001). Major formulations of fundamentalist principles began as a prod "designed to stir lethargic churchgoers into action" (Bendroth 1999: 2)—an action which in so doing drew the boundaries of religious adherence more tightly than before (Bendroth 1999). Issues such as the role of women and children in families, controversy over the place of religion in schools and laxity among mainstream religions are signs of the battle against modernity which fundamentalists fear they are losing (Bendroth 1999). One of the contradictions Bendroth points out is that the U.S. was seen as both the promised land, or Zion, even while it also represented the excesses of Babylon. Bendroth concludes, "fundamentalists never gave up hoping to redeem the nation from corruption, even as they waited impatiently for its downfall" (1999: 2).

A significant point made by van der Vyver is that even though fundamentalists profess to be upholding religious orthodoxy and "preserving traditions from erosion, they in fact embark upon ideologies, practices and organization structures that are quite new and unprecedented in established or mainstream religions" (1996: 1). To preserve the traditions, the past is glorified and the present condemned; there is a spirit of "repristination" (van der Vyver 1996: 1), which is said to restore the benefits of a pristine past, which never really existed in the way it is now being described. Bendroth (1999) argues that in the history of faith traditions and the family, the fundamentalist pro-family movement is only a recent development, beginning after World War II and accelerating in the 1970s. What is seen as an essential part of Christian teaching from the beginning is really a response to secular pressure among the faithful. The emphasis of the family formation with a strict male/female role alignment serves the needs of fundamentalist conformity more than historical accuracy.

Disrupted Identities

I would like to return to the example cited earlier in which the recitation of school prayer in Saskatoon public schools was found to be discriminatory. The case illustrates the shifting nature of social identifications and the problem of a closed history in describing how things used to be. The historic reality is that schools were permitted a limited form of religious observance, including recitation of the Lord's Prayer, dating from the inception of the Province of Saskatchewan. One of the reasons that human rights judge Halvorson declined to sanction the recitation of the Lord's Prayer was that for the last several years the event had been recognized more often in the breach than in the observance (Watkinson 1999). Besides the significant factor that the recitation was judged as discriminatory, it would have been very difficult to prescribe the use of this social custom that had fallen away in a great many schools. Indeed, the loss of school prayer had not previously provoked any interest. Reinstating the prayer would have amounted to revisiting a past that never was, a repristination. Taking the schools back to their pristine past would have been at the least impractical.

The controversy that surrounded the case was an indication that cultural and social norms had been challenged—and school prayer was the symbol. What were the unspoken norms and identifications that were suddenly at risk in the challenge to inclusive practice? As schools are key places of ideological struggle, access to them represents nothing less than publicly legitimated space for private acts of worship. In a white settler society, however, the claim of historic primacy will always be contested, especially as the claim is little more than a hundred years old and neglects mentioning First Nations peoples. The demise of Christianity as a publicly legislated expression challenges its religious and historic supremacy and, by association, the presumed entitlement of its adherents.

To Belong or Not to Belong?

Fundamentalists attempt to resolve their ambiguous position of not/belonging by linking themselves more closely to the nation in which true Canadians are Christian. If their claim to public space for Christian prayer cannot be made strictly on religious grounds, it will be advanced in the name of the nation and its traditions. In letters to the editor, the connections between citizen identity and Christianity are made regularly: Christianity is the "foundation stone of our society" (*Star Phoenix* 1999c: A10). Consequently, the removal of Christian prayer in public schools has become a touchstone for a list of moral ills: "bringing in guns, condoms, and drugs won't help our children" (*Star Phoenix* 1999a: A10). Linking these issues with lack of prayer—already decried as a moral ill—suggests some kind of emergency that is said to be plaguing the community and the nation.

Most of the discourses describing the actions of true Canadians and their threatened values employ a dichotomy of insider/outsider representation. On the one hand, there are Canada's "good immigrants" (Honig 1998), who believe in God, versus non-Christians, who are assumed to be more recent immigrants and not of European origin. This is a triumphalism that is typical of white settler societies (McClintock 1995). The tension to be resolved is that Canada may not be the welcoming nation it claims to be or perhaps never was, even when the majority of immigrants were from European countries. How do fundamentalists resolve the ambiguity of themselves as good citizens and the contradictions of their own discriminatory stand towards non-Christians? They establish a link between Christianity and an innocent and generous Canadian identity: "Most Canadians have a rich Christian heritage which has nurtured them to become what they are today—just, benevolent and tolerant" (*StarPhoenix* 1999d: A8). There is a confident assertion that God is on the side of Christians in this debate and in this country. This confidence asserts that Christian values are representative of Canadian values.

This construction of Canadian society is a commonplace national activity in which citizens are positively predisposed toward their country. Ghassan Hage (2001) also describes a nation-building process in Australia that goes beyond simple patriotism; the comparison to Canada is apt. Hage argues that the way of speaking about the nation established in public statements of Australian Prime Minister John Howard constitutes a type of national fundamentalism. This fundamentalism is characterized by the existence of a national "social essence" (Hage 2001: 27) that is an "historically unchanging reality" (28) as well as a "causal essence" (28) for national and political action.

In speaking about national fundamentalism in Australia, Hage describes the way in which Howard maintains the image of the country as unfailingly good. As in Canada, "tolerance and harmony" (2001: 28) are Australian values and are considered an "unchanging core [that is] quasi-genetically acquired by good nationals" (28). Howard claims unfailing national goodness while simultaneously admitting to the negative aspects of his country's history. Proof of current goodness, as well as evidence that it has always been good, comes out of the country's being stronger for what was wrong in the past.

These claims (of the good nation) are common terms favoured in liberal democracies. The terms are not exclusive to Australia, being found in other societies, for example, the U.S., as JoAnn Jaffe points out elsewhere in this volume. The point Hage is making is that the claim of goodness forestalls any other claims of what else the nation may be. The insistence on goodness limits any thinking or critical discussion about the degree to which the nation might indeed make this claim and the ways it might not always be true. When the nation is constructed overwhelmingly in idealist terms with an imagined sense of a united people, it is difficult to raise or even imagine questions about restrictive national policies such as immigration. Instead, there is a sentimentality that the imagined community of fellow citizens is essentially a fair-minded, likable group of people of whom we would approve for the simple reason that if we were to meet them we would be delighted to discover they are just like us. As in the Canadian example, the "we who built this country" are presented as a homogeneous group who are different and separate from more recent immigrants. As Hage says, "fundamentalism always offers a normative conception of society as a coherent projection of complementary values" (2001: 29). J.M. Swomely says that the sentimentality of complementary values appeals to a mythology of a unified nation of homogeneous, like-minded people. Quoting from a 1970 international seminar on fascism, Swomely explains: "sentimentality ... glorifies the simple, intimate, human forms of living together—the family, the folk community—and so on" (1995: 5–6).

The meaning of national mythologies and what they represent is almost impossible to examine. As Homi Bhabha says: "the natural(ized), unifying discourse of nation,' 'peoples,' 'folk' tradition—these embedded myths of culture's particularity—cannot be readily referenced"(1995: 49). Consequently, outsiders of the nation, peoples, folk tradition are simplistically regarded as oppositional forces and treated with great suspicion. Hage provides an example from Australian Prime Minister John Howard, who says that intellectual discourses that describe the shortcomings of the nation should be viewed suspiciously because they are at odds with the telling of the "nation as good." "Good" in the sense of traditional stories of the historical and unified people, is at risk from multiculturalism and open immigration. One of the most important processes for designating exclusive insider status is the necessity of the outside other. "Fundamentalist politics is always about recovering the Good people who are ... silenced/oppressed/repressed, etc. ... by the Bad people" (Hage 2001: 29). The "folk" and the "peoples" can only recognize themselves through the presence of an outsider described in dialectically opposite terms.

In Saskatoon, prayer advocates refer to the removal of prayer in schools in strictly negative terms: activist human rights, tyrannical social engineering, multicultural chaos, human rights ideologues, humanists, secular humanists, liberal Christians, moral disintegration, government control, totalitarianism. Ethnic and religious minority claims are framed as if the people who make those claims are unreasonable, outrageous or violent—certainly a threat to a good nation. Alternative discourses may enter the discussion only as outside voices who do not understand how "we" do things. Bannerji says that it is in these "diffused normalized sets of assumptions, knowledge, and so-called cultural practices" (1995: 45) that is racism in its most powerful, pervasive form.

As outlined by Wetherell, the discourses that are exchanged in such debates are a consequence of speakers "making sense in light of the collective interpretive resources of their local culture" (1998: 267). In this case, the performance of Christian rituals in schools is taken as evidence of Christian dominance and superiority. Christian respectability and the nation are tested by the demands of an unreasonable minority who push the tolerant beyond what they can reasonably be expected to bear. The discourses that speakers are able to access are informative of the culture in which they are produced. Describing the process of othering and discrediting with the simplistic division of us and them illustrates the discourses that are available in the community and the nation. That fundamentalist prayer advocates can access them is a marker of their insider status. As a way of asserting their influence over public policy, however, having access to recognizable discourses proves insufficient for prayer advocates when their position is found outside of the Human Rights Board ruling.

Clear-cut boundaries that might mark a fundamentalist identity slip even further in the competing attempts to be both exclusionary and universal. M.L. Bendroth explains this process in tracing the rise of the focus on the family in religious fundamentalism. She states: "fundamentalists became outsiders through a complex historical process. The movement arose in the late nineteenth century among Protestants who found themselves intellectually and spiritually—but not economically or politically—disenfranchised from white, middle-class culture" (Bendroth 1999: 2). Becoming outsiders was not necessarily what fundamentalist adherents intended as they attempted both to influence public life and withdraw from mainstream norms at the same time. The balancing act necessitated by conflicting desires resulted in insecure positioning such that "the need to be left alone and the fear of being ignored has been a tension within the conservative wing of American Protestantism for the past hundred years" (2).

The ambivalence in fundamentalist practices is seen in the desire to occupy the space of the exclusive faithful remnant and at the same time to influence public policies and shift the boundaries of what is considered normative and good. "Surrounded by a world they perceive as hostile, fundamentalists often plan a counter-offensive, resolved to drag God and religion from the sidelines in secular society and bring them back to centre stage" (Armstrong 2001: 17). All but the most extreme fundamentalists wish to be both of central influence in the social and national communities as well as to retain a distinction that separates them from the increasingly secular norms. Shifting social values and the right to influence public schooling collide in the Saskatchewan ruling that the Lord's Prayer in public schools must cease. When challenged by the shifting of normative social values, as characterized by the ruling of the Human Rights Board, fundamentalist believers find that some of their firmly held beliefs render them as outsider or other, a designation they resist. Their desire to see themselves on the side of what is good is in conflict with the ever-evolving nature of social norms influenced by human rights legislation.

Schools are highly contested sites for their real and symbolic power to designate respectability within a community. It is a designation that includes having one's "way of living," in all its complexity, taken up as "how to live" (Foucault 1990; Stoler 1995). How things come to be defined as legitimate and respectable in a community are not arbitrary or *ad hoc* processes; legitimacy is too important for that. Rather, the process of gaining a "toehold on respectability" (Fellows and Razack 1998), accomplished through hierarchical power relations, identifies the citizen who has the right to govern and arbitrate social values. It is not merely an insult to one's sensibilities when ethical and moral practices to which one subscribes constitute acts of discrimination. What is at stake is that one's identity and way of living are no longer understood as superior or as *the* way of living; one's social identification is not the unquestioned model of the ideal citizen. Even more unsettling: there is no longer an unambiguous race, ethnic or religious identity that represents the quintessential Canadian citizen.

Who Are "We"?

An examination of the public discourses of the Saskatoon case indicates that the fluid nature of identity construction has become so unsettling that speakers cannot recognize themselves. The conservative Christians in this debate alternately claim both dominant and subordinate status although, for the most part, they have enjoyed long-standing recognition as predominant members of the community. It is their dominant identifications and social authority that make sense of their demands for others to accept how "we" do things. On the other hand, they are non-dominant with respect to being publicly confessing, fundamentalist Christians, which is an increasingly marginalized positioning in Canadian society. They distinguish themselves from the majority of Christians by calling the others liberal, which is to indicate a broad and less exclusive interpretation of Christianity. Their fundamentalist religious positioning allows them to consider themselves as defenders of religious purity and opponents of a secular legal decision.

I realized there was more to this question of one group opposing the human rights of another when I could not easily distinguish which side was making which argument in the letters to the editor. What is going on when the rhetoric of the fundamentalist Christian sounds like the rhetoric of the original complainants who brought the suit? For example, which position is being described in the following?

> The decision shows that there are two sides to the coin of tolerance. One side is a specific religion imposed on all, without freedom of conscience or personal belief; the other side of the same coin is that certain religious ideas and concepts are disallowed for public examination. (*Star Phoenix* 1999e: A13)

The rest of the letter from which this excerpt was taken indicates that its author is a fundamentalist Christian supporter writing about local conditions. In this context, "a specific religion" refers to the varied ideological positions of those who petitioned to remove the Lord's Prayer. The "religious ideas and concepts that are disallowed" refers to Christianity. Even though fundamentalist Christians, as part of the majority—the "all" on whom a specific religion is being imposed—can refer to normative practices about how things ought to continue, they nevertheless find themselves on the wrong side of human rights legislation.

The notion of a fluid and non-essentialist identity construction is usefully employed: fundamentalist Christian supporters retain honour and respectability by identifying themselves alternately as upholders of majority rules and as a victimized minority. From a minority positioning, prayer advocates protest that their rights are being denied. "I consider my rights to be trampled on by those who would take religion out of our schools" (*Star Phoenix* 1999b: A11). In this shape-shifting, fundamentalists become the beleaguered minority whom human rights principles should defend.

Although the court ruled that the Lord's Prayer in public schools is discriminatory, these Christians must reject this decision if they are to remain true to their particular interpretation of a faith whose profession is love: it is a contradiction in terms to be an uncharitable Christian. The contradiction lies between the image of the Christian who champions the Lord's Prayer and the one who discriminates against and rejects the rights of particular school children. In the face of an ambivalent, shifting identity construction, the supporters—as ostensible defenders of the national heritage—cannot recognize themselves as a group who discriminates. Their dilemma is resolved in a fantasy of self-sacrifice, persecution and innocence. Therefore, fundamentalist Christian supporters position themselves as the aggrieved minority whose only choice is to reject the human rights decision.

Finally

In post-modern times it is no longer possible "to speak of the social agent as if we were dealing with a unified homogeneous entity" (Chantal Mouffe, cited in Wetherell 1998: 394). What is challenging to fundamentalists (and others as well) is that social identifications are contingent and precarious; similarly, the way a nation articulates itself is a constantly changing process. Social meanings are not bound by holy writ or the national charter—which itself is subject to on-going revision and interpretation. The shifting nature of social fabric and the nation, as exemplified in changes to school prayer, is at the heart of fundamentalist anxiety. This lack of fixed meaning must be especially unsettling for people accustomed to uncompromising principles and the authority of a sacred text. The title of the familiar hymn, "How Firm a Foundation," if applied to fundamentalists' recognition of themselves as the quintessential Canadian identity, is no longer a statement in the affirmative. Instead, the title has become more of a question for those whose self-recognition depends on insider status. That insider/outsider status is capable of changing at all may come as an unwelcome surprise to many.

The problem of producing and sustaining a secure and respectable citizen identity is at the heart of the hearings and the discussions about whether Christian prayers will be allowed in public schools. The problem is much more than a public debate over whether particular social practices should be continued. Rather, the impassioned letters to the editor and presentations to various public boards attest to the shifting nature of public identity and the uneasy changes taking place in the nation. The social rupture caused by fundamentalists' dilemma provides insight into the formerly unexamined assumption of citizen identity and the nature of social and religious observance that can be considered public. Christian fundamentalists can no longer count on public sponsorship of their religious views that seemed, at one time, to coincide with quintessential citizenship status. What is at stake is a loss of prestige that favours a particular way of living as well as automatic entitlement to the good, respectable citizen identity.

The first chapter in this book says that one reason to pay attention to fundamentalist practices is for those moments of intervention that might otherwise be missed. The contingent nature of social relations that causes anxiety for fundamentalists also provides impetus for action as well as spaces in which to challenge taken-for-granted privileges. The impetus for action also allows possibilities for naming and interrupting the familiar language of entitlement; for it is familiar everyday phrases, in their appeal to God and country, that render the fundamentalist claims plausible and even desirable to casual citizen observers. Ruptures to the social fabric found in public discourses afford opportunities for challenging the rigid ideas of inclusion and exclusion on which fundamentalist systems depend. As fundamentalists discover, however, it is their exclusivity that invites public scrutiny and their unwillingness to be inclusive that renders their position at odds with basic human rights. Ironically, a fundamentalist system is undermined by its own rigidity.

Notes

1. "This discriminatory practice is not constitutionally excused and must yield to the [Saskatchewan Human Rights] Code. It is ordered that the Board of Education cease sanctioning the Lord's prayer at assemblies in public schools" (Saskatchewan Human Rights Board of Inquiry 1999: para. 85).

References

Armstrong, K. 2001. "Cries of rage and frustration." *New Statesman (1996)*, 130(4556). Available at http://web1.infotrac-custom.com/pdfserve/get-item/1/S552c20w1_1/SB856_01.pdf [accessed Oct. 3, 2003].

Bannerji, H. 1995. *Thinking Through: Essays on Feminism, Marxism and Anti-racism*. Toronto: Women's Press.

Bendroth, M.L. 1999. "Fundamentalism and the Family: Gender, Culture, and the American Pro-family Movement." *Journal of Women's History* 10(4). Available at http://web2.infotrac-custom.com/pdfserve/get_item/1/S3426dfw7_1/SB823_01.pdf [accessed Oct. 3, 2003].

Bhabha, Homi K. 1995. "Freedom's basis in the indeterminate." In J. Rajchman (ed.), *The Identity in Question*. New York: Routledge.

Byfield, T., and V. Byfield. 2000. "Defining the elusive 'fundamentalist'—Susan Riley and Lois Wilson take on the job." *Alberta Report* 27(2). Available at http://web2.infotrac-custom.com/pdfserve/get_item/1/S3426dfw7_3/SB823_03.pdf [accessed Oct. 3, 2003].

Fellows, M.L., and S. Razack. 1998. "The race to innocence: Confronting hierarchical relations among women." *The Journal of Gender, Race and Justice* 1(2).

Foucault, M. 1990. *The History of Sexuality: An Introduction* (translated by R. Hurley, Volume 1). New York: Vintage Books.

Hage, Ghassan. 2001. "The Politics of Australian Fundamentalism: Reflections on the Rule of Ayatollah Johnny." *Arena Magazine* 51. Available at http://web2.infotrac-custom.com/pdfserve/get_item/1/S5a890bw6_1/SB323_01.pdf [accessed Oct. 3, 2003].

Honig, B. 1998. "Immigrant America? How foreignness 'solves' democracy's problems." *Social Text* 16(3).

McClintock, A. 1995. *Imperial Leather: Race, Gender and Sexuality in the Colonial Contest*. New York: Routledge.

Saskatchewan Human Rights Board of Inquiry. Halvorson Decision. July 23, 1999.

Star Phoenix, Saskatoon. 2003. "Public schools have lost moorings." February 21.

_____. 1999a. "Columnist wrong in assessment that most Christians are hypocrites." Saskatoon, July 22.

_____. 1999b. "Education needs moral basis." July 29,

_____. 1999c "Best to rethink prayer decision." July 31,

_____. 1999d. "School board took right stand." August 4,

_____. 1999e. "Human rights protection applied unequally." August 5.

Stoler, A.L. 1995. *Race and the Education of Desire: Foucault's History of Sexuality and the Colonial Order of Things*. Durham: Duke University Press.

Swomley, J.M. 1995. "Neo-fascism and the religious right." *The Humanist* 55(1). Available at http://web1.infotrac-custom.com/pdfserve/get_item/1/S552c20w1_2/SB856_02.pdf [accessed Oct. 3, 2003].

van der Vyver, J.D. 1996. "Religious fundamentalism and human rights." *Journal of International Affairs* 50(1). Available at http://web1.infotrac-custom.com/pdfserve/get_item/1/S552c20w1_3/SB856_03.pdf [accessed Oct. 3, 2003].

Watkinson, A.M. 1999. *Education, Student Rights, and the Charter*. Saskatoon: Purich Publishing Ltd.

Wetherell, M. 1998. "Positioning and interpretative repertoires: Conversation analysis and post-structuralism in dialogue." *Discourse & Society* 9(3).

Index